Legal Aspects of the Information Society

Ian Lloyd LLB, LLM PhD

*Professor of Information Technology Law,
University of Strathclyde*

Butterworths

London, Edinburgh, Dublin

2000

United Kingdom	Butterworths, a Division of Reed Elsevier (UK) Ltd, Halsbury House, 35 Chancery Lane, LONDON WC2A 1EL and 4 Hill Street, EDINBURGH EH2 3JZ
Australia	Butterworths, a Division of Reed International Books Australia Pty Ltd, CHATSWOOD, New South Wales
Canada	Butterworths Canada Ltd, MARKHAM, Ontario
Hong Kong	Butterworths Asia (Hong Kong), HONG KONG
India	Butterworths India, NEW DELHI
Ireland	Butterworth (Ireland) Ltd, DUBLIN
Malaysia	Malayan Law Journal Sdn Bhd, KUALA LUMPUR
New Zealand	Butterworths of New Zealand Ltd, WELLINGTON
Singapore	Butterworths Asia, SINGAPORE
South Africa	Butterworths Publishers (Pty) Ltd, DURBAN
USA	Lexis Law Publishing, CHARLOTTESVILLE, Virginia

© Reed Elsevier (UK) Ltd 2000

A CIP Catalogue record for this book is available from the British Library.

ISBN 0406 929 580

Typeset by Doyle & Co, Colchester
Printed by Cromwell Press Ltd, Trowbridge

Visit us at our website: http://www.butterworths.co.uk

Preface

It used to be commonplace for Internet enthusiasts to regard cyberspace as territory which was not, and should not be, subject to legal regulation. Given that in a recent Internet libel case, a headline settlement figure of £245,000 turned out to consist of damages of £15,000 and legal costs of £230,000, it is easy to see why the involvement of law and lawyers should be regarded unfavourably.

As Internet usage has expanded and the network has become a key component of the much vaunted 'Information Society', so it has become increasingly clear that it cannot be a law unto itself. Unfortunately, much of the emphasis of the law and legal systems to date has been concerned with the allocation and protection of rights in physical property. Principles derived from the age of the industrial revolution are not necessarily appropriate for a post-industrial age.

Whilst there is considerable room for debate concerning the suitability of law, people ignore its impact at their peril. In recent years, employers have been held liable to the extent of several hundred thousand pounds in respect of the improper use made of email by their employees. The Data Protection Act imposes stringent controls over the use which may be made of personal data. Owners of intellectual property rights are becoming increasingly vigilant in prosecuting instances of copyright infringement. In all these cases, penalties may be severe for those who unwittingly transgress legal requirements. Perhaps above all else, the explosion of interest, if not yet in consumer activity, in the field of electronic commerce raises a whole host of legal rights and liabilities.

It is hoped that this book may serve two purposes. For non-lawyers it introduces basic legal concepts and explains how these might be applied in the context of Internet-based activities. For lawyers, the book describes some of the areas of technology in which the law is required to operate. Information technology is changing the world and the law is no more immune from that process than any other aspect of life.

Any book is always the product of more than one set of digits on a computer keyboard. I am grateful for the skilful work of the editorial staff at Butterworths, to Carol Hutton who has kept many other distractions and distractors at bay whilst I have been attempting to complete too many projects, and to Chirsty McSween, a law librarian without peer. Most of all, thanks are due and given to Moira Simpson.

Contents

Table of Statutes

List of Cases

Chapter 1

Key legal concepts

Introduction

1.0 The purpose of this chapter is to provide non-legal readers with a brief introduction to some of the legal concepts which will be discussed in more detail in the following chapters. It sets out the nature of law, indicates its main sources and describes the main features of those areas of law which are of particular relevance to the information society. It appears to be an immutable legal principle that every rule is subject to exceptions and the reader should not be surprised if the detailed picture is not entirely consistent with this general overview.

1.1 Although a basic understanding of the various sources of law is necessary, a more important issue concerns the nature of the role played by the law. Again, a range of categories can be identified. The criminal law exists to deter and, that failing, punish forms of conduct which are regarded as detrimental to the interests of society. Private law, sometimes also referred to as civil law, is in many respects less judgmental, being designed primarily as a mechanism for resolving disputes between individuals. Often this boils down to the task of determining where losses should fall. A simple example might see a person visiting a shop accidentally knocking a piece of china off a display and causing it to break on the floor. Few people would argue that the conduct was criminal but a vase worth perhaps £50 has been rendered valueless. If the matter should reach the courts, the task for the law will be to determine who is responsible for the accident and for what losses liability should accrue.

1.2 Other cases may be far more complex and involve a multiplicity of parties. A perhaps apocryphal story suggests that a bank required to be knocked down and rebuilt because of a fault in a microprocessor built into the door of its safe controlling the times when the door can be opened. The chip could not be reached without destroying the vault and the structural integrity of the building would therefore be compromised. A moment's thought will identify a range of issues which will have to be resolved in order to determine who might be required to bear any losses. Should the architect of the bank have allowed it to be vulnerable to a single point of failure? Should the bank have specified its requirements more clearly? Should the builders have worked differently? Should the chip designers have designed the object differently? Litigation in such a case might be extensive, prolonged and expensive. As will be discussed, an important distinction can be drawn between situations where parties are acting in the course of an agreement or contract between themselves and those where there is no such agreement. In the case of the bank example, the bank might have a contract with the architect and the main building contractor but not with sub-contractors and the chip manufacturer.

Nature and sources of law

1.4 The word 'law' has a wide variety of meanings. The Encarta dictionary gives the word no fewer than 13 interpretations, ranging from a colloquial description of the police to the fundamental rules of physics. For present purposes the most appropriate definition refers to 'a rule of conduct or procedure recognized by a community as binding or enforceable by authority'. The essence of a law is that it both prescribes standards of conduct and provides for an enforcement mechanism.

1.5 The question obviously arises, where does law come from? Although reference is often made by legal theorists to notions of natural or divine law as encompassing principles and rules which are so fundamental to life that they need not be formally stated, the modern day reality is rather more prosaic. Laws, in the form of binding rules, are created from a limited number of sources. The most important sources are:

- statute law;

- judge made (common) law;

- European Union legislation and international treaties.

Statutue law

1.6 The UK Parliament (and the Welsh and Northern Irish Assemblies and Scottish Parliament) possess law making powers. In theory, the UK Parliament (although not the national legislatures) can enact any law it wishes and the courts will be obliged to give effect to it. This contrasts with the situation applying in most democracies where the law making powers of parliament are subject to the provisions of a written constitution and where a special constitutional court will declare invalid any laws which do not conform with constitutional requirements. A relevant example of this occurred in Germany. In 1983 the West German legislature made provision for a national census. The Census Act identified items of information which would be required from citizens and also made provision that elements of the data gathered might be transferred from the census authorities to other public authorities in connection with the performance of their prescribed functions. The transfer possibilities envisaged in the legislation led to the statute being struck down as unconstitutional by the Constitutional Court, which held that the proposal breached arts 1 and 2 of the German constitution, which require the state to respect and promote the 'dignity of man' and to guarantee the 'free development' of the individual's personality. Whilst recognising the need of the state to gather information, the court held that the processing power contained in computer systems posed substantial threats to individual liberties. It held that:

> The possibilities of inspection and of gaining influence have increased to a degree hitherto unknown and may influence the individual's behaviour by the psychological pressure exerted by public interest ... if someone cannot predict with sufficient certainty which information about himself in certain areas is known to his social milieu, and cannot estimate sufficiently the knowledge of parties to whom communication may possibly be made, he is crucially inhibited in his freedom to plan or to decide freely and without being subject to any pressure/influence.

Particular dangers identified were that individuals might be reluctant to participate in an 'assembly or citizens' initiative' if they were uncertain whether details of their actions might be recorded and used for other purposes.

1.7 In reality, constraints do exist on Parliament's powers. The European Community Act 1978 provides that some forms of European legislation are to take precedence over conflicting UK provisions. More recently, the Human Rights Act 1998 seeks to ensure that future UK legislation will comply with the requirements of the European Convention on Human Rights. In theory it will be open to any future UK Parliament to repeal the Human Rights Act. Politically, however, such a move might be more difficult.

1.8 Laws adopted by Parliament can be placed into two categories: statutes and statutory instruments, sometimes referred to as secondary legislation. A statute, otherwise referred to as an Act of Parliament, becomes law following extensive procedures and debates in both the House of Commons and the House of Lords. Limits exist on the power of the House of Lords to oppose legislative proposals but, generally,

measures have to be debated and approved by both Houses of
Parliament before they become law.

Procedures for adoption of an Act of Parliament

1.9 Legislative proposals, referred to as Bills, can be introduced into
either House of Parliament. By convention, significant or controversial
measures are normally introduced in the House of Commons, whilst
less contentious or more technical measures often begin in the House
of Lords.

1.10 Assuming that a Bill starts life in the House of Commons, its
formal introduction is referred to as the First Reading. There is no
debate or discussion at this stage. Some time later, the Second
Reading provides an opportunity for Members of Parliament to
discuss the principles of the Bill. At the conclusion of the debate, a
vote is taken whether the Bill may proceed. Assuming the vote is in
favour, the Bill enters its Committee stage. Here the Bill is discussed
(normally by a committee of 15-20 MPs) and voted on on a line by line
basis. Frequently amendments are made, some correcting defects in
the original wording and others of more substance. At the conclusion
of the Committee stage, the Report stage sees the changes made being
voted upon by the whole House. Further amendments may also be
introduced at this stage. In the case of the Data Protection Act 1998,
for example, more than 100 amendments were tabled on behalf of the
government at the Report stage. There then follows the Third Reading,
which provides a final opportunity for Members to discuss and vote
on the principles of the legislation.

1.11 Having passed through the House of Commons, a Bill will
follow the same procedure in the House of Lords. One difference is
that the Committee stage in the House of Lords can be attended by any
member of the House. It is quite normal for other amendments to be
made to the Bill in the House of Lords. After its Third Reading,
therefore, there will be different texts as approved by both Houses.
Processes exist whereby the Houses of Parliament can agree on a
single text. If this does not occur the measure will be lost.

1.12 The final stage in the law making process sees the text as
approved by Parliament being submitted for what is referred to as the
Royal Assent. This process dates back to the battles for legislative
supremacy between the Crown and Parliament in the Middle Ages.
Today, the sovereign's role is purely symbolic and the grant of Royal
Assent is a procedural formality.

1.13 As the description given above indicates, the procedure is a complex one. Although, in cases of emergency, it has been known for the process to be compressed into one or two days (often demonstrating the truth of the adage 'act in haste, repent at leisure') a period of six to eight months is normally required. Relatively few statutes are enacted in any given year. In the parliamentary session 1998/9, 35 Acts of Parliament became law. Most of these were brought forward on behalf of the government, although each year some time is allocated for Bills proposed by individual Members of Parliament. The Computer Misuse Act 1990, which constitutes the major legal response to activities such as computer hacking, was such a measure.

1.14 For most areas of law, major statutory reform occurs at lengthy intervals. In the field of intellectual property, for example, only three major copyright statutes have been enacted this century (in 1911, 1956 and 1988). Although smaller pieces of legislation have been introduced in the field, there is an increasing perception that aspects of this branch of the law are ill suited for the needs of the information society. The validity of this perception will be considered in more detail below, but the point may be noted that relatively few statutes can be enacted in any year and that considerable time may pass before any amendments can be made. In large part, these factors have been responsible for an increase in the use of statutory instruments. To put the figures into perspective, in 1999, 3,474 statutory instruments were adopted, a ratio of almost 100 statutory instruments per Act of Parliament. Although many instruments are of peripheral and transitional significance, others are considerably more important.

The nature of secondary legislation

1.15 In contrast to the ability of Parliament to legislate in any form it thinks fit, secondary legislation may be introduced only when it is authorised by an Act of Parliament. The legislation will be made by a government minister. Having been made the legislation will be presented to Parliament for approval. This may take a variety of forms. Most statutory instruments are subject to what is referred to as a 'negative resolution' procedure. Under this, the measure is tabled before both Houses and will enter into force after a period of 40 days unless either House votes against its adoption. The 'affirmative resolution' procedure, as its name suggests, requires a positive vote in both Houses of Parliament before the measure enters into force. Even where affirmative resolution is required, the process is much quicker than that associated with a statute.

1.16 Many modern statutes make extensive provision for the adoption of secondary legislation. In many cases the legislation itself will not enter into force until this legislation is made. The Data Protection Act 1998, for example, required the making of some 20 statutory instruments. Although the Act became law in July 1998, it did not enter into force until March 2000, the drafting of the necessary statutory instruments proving a more complex task than was originally estimated. In such cases, the statute provides what might be regarded as the framework which requires to be filled in by secondary legislation.

1.17 Taking the Data Protection Act as an example, a range of roles can be identified for secondary legislation. Some matters of detail might date relatively quickly. Fees are payable in respect of many actions taking place under the Act, for example obtaining access to personal data. Were the Act to prescribe the level of fees, inflation might soon erode their value. The Act provides accordingly that fees may be fixed and amended by statutory instrument. A similar approach was adopted under the Data Protection Act 1984. Many of the fees were increased on three occasions between 1984 and 1998.

1.18 A second category of application occurs when it is considered that changes in circumstances, perhaps brought about because of other legislation, might call for updating. One of the key rights conferred under the Data Protection Act enables individuals to obtain information about data held on computer. The right is subject to a number of specific exceptions laid down in the Act (data held by the police, for example, indicating that an individual is suspected of the planning of or involvement in a criminal offence, need not be disclosed). In addition to the list of specific exemptions it is provided that:

> The Secretary of State may by order exempt from the subject information provisions personal data consisting of information the disclosure of which is prohibited or restricted by or under any other enactment if and to the extent that he considers it necessary for the safeguarding of the interest of the data subject or the rights and freedoms of any other individual that the prohibition or restriction ought to prevail over those provisions.

1.19 It will be seen from this that the Secretary of State does not have unfettered power to exempt data from the subject information provisions. There needs to be a factual conflict with the provisions of another statute and a value judgment made which provisions should prevail. It is open to any person affected by such a statutory instrument to bring a challenge before the courts claiming either that the legislation was misguided on factual grounds or (much more difficult to establish) that the judgment made was one which no reasonable minister could have made.

1.20 A final area where statutory instruments are often relied upon is when detailed provision needs to be made for a particular form of activity. In the case of the Data Protection Act, for example, those processing personal data are required to notify details of the processing to an independent authority, the Data Protection Commissioner, charged with overseeing the operation of the legislation. The approach adopted in the legislation has been to define a number of basic requirements but leave the detailed implementation to be prescribed by statutory instrument.

1.21 In general terms, statutes and statutory instruments may both require to be taken into account in seeking to identify the law relating to a particular topic.

Common law

1.22 Although the volume of law made by Parliament is expanding continually, it is not the only source of law emanating from the UK. Account must also be taken of the role of the courts and judges in determining disputes between parties.

The court structure and judicial precedent

1.23 Many simple disputes will be dealt with in the County Court (in Scotland the Sheriff Court) and may well utilise some form of small claims procedure. More extensive and extensive disputes will reach the higher courts and here the doctrine of judicial precedent provides that legal rulings may be binding on other courts in future cases. There are three tiers of courts. Disputes will be raised in one of the Divisions of the High Court (in Scotland, the Outer House of the Court of Session). An appeal may be made to the Court of Appeal (the Inner House of the Court of Session in Scotland) and a final appeal to the House of Lords.

1.24 Decisions of the High Court are of what is called persuasive authority. They may be referred to in future cases where the same legal points are at issue and may influence the judge in his findings. Decisions of the appeal courts laying down a point of law must be followed in later High Court cases. A decision of the Court of Appeal will be binding on itself and on all lower courts. A decision of the House of Lords, the highest court in the land, will be binding on all other courts although it may be overturned by a later decision of the House of Lords. As will be seen throughout this book, the decisions handed down by the courts are recorded and published either in paper form in what are referred to as Law Reports or, increasingly, on the

Internet. All judgments of the House of Lords, for example, are available on the Internet as are all decisions of the High Court and Court of Session in Scotland.

A note on terminology

1.25 Cases are reported by reference to the names of the parties involved. The party initiating an action is referred to as the plaintiff (in Scotland the term pursuer is used). The other party is the defendant (defender in Scotland). In the event an appeal is brought against the decision of the first court terminology changes somewhat. The party bringing the appeal is the appellant and the other party is the respondent.

How do judges make law?

1.26 Judges can be seen as making law in two situations. The first applies when a court is called upon to interpret a statute (or statutory instrument) in the context of a particular dispute. To give an example, the Sale and Supply of Goods Act 1994 provides that goods must be of 'satisfactory quality'. An individual may buy a new car and discover some weeks later that the engine is suffering from an oil leak. If the seller refuses to take any remedial action, the courts may well be called upon to determine whether the car is of satisfactory quality.

1.27 As well as cases where the courts are called upon to determine the meaning of a statute, there remain areas of the law which are not regulated by statute law and where the courts will have to look to the body of legal principles and doctrines that is referred to as the common law. In Scotland, for example, very few criminal offences are established by statute; most have been developed by the courts over a period of centuries and there remains a power vested in the High Court to declare criminal any conduct which, although not previously so regarded, ought to be prosecuted in the public interest. The last occasion when this power was exercised concerned a case when a shopkeeper had sold solvents to children knowing that these would be used for their narcotic effects. The High Court declared that this conduct should be criminal and sentenced the shopkeeper to a term of imprisonment.

1.28 Views can be expressed both in favour and against such an approach. The technique is a flexible one and in the case referred to enabled the Scottish courts to punish what was widely regarded as unacceptable conduct. Against this, in the United Kingdom judges are appointed rather than elected and, at least in the case of more senior appointments, can be removed from office only in the most extreme circumstances. Such security is seen as being necessary in order to enable the judiciary to demonstrate independence of government but it does raise questions about law being made by unelected and unaccountable individuals. More fundamentally, perhaps, although the judges would argue that they are merely applying in a concrete case legal principles that had not been previously been specifically expressed, it is much harder for an individual to assess the nature and extent of rights and obligations against the amorphous mass of the common law than with regard to a specific statute or statutory instrument.

1.29 In a number of areas, notably that relating to the law of privacy, judges have been unwilling to develop new rights, arguing that such a reform should be a matter for Parliament. In the case of *Malone v Metropolitan Police Commissioner (No 2)* [1979] 2 All ER 620. Malone's phone had been tapped by the police in the course of a criminal investigation. This act, it was claimed, infringed his right to privacy. Today, the interception of communications is governed by the Interception of Communications Act 1985. The case, however, was brought in 1983, at which time there was no statute dealing with telephone tapping. Malone argued that the court should intervene to protect people in his situation. The judge disagreed stating that '[i]t is no function of the court to legislate in a new field. The extension of existing laws and principles is one thing; the creation of an altogether new right is another'. A similar approach was adopted in a case brought before the Court of Appeal in 1990, *Kaye v Robertson* [1991] FSR 62. Kaye, a well-known actor, had suffered severe head injuries and had been hospitalised. A reporter and a photographer secured access to his hospital room and took photographs of the injured person. It was intended that these should form the basis of a feature in a Sunday newspaper. The action alleging infringement of privacy failed although all the judges expressed regret at the state of the law. The comments of Lord Justice Bingham are typical:

> If ever a person has a right to be let alone by strangers with no public interest to pursue, it must surely be when he lies in hospital recovering from brain surgery, and in no more than partial command of his faculties. It is this invasion of privacy which underlies the plaintiff's complaint. Yet it alone, however gross, does not entitle him to relief in English law.

The passage of the Human Rights Act in 1998 might go some way to providing a right of privacy although, as is frequently illustrated, a difficult balance requires to be struck between an individual's demand to be let alone and the media interest in exposing wrong-doing.

European law

1.30 With the UK's entry into the European Community in 1973, a new source of law came into existence. Today, laws developed within what is now the European Union's law making process form an increasingly important part of UK domestic law. European law is an especially important component of the law in many aspects relevant to the information society with, data protection, electronic commerce and intellectual property laws all deriving from European initiatives.

1.31 European law can take a variety of forms. The principle measures are:

• regulations;

• decisions;

• directives.

A regulation is a legal instrument which applies throughout the EU and becomes part of national law without the need for any further action by the national authorities. Decisions possess a similar status, known as 'direct effect' but will be addressed to a smaller audience; perhaps one member state. The concept of the directive is perhaps the most complex. In common with regulations, directives are binding throughout the EU. They operate, however, at a more general level, binding member states as to the results to be achieved but leaving a degree of flexibility as to the manner in which this is accomplished. A good example of the legislative phenomenon can be seen in the field of data protection. In October 1995, following a law making process extending through five years, the European Union adopted a directive 'on the protection of individuals with regard to the processing of personal data and on the free movement of such data' (the Data Protection Directive). This directive contains some 12,750 words in 34 articles and required to be implemented in the member states within a period of three years, expiring in October 1998. The Data Protection Act 1998 was the first step in the UK's response. To give an initial point of comparison between the directive and the Act, the latter contains some 38,000 words in 75 sections. The Act, therefore is around three times the length of the directive, a ratio which will increase further when the associated secondary legislation is made.

1.32 Implementation of directives can prove a difficult matter. In part this is due to different legislative philosophies between the UK and the rest of Europe. The UK approach has sought to ensure that a statute provides for every eventuality. In theory, although seldom in practice, the task for the courts should be to apply rather than to interpret the law. The continental and EU systems tend to frame legislation at a greater level of abstraction, prescribing principles which will then be interpreted by the courts in particular cases. On occasions, also a directive's text may use terms which do not fit easily into a domestic context. An example might be taken from art 13 of the Data Protection Directive. This provides that:

> Member States shall guarantee every data subject the right to obtain from the controller—
> (a) without constraint at reasonable intervals and without excessive delay and expense (information about the data held concerning the subject)

The contentious phrase in this article is 'without constraint'. In most cases, that phrase would be interpreted in the sense of 'without impediment' or 'without restriction'. Analysis of the background to the legislation reveals a different sentiment. There is some evidence to suggest that, in most cases where individuals seek access to personal data, the request is not spontaneous but follows a demand from a third party. Typically, an employer may require potential employees to seek access to their criminal record (if any) and reveal the results to the employer. The directive seeks to outlaw the practice of requiring individuals to exercise rights of access against their wills and the term 'without constraint' is intended to achieve this. Such an interpretation might be seen as stretching unduly the flexibility of the English language.

European law is frequently applied in domestic courts. The ultimate authority on questions of its interpretation is, however, the European Court of Justice based in Luxembourg.

Branches of law

1.33 As with any subject, law is divided into a number of categories. In many cases the distinctions are somewhat artificial and there is often considerable overlap. Initially, it may be helpful to draw a distinction between criminal law and civil law.

Criminal law

1.34 The purpose of the criminal law is to involve the state in the punishment of conduct which is seen as being undesirable in the general public interest. Originally, a significant reason for the state's involvement was to avoid the prospect of individuals seeking their own vengeance for wrongs conducted against them or their families.

The role of the criminal law has expanded subsequently and generally it may be stated that criminal sanctions are applied when it is considered necessary to deter and punish certain forms of conduct. The UK makes perhaps more use of the criminal law than most other countries. Whilst many states draw a distinction between crimes and more minor misdemeanours, in the UK the act of parking a car on a yellow line is just as much a crime as the most heinous case of mass murder.

1.35 Until the advent of the computer, the criminal law played a very limited role in relation to information. Much of the criminal law is based on the concept of offences against the person and offences against property. Artificial intelligence notwithstanding, computers are not yet regarded as possessing personality. More significantly, information has not generally been regarded as constituting property, save where it is connected to some tangible object. In many respects this view is entirely logical. The English law of theft, for example, requires that the owner of property be deprived of its possession on at least a quasi-permanent basis. If my copy of *Legal Aspects of the Information Society* is stolen, it is clear that this condition has been satisfied. I have lost pieces of paper with text printed on them. If someone reads through the book without my consent and retains a memory of the text (or puts the book on a photocopier), they may obtain much the same benefit but it is difficult to identify anything that I may have lost.

1.36 Such an approach was of little practical consequence in an era when information generally required to be fixed to some tangible object. Clearly, as the mass of books and films concerned with the world of espionage demonstrates, some information, whether industrial or state secrets, is considered to be of substantial value. As such, it would be maintained under some form of security with the legal consequence that any secret agent seeking to obtain access to the information would be likely to commit an offence in relation to unauthorised access to property.

1.37 In the information society, information is becoming an increasingly valuable commodity. As was said in the leading Canadian case, *R v Stewart* 149 DLR (3d) 583:

> Compilations of information are often of such importance to the business community that they are securely kept to ensure their confidentiality. The collated, confidential information may be found in many forms covering a wide variety of topics. It may include painstakingly prepared computer programs . . . meticulously indexed lists of suppliers . . . For many businessmen their confidential lists may well be the most valuable asset of their company. Their security will be of utmost importance.

As can be seen in the spiralling numbers of Internet companies, very often information is the only significant asset of the company.

1.38 With the emergence of the Internet, information has been freed to a considerable extent from the need to be recorded on some tangible storage device. Likewise, as the phenomenon of computer hacking demonstrates, it is possible for electronic spies to obtain access to data held on computer without the need to enter the premises or even the continent on which the data is held.

1.39 A variety of measures have been taken to enhance the protection afforded by the criminal law to the keepers of information. Many countries have introduced computer crime statutes which criminalise activities such as hacking and the dissemination of computer viruses. These will be discussed in more detail in subsequent chapters. Another legislative trend which will be discussed has seen an extension of criminal provisions into the law of copyright. Copyright constitutes the main legal vehicle for protection of an author's (or publisher's) interests in a literary, artistic or musical work. Until the 1980s, breach of copyright was primarily a matter for the civil law but it may now attract significant criminal penalties, in the UK extending to a two-year term of imprisonment.

1.40 In general, therefore, we can identify an increasing involvement of the criminal law in the field of information. This reflects the perception of the legislature that, as was said *in R v Stewart* 149 DLR (3d) 583 by Cory JA:

> If questioned, a businessman would unhesitatingly state that the confidential lists were the 'property' of his firm. If they were surreptitiously copied by a competitor or outsider, he would consider his confidential data to have been stolen. The importance of confidential information will increase with the growth of high technology industry. Its protection will be of paramount concern to Members of industry and the public as a whole.

In such circumstances, it is not sufficient to allow individuals and organisations to resolve disputes between themselves. The interest of the public at large is such that public intervention is required initially to deter those contemplating activities which will adversely affect those holding or using information and, if deterrence fails in a particular case, to impose punishment.

Civil law

1.41 The term 'civil law' encompasses a range of topics with the common factor that the law establishes a framework defining rights and obligations. In the event of any dispute concerning these, the individuals or organisations concerned will bring and defend proceedings in court.

1.42 Although the civil law is distinct from the criminal law, there may be circumstances in which a single act or omission may incur both criminal and civil liability. If a car driver, for example, consumes an excessive amount of alcohol and subsequently drives carelessly so as to knock down and injure a pedestrian, criminal sanctions may be incurred, with the pedestrian also claiming damages under civil law in respect of the injuries incurred.

Contractual and non-contractual liability

Introduction

1.43 In talking of rights and liabilities enforceable under some branch of civil law, a basic distinction can be made between those which arise pursuant to some agreement between the parties and those which arise independent of any agreement. These are generally referred to under the headings of contractual and non-contractual liability. Examples of the former category would include the purchase of a bus ticket, or entering into a contract of employment or of marriage. In all of these cases the parties have, at least in theory, freedom to decide whether to enter into the agreement. The notion of freedom of contract is one of the traditional cornerstones of the law. Under this doctrine the role of the law is one of determining what the parties have agreed, and either of giving effect to that or providing a remedy, normally in the form of an award of financial compensation, in the event that a party fails to meet its obligations.

1.44 One important point which arises from this is that the concept of fault or negligence is generally irrelevant under the law of contract. One party will offer to act in a particular way, the other will accept this offer. In many cases there may be a series of negotiations leading up to the stage where the parties reach full agreement. Once agreement is reached, save where external and unforeseeable circumstances render performance impossible, each party must perform as promised or face the legal consequence.

1.45 In many cases parties may come into contact in the absence of any specific agreement. The example of the car accident cited above provides a good illustration. It is unlikely in the extreme that the driver and pedestrian had entered into any agreement regulating the manner in which they would behave towards each other, yet rights and obligations flow from the nature of their relationship. The basic duty is to take care to avoid acts or omissions which are likely to injure another. Here the basis for liability is rooted in the notion of fault or negligence.

1.46 A new arrival on the legal scene is the concept of product liability. This may be seen as a halfway house between the systems of contractual and delictual liability. Under its ambit, producers will be held liable for certain forms of damage caused to users of their products unless it can be shown that the product was not defective.

Contractual liability

1.47 The concept of contract can be explained fairly simply. Practical matters are not always so straightforward and considerable modifications have had to be made to the concept of freedom of contract. Two major problems have to be addressed. In many cases, parties may contract on a very informal basis. To give a simple example, a person may enter a supermarket, place goods in a shopping trolley, proffer payment at the checkout and leave the premises with the goods all without a word being exchanged with any member of staff. There is no doubt that a valid contract has been entered into. Suppose, however, that included in the customer's purchases is a light bulb. On returning home and fitting the light bulb into an electric socket, the customer discovers that it does not work. What rights might the customer have? Nothing, after all, was explicitly agreed concerning the quality of the light bulb.

1.48 Under English law as it developed until the nineteenth century, the question would have been answered by reference to the doctrine still referred to by its Latin term *caveat emptor* (let the buyer beware). Legal analysis of the transaction would have proceeded along the lines that the customer bought a particular object; nothing was said concerning its condition and therefore nothing was to be assumed concerning its quality or fitness for purpose. Such a view now seems outlandish. In fairness to the early law makers it should be pointed out that the doctrine developed at a time when the comparatively few products which were offered for sale were simple in nature and susceptible to inspection and testing by the average customer. If a customer did not notice that the legs on a wooden table were uneven in length or were insecurely fashioned, it could well be argued that the fault lay at least as much with the buyer as the seller.

1.49 With modern products, which are frequently complex in nature and often sold pre-packed, such an approach is not realistic. Even were the buyer to possess the necessary technical skill, the reaction of an electrical retailer can readily be predicted were a customer to ask to disassemble a television set prior to deciding on a purchase!

1.50 The concept of the implied term has been developed to handle such situations and in terms of the contract for the sale of goods can be traced back to the nineteenth century, when the development of systems of mass production began to increase dramatically the range and complexity of goods available to the average person. Most readers will be familiar with the requirements of the Sale of Goods Act 1979 that goods should comply with any description attached to them, be of satisfactory (formerly known as merchantable) quality and reasonably fit for any particular purpose for which they are supplied. Seller and buyer need say nothing about these matters, the terms will be implied into their contract.

1.51 Implication may not itself prove sufficient. As a general rule, something which is implied will be overruled by a contrary express stipulation. If I buy a table and the seller expressly points out to me that it has only three legs and is incapable of standing upright, it would be absurd if I could subsequently complain that the table was not of satisfactory quality as it would not stand upright. With simple products and with clear disclaimers of this nature, there are few problems in accepting that the express term should overrule its implied counterpart. Difficulties arise, however, where there is an imbalance in bargaining power between parties so as to render the notion of freedom of contract a sham. Another simple example may illustrate the problem. A person may wish to travel by train. A ticket may be purchased at the station. This will include reference to the train operator's terms and conditions. This will almost certainly seek to exclude liability for any form of delay or discomfort encountered by the passenger.

1.52 There have been a considerable number of legal judgments concerned with what are referred to as 'ticket cases'. These revolve around the question whether the terms of the contract were brought to the notice of the customer prior to his deciding to enter into the transaction. In effect, what the judges were attempting in these cases was to apply the doctrine of freedom of contract in such a way as to maximise the opportunity for the customer to become aware of the conditions. What could not be taken into account was the very real possibility that the customer would have no option other than to accept the terms. Transport operators and many other commercial organisations go to considerable lengths to ensure that transactions can only be entered into on the basis of their standard terms and conditions. Even where competition exists between suppliers, it is likely that similar terms will be used. Anyone purchasing software will be all too familiar with the exclusion clauses which tend to appear in every software licence. The consumer's choice often lies between accepting the supplier's terms or doing without the goods or services sought.

1.53 What we see with the Sale of Goods Act – and a range of other statutes which will be discussed in the following chapters – is the legislature intervening so as to prescribe the conditions under which individuals and organisations should conduct their activities. In a rather more limited respect, there is also recognition that in some cases non-consumer parties can be in a weak position in their dealings with suppliers and again the law may intervene to protect the weaker party.

Privity of contract

1.54 For many years it has been a cornerstone of English law that only those persons who are party to a contract can rely upon its terms. In many respects, such a view is appropriate. Agreements are personal to the parties involved. In practice, the doctrine may produce results which appear at variance with general expectations. An obvious example concerns the sale of goods. A customer choosing to buy a new car will normally decide on a particular make and model. The vehicle will generally have to be acquired through a dealer. In many cases the identity of the dealer will be a matter of minor importance but when the transaction is assessed in legal terms, the customer's contract is with the dealer rather than the manufacturer. Customers complaining of a defect in a product are frequently told by retailers that the matter should be taken up with the manufacturer who has offered some form of guarantee. In legal terms, this advice is inaccurate. The customer's contract is with the retailer; responsibility for any breach lies with that party and the existence of a guarantee is a legal irrelevance.

1.55 In the example of a motor vehicle, there is likely to be a significant role for a dealer in preparing the vehicle for delivery and it might be argued that there is the opportunity for defects to be identified and cured. In many other situations, however, the dealer is a mere conduit for the supply of goods packaged by the manufacturer and opened by the customer.

1.56 Some change to the rigours of the doctrine of privity of contract (which is not a feature of Scots Law) have been introduced as a result of the Contracts (Rights of Third Parties) Act 1999. This provides that where the purpose of a contract is to benefit a third party, that party can take action to enforce it. At a simple level, the effect will be that if party A agrees with party B that (in return for payment by A) the latter will deliver a bunch of flowers to C, C will be entitled to take legal action against B in the event the flowers do not comply with the contractual requirements relating to quality.

The extent of liability

1.57 Great (or disastrous) events often have their origins in trivial incidents. A student, for example, might purchase a computer for the purpose of preparing course work. A failure of the computer might result in a deadline being missed, the student failing a class and being required to withdraw from the university, thereby losing the offer of a highly paid job which was conditional upon the obtaining of a degree. The sorry saga could go on and on. Whilst identifying the consequences of acts or omissions is often an interesting intellectual activity the law tends to adopt a more pragmatic and restrictive view.

1.58 Assuming that it can be shown that a breach of contract has occurred, that the computer was not of satisfactory quality, the supplier will be liable for losses which can be shown to have arisen directly in the normal course of events following the breakdown. Additionally, suppliers will be liable for any additional risks known to and accepted by them.

1.59 It will be a question of fact which losses fall into these categories. In the example hypothesised, the student will be entitled to compensation for the cost either of repairing the computer or, if this cannot reasonably be done, of obtaining a new model. It is unlikely that any additional compensation will be forthcoming. Even if the supplier (or more likely a employee of the supplier) were to be aware that the computer was being purchased for the preparation of course work, it is most unlikely that there would be any acceptance of such risks. A further refinement to the scenario might see a street-wise student informing the employee of the risks and securing some form of acceptance of risk. Such tactics will seldom work. In many cases suppliers will deal under standard terms and conditions which state explicitly that no member of staff is authorised to vary the terms in any way. Even if this is not the case, the actions of an employee will bind the employer only if the employee is in such a position of authority that it might reasonably be expected that there should be the power to negotiate on the employer's behalf. It might be reasonable, for example, for a store manager to offer some additional assurances but not for a part-time shop assistant.

Non-contractual liability

1.60 Many of the issues discussed above remain relevant in the non-contractual field. The underlying principle behind non-contractual liability was perhaps expressed by Lord Atkin in the celebrated case of *Donoghue v Stevenson* [1932] AC 562. The case provides an excellent illustration of some of many of the issues we have been discussing and may be described briefly.

1.61 Mrs Donoghue, accompanied by a friend, visited a café in the Scottish town of Paisley. Her friend, heedless of the hard-earned reputation of the citizens of Paisley for meanness, purchased a ginger beer for Mrs Donoghue. The drink was contained in a stone bottle. Some of the drink was poured into a glass and consumed. When the remainder was poured, the remains of a decomposing snail allegedly accompanied the ginger beer. The realisation of what she might have consumed made Mrs Donoghue ill, she consulted a solicitor and legal proceedings followed. The case proceeded from the Sheriff Court in Paisley through the Court of Session in Edinburgh before reaching the House of Lords. The reason why such a simple tale should have such profound and expensive legal consequences lay in the fact that Mrs Donoghue had not purchased the ginger beer. If she had, the action would have been straightforward and a claim could have been brought against the café owner with every prospect of success. In the absence of a contract, her claim required to be brought on a non-contractual basis. As has already been mentioned, in many cases a party bringing proceedings on a non-contractual basis will be required to establish negligence. In this case one might identify three parties who Mrs Donoghue might have sued; the friend who gave her the drink, the café owner or the manufacturer of the ginger beer. It is difficult to identify any fault on the part of the first two candidates and indeed the action was brought against the manufacturer, Stevenson.

1.62 Lakes of ink and forests of paper have been consumed in the course of legal discussion of *Donoghue v Stevenson*. This is because, until the House of Lords delivered its opinion (by a majority of 3-2), the view had been that a manufacturer owed no duty to the end-user of the product. Such a view might seem incredible today but until the 1930s it was reality. The speech of Lord Atkin laid down a new doctrine, often referred to as the 'neighbour principle'. He stated ([1932] AC 562 at 580):

> The rule that you are to love your neighbour becomes in law, you must not injure your neighbour; and the lawyer's question 'Who is my neighbour?' receives a restricted reply. You must take reasonable care to avoid acts or omissions which you can reasonably foresee would be likely to injure your neighbour. Who then in law is my neighbour? The answer seems to be – persons who are so closely and directly affected by my act that I ought reasonably to have had them in contemplation as being so affected when I am directing my mind to the acts or omissions which are called into question.

1.63 There is obviously an element of artificiality about this test. In most cases, the reason why an accident occurred is that a party did not give due thought to the possible consequences of an act. Mention might be made of the reference to liability for omissions. This is interpreted in a very restrictive fashion. In general, and unlike the position applying in countries such as France, a person is under no duty to offer help to his neighbour. Certainly, if a motorist sees a pedestrian crossing the road and omits to brake, liability may result. In this situation, the omission by the motorist has put the pedestrian in danger. Generally, however, if a person sees another in danger through no fault of his own – a passer-by seeing a child drowning in a shallow pond – an omission to offer help will not attract liability. The good neighbour is not to be equated with the Good Samaritan. Applying the test, Lord Atkin held that a manufacturer should foresee that carelessness in the manufacturing process might ultimately result in injury to a user of the product.

The concept of the reasonable man

1.64 The term 'reasonable' or 'reasonably' appears three times in the passage from Lord Atkin's judgment quoted above. Although there are a number of areas in non-contractual liability – most relevantly that relating to liability for copyright infringement and for defamation where liability arises independently of any fault, in most cases a party will escape liability if it can be shown that actions were reasonable in the circumstances. The test might also be expressed in terms of fault or negligence.

1.65 Determining whether a party has acted in a negligent manner requires that conduct be compared with that reasonably to be expected of a person in the same situation. In many instances reference is made to the concept of the reasonable or average man – the 'man on the Clapham omnibus'. This test will work quite adequately for everyday activities such as driving a car but requires to be modified for more specialised undertakings. If the question before a court, for example, is whether a surgeon is liable for the negligent conduct of an operation, it would not be helpful to consider what level of performance could have been expected from an ordinary person brought in from the street. In such cases, the appropriate standard must be that of the reasonable member of the profession. This may raise an issue in the IT sector. Whilst more established professions, such as medicine and law, have recognised professional bodies, membership of which is a prerequisite for working in the field, the same cannot be said of IT. Although it is normal for expert witnesses to disagree as to the level of conduct expected of a member of a profession, in most cases the area of disagreement is at the margins.

Disagreements between expert witnesses in IT cases often concern matters at the core of the dispute. In the case of *Missing Link Software v Magee,* a case concerned with alleged infringement of copyright, the expert witnesses' disagreements prompted the judge to comment of one report where the expert had indicated that he had attempted to express his views in as moderate a fashion as possible:

> In the course of eight or nine pages the following expressions may be found: 'effect of misleading the court in a major way'; 'fundamental errors'; 'conclusions which are at best fanciful and in my opinion not worthy of serious consideration'; 'no grounds whatsoever for the conclusions reached'; 'no person of reasonable common sense'; 'displays an inability to read a program'; 'cannot distinguish between'; 'this is a ridiculous inference to draw'; 'an error of which even a schoolboy would be ashamed'; 'attempting to mislead the court'; 'this is another absolutely basic error'; 'paragraph 17 and 18 are of course based on the same fundamental error'; 'sheer and utter nonsense' . . . One shudders to think what he might have said if he had really let himself go.

1.66 The absence of a consensus regarding even basic aspects of software development must render difficult the task of a judge in determining whether any aspect of the work might have been tainted by negligence. The sheer pace of technological development also creates substantial problems. To give a topical example, it would almost certainly constitute negligence today to supply a software system which is not 'year 2000 compliant'. It is very likely also that such a system would not be considered fit for its purpose. It was only in the final years of the twentieth century, however, that attention became focused on this problem and it may well be that no negligence could be ascribed to a party who supplied exactly the same system in 1996.

Product liability

1.67 In most instances, liability will only exist on a non-contractual basis where fault can be demonstrated. In a number of situations this rule is relaxed. Where a private individual (a consumer) is injured or has his property damaged by the operation of a product, the producer will be liable unless it can be demonstrated that the product was not defective. This doctrine was introduced into the UK in 1987 as result of the European Union's product liability directive. The rationale for the change was described as follows:

> Liability without fault on the part of the producer is the sole means of adequately solving the problem, peculiar to our age of increasing technicality, of a fair apportionment of the risks inherent in modern technological production.

The validity of this assertion appears beyond doubt. Many modern products are made up of components sourced from a variety of suppliers who may in turn buy components from other parties. A failure may well result in the destruction of the object. In such circumstances it would be verging on the impossible to identify which component failed and whether this was due to negligence on the part of a specific party. In many respects the product liability regime can be seen as requiring the producer of the final product to act almost as an insurer. The approach is justified on policy grounds rather than on any abstract notion of fairness.

1.68 The product liability system is a relatively new addition to UK law. Two other areas of considerable relevance to the information society have, over a period of centuries, operated on a similar no-fault basis are defamation and intellectual property law.

The extent of liability

1.69 In principle, damages may be claimed under the law of tort in respect of any form of damage. During the 1970s and early 1980s the distinction between contractual and tortuous liability appeared to be steadily eroded. In the case of *Junior Books v Veitchi* [1983] AC 520 at 545 Lord Roskill commented:

> I think today the proper control lies not in asking whether the proper remedy should lie in contract or instead in tort, not in somewhat capricious judicial determination whether a particular case falls on one side of the line or the other, not in somewhat artificial distinctions between physical or economic loss when the two sometimes go together and sometimes do not (it is sometimes overlooked that virtually all damage including physical damage is in one sense financial or economic for it is compensated by an award of damages) but in the first instance in establishing the relevant principles and then in deciding whether a particular case falls within or without those principles.

1.70 The effect of such an approach was at least to accept the possibility that damages might be awarded in tort in respect of defects which served to diminish the value of a product rather than requiring that the product cause injury damage to persons or property. More recently, however, the courts have retreated substantially from such a proposition. In the case of *CBS Songs Ltd v Amstrad Consumer Electronics plc* [1998] 2 WLR 1191 the House of Lords considered and rejected the proposition that the manufacturer of audio equipment, in this case a hi-fi unit with two cassette decks, owed a tortious duty of care to the owners of copyright in musical works whose interests, it was alleged, would be adversely affected in the event that users of the equipment used its facilities to make unauthorised copies of pre-recorded cassette tapes. Delivering the judgment of the court, Lord Templeman was critical of the approach in *Junior Books* and the earlier case of *Anns v Merton London Borough Council* [1978] AC 728, stating that since these decisions:

> . . . a fashionable plaintiff alleges negligence. The pleading assumes that we are all neighbours now, Pharisees and Samaritans alike, that foreseeability is a reflection of hindsight and that for every mischance in an accident-prone world someone solvent must be liable in damages.

1.71 In particular, the courts are today extremely reluctant to award compensation for economic loss. The concept of economic loss is not susceptible of easy or precise definition. It may consist of a sum representing the diminished value of a product which is considered to be defective or it may represent lost profits resulting from an inability to perform what would otherwise be a profitable activity. An example might be found in the case of a person who negligently cuts off a factory's electricity supply causing cessation of production. Certainly the party will be held liable for any form of physical damage which may be caused to the factory or its assets, but will not be held responsible for the lost profits which may result from the breakdown in production. Although the case of *Junior Books* remains as precedent for the proposition that economic loss might be compensated in the event that the relationship between the parties is akin to one based in contract, it must be questioned how far this approach will be followed in any future decisions.

1.72 In many instances the arguments that have persuaded the courts to backtrack from the award of damages for economic loss outside the contractual relationship will apply with particular force to information technology. Comparatively few products operate in the safety-critical field, most being concerned with more mundane tasks where the consequence of a failure will be some form of economic loss. Thousands of copies of such a product may be sold, they may be used in a large number of situations and their operation may result in exposure to a great variety of risks ranging from minor inconvenience to the substantial losses referred to in the example. In this and in many other situations it might be unreasonable to hold the producer liable. Another example cited from the United States may further evidence the point. In this, proceedings were initiated against the Lotus Corporation, alleging that a defect in its spreadsheet had resulted in a building contractor submitting a tender which was too low. The contract was awarded, only for the contractor to discover that the work could be carried out only at a loss.

1.73 This action was withdrawn before trial but the case provides some evidence of the range of situations in which a basic software product might be used and of the impossibility for the producer to anticipate the extent of potential losses. A final example might be cited from the author's own experience. Students on a postgraduate course were required to submit a sizeable number of items of assessment. The marks attained were entered into a spreadsheet program to calculate the final mark. Two different departments used two different makes of spreadsheet. When the figures were rounded up or down to the nearest whole number, the result in the case of one student was that there was a disagreement between the spreadsheets. One gave a pass mark of 50% and the other a fail at 49%. Analysis of the possible legal consequences of such a result might occupy most of this book. Could either of the spreadsheets be considered wrong? Should the users have been aware of this possibility? Should all marks be double-checked? Assuming the student was denied a degree because of an incorrect output, would any form of compensation be available? Fortunately for the student, and unfortunately for the legal profession, this incident ended with the higher mark being selected.

Vicarious liability

1.74 In all of the situations discussed above, a party has been held liable for the consequences of his or her own actions. The doctrine of vicarious liability provides that in certain cases a third party may be held liable for such wrongful actions. The classic illustration of this principle is seen in the employment relationship. Here an employer will be held liable for acts of an employee conducted in the course of employment. There are often sound practical reasons why an injured party may wish to bring action against the employer rather than the employee responsible, not least in that the employer is likely to have more resources than the employee. The principle of seeking to take action against the party with the deepest pockets is seen in other areas of activity, and special reference will be made in subsequent chapters to the extent to which Internet service providers might incur liability in respect of material posted on or transmitted through their services by a third party. The two areas of law where this is of particular relevance are copyright and defamation.

Conclusion

1.75 Almost every action will have some legal consequences. Although there are occasions when it is difficult to identify the nature and extent of these, the major legal pitfall tends to lie in a failure to give consideration to legal matters before an incident occurs. Numerous cases have been brought under the law of contract in situations where parties have contracted for the development of software. The prime reason why the parties have ended up in court has been that insufficient thought was given to what each party was due to contribute to the development process. Typically, the supplier may argue that the customer was provided with what was asked for, with the counterclaim being that what was supplied was not what the buyer needed. Where the contract is either silent or ambiguous on these matters, the end result may be a judicial interpretation which satisfies neither party. In the law, as with much of life, a little preparation can save a great deal of time, expense and pain.

Chapter 2

The emergence of the information society

A short history of cyberspace

2.0 The space race has been identified as a catalyst for the development of personal computers, the argument being that the United States required to minimise the size and weight of onboard computers in order to compensate for the greater power of Soviet rockets. The connection between the space race and the Internet is less well known but is likely to prove of greater long-term significance.

2.1 The first artificial satellite, Sputnik, was launched in 1957 to great consternation in the US defence establishment. As part of its response, the Advanced Research Projects Agency (ARPA) was established under the auspices of the Department of Defense with a remit of establishing US leadership in areas of science and technology which might possess military applications.

2.2 The concept of a decentralised network had been considered in a number of countries, including the UK, but it was with the provision of substantial funding from ARPA in 1964 that a practical implementation was developed. The project was based upon ideas drawn up by Paul Baran of the RAND Corporation, an organisation described as 'America's foremost Cold War think-tank'. Its genesis lay in the desire to find a method of enabling the US military and government to maintain communications after a nuclear war. The assumption was that telecommunication control centres would be a prime target for attack and that traditional telecommunications networks would be rendered unusable. The solution lay in reversing the conception that a telecommunications network should seek to be as reliable as possible by building in the assumption of unreliability. From this start point, the system should be designed in such a way as to enable messages to overcome obstacles. The system would link a number of computers or 'nodes'. Every message would be divided up into a number of segments called 'packets'. Each packet would be labelled with its intended destination and with information as to its position in the message as a whole. The packets would be sent on their way and would pass from node to node until they all arrived at the intended destination where they would be reassembled to indicate the complete message. Although packets would be forwarded in approximately the correct direction, the particular route taken by a packet would be dependent upon chance and network availability. If one section of the network had been damaged, the packets would be routed via other sections. A helpful illustration might be to analogise the system with the road network of the UK. The motorway network might be compared with a telecommunications network. It provides high capacity and (the M25 possibly excepted) high speed transport links. Disruption at a few key locations – by nuclear attack or less dramatic incidents – would render the system unusable. The Internet might be compared with the non-motorway road network. Travel may be slower and more circuitous but the sheer variety of routes would make total disruption of service a most unlikely event.

2.3 The initial network, which was named after its sponsors, was installed in 1969 with four nodes or points of connection. By 1972 this figure had grown to 37. One of the next major developments was the development of the communication standard TCP/IP (Transmission Control Protocol/Internet Protocol). The TCP component is responsible for converting messages into streams of packets whilst the IP is responsible for addressing and routing the packets to their intended destination. The TCP/IP protocols were developed in the 1970s but it was with their adoption as the basis for ARPANET on 1 January 1983 that the Internet could be said to have originated.

2.4 A feature of the TCP/IP protocols is that they enable any user to connect to the Internet. There are no social or political controls over the making of such a connection and the cost implications are minimal. It is somewhat ironic that a system which was designed to enable the authorities to retain control over a nuclear wasteland should have metamorphosed into a system which is almost a byword for anarchy. From their introduction the rate of growth in the Internet has proceeded apace.

2.5 Although the size and usage of the Internet grew very significantly in the 1970s and 1980s it remained predominantly a tool for the academic community. Although effective as a mechanism for transferring large amounts of data, its use, in common with most computers of the time, required a considerable degree of technical competence. In the early 1990s more user-friendly navigational tools were introduced in the form of Archie, Gopher and Veronica. In 1991 for the first time the National Science Foundation (NSF), which funded the Internet infrastructure in the United States, relaxed its ban on commercial applications. The most significant technical innovation was undoubtedly the introduction of the World Wide Web (WWW) in 1992. Developed by Tim Berners-Lee, a physicist at the nuclear physics research centre, CERN, the WWW uses the system known as hypertext to create links between documents. A user need only 'click' on a marked link to move to the other document. The addition of browsers, such as Mosaic, Netscape Navigator and Microsoft Explorer, served to complete the transformation of the Internet from a text-based network of elusive resources to what has been described as 'a multimedia tapestry of full-color information'.

2.6 Taking figures as of mid-1999, there are estimated to be some 43 million Internet sites in the world and 3 million WWW sites. 170 million persons in more than 200 countries are estimated to have access to the Internet and WWW. Although the rate of development of the Internet (90% compound growth during the period 1990-97) and the raw statistics seem impressive, we remain a long way from the global network that is sometimes depicted. 170 million users represent less than 4% of the world's population. The Internet remains very much a North American-centred phenomenon. There are more Internet hosts in New York than in the whole of Africa. The US, Canada and Europe are responsible for more than 88% of Internet hosts. More than 80% of WWW sites are in English. In 1995 more than 50% of commercial telephone traffic in the US was made up by communications between computers. In 1996 more messages were carried in America by e-mail than by US Mail. In the UK it has been estimated that some 18% of local telephone traffic is made up of connections to the Internet. The fact that local telephone calls are typically free in the US is one factor which undoubtedly influences the difference in rate of usage between the two countries.

2.7 For users in the developed world, the Internet is becoming a feature of our everyday lives. It is rare to find a newspaper which does not contain some feature on the Internet. Most newspapers and many television and radio programmes maintain an electronic presence on the Internet. Many advertisements and publicity documents refer readers to an Internet site for further information.

2.8 The Internet and the WWW are but one manifestation of a radical change in the nature of society which has been brought about by the computer. It is now trite comment to say that we live in an information society. The questions arise: what is the nature of this beast? and how should it be regulated?

Regulation of communications

2.9 The existence of the Internet is having profound changes on all aspects of society and has also changed dramatically the nature of the computer revolution. A report produced to mark the completion of the ARPANET commented that:

> the promise offered by the computer as a communications medium between people, dwarfs into relative insignificance the historical beginnings of the computer as an arithmetic engine.

2.10 The seemingly remorseless advance of the Internet (and the WWW) is challenging many existing models of society and forms of regulation. Traditionally, all forms of communication have been subject to some form of official control. Often the initial response has been to attempt to operate a strict system of licensing. When the printing press was first introduced, for example, in the sixteenth century the initial reaction of the English authorities was to require that those operating a press should be licensed. Licensing extended even to each individual document printed. The controls over the printed word have been weakened very significantly in the intervening centuries and, although legal actions may be brought in respect of the contents of publications, there is no requirement to seek authorisation in advance of publication.

2.11 As other forms of recording and communication technologies have developed systems of licensing have tended to follow within a short period of time. Radio, television and cinematographic films are all subject to statutory controls. As well as seeking to regulate content, a prime purpose of licensing has been to ration access to and use of scarce resources. In the days of analogue broadcasts emanating from terrestrial transmitters, limitations on the range of frequencies available justified the operation of a strict system of licensing of operators. As developments in broadcasting technology have occurred, the rationing rationale has been steadily eroded. Another factor which is increasingly relevant has been the growth in satellite broadcasting. With terrestrial systems, broadcasts can generally be confined broadly within national boundaries. Although there will always be an overlap in border regions, the range of transmitters is generally limited. Although international agreements exercise some control, satellite broadcasts pay little regard to national boundaries. What is occurring is a shift from nationally based broadcasting systems to global operations with limited prospect of national regulatory controls proving effective. In a number of cases the UK authorities have attempted to prevent satellite broadcasts containing hard core pornography. One well-publicised case concerned the satellite channel 'Red Hot Dutch'. Here an order was made under the provisions of the Broadcasting Act 1990 which had the effect of prohibiting the supply of the decoders necessary to receive the offending signals. Enforcement problems are compounded by the fact that in many respects the UK's legal controls are more restrictive than those applied in other states, including some which are members of the European Community. Where material would be lawful in its country of origin, it is difficult to see how effective enforcement might be undertaken against its producer or disseminator.

2.12 Similar regulatory tendencies can be identified within the telecommunications sector. The origins of the modern telecommunications networks can be seen in the establishment of the telegraph system, principally in the second half of the nineteenth century. In the US the operation of the telegraph system remained the province of the private sector. In most European states, however, state control was exercised from the beginning. In the UK, although services were initially provided by private companies, the Telegraph Acts of 1868 and 1870 provided for the nationalisation of the telegraph system. The rationale behind the move lay not in any form of ideological belief but rather in the recognition that the telegraph was acquiring a status similar to that of the mail system. Here the famous 'Penny Black' stamp provided assurance to inhabitants of any part of the Great Britain that letters could be sent to any other part for a standard fee. The provision of such universal service was seen as requiring legal protection against competitors who might target their business on lucrative areas, for example, mail within and between large conurbations and therefore be able to undercut standard rates. The approach adopted in respect of the mail and telegraph systems was to provide that the Postmaster General – the government minister responsible for communications – would possess a monopoly right to provide postal and telegraph services together with the obligation to provide these throughout the country at uniform charges.

2.13 A somewhat different pattern applied for the development of the telephone network. Here the government was involved from the early stages in providing funding for the development of a national network. Its role was, however, seen as being the provision of the connecting lines between towns and cities whilst the provision of services within these areas would be licensed to local authorities or private companies. As a historical anomaly, such a situation remains in the area of Kingston upon Hull. This situation came to an end with the Telephone Transfer Act 1911, which gave the Postmaster General the power to acquire private systems. Until 1969, public telephone services were provided as a state monopoly under the auspices of the General Post Office.

2.14 The liberalisation process can be seen as having started in 1969, with the grant of a measure of independence to the GPO with a change in status from government department to statutory corporation. It was to be the 1980s, however, with the election of a Conservative government committed to a process of denationalisation or privatisation that significant changes were to come about. OFTEL maintains a good chronological history of recent developments. The GPO was divided into separate postal and telecommunications divisions, with British Telecom being established to provide telecommunications services under licence. A licence was also issued to Mercury Communications (now part of the Cable and Wireless company) to establish a competing network. It was announced in 1983 that no further licences would be issued to long-distance fixed-link operators for a period of seven years. The move, therefore, was one from monopoly to duopoly, although it was recognised that the emerging market in mobile communications would provide alternatives to traditional fixed link operations.

2.15 The enactment of the Telecommunications Act 1984 is the major landmark in recent telecommunications history. Its long title proclaims it as a measure to:

> provide for the appointment and functions of a Director General of Telecommunications; to abolish British Telecommunications' exclusive privilege with respect to telecommunications and to make new provision with respect to the provision of telecommunication services and certain related services; to make provision, in substitution for the Telegraph Acts 1863 to 1916 and Part IV of the Post Office Act 1969, for the matters there dealt with and related matters; to provide for the vesting of property, rights and liabilities of British Telecommunications in a company nominated by the Secretary of State and the subsequent dissolution of British Telecommunications; to make provision with respect to the finances of that company; to amend the Wireless Telegraphy Acts 1949 to 1967, to make further provision for facilitating enforcement of those Acts and otherwise to make provision with respect to wireless telegraphy apparatus and certain related apparatus; to give statutory authority for the payment out of money provided by Parliament of expenses incurred by the Secretary of State in providing a radio interference service; to increase the maximum number of members of British Telecommunications pending its dissolution; and for connected purposes.

2.16 Three main tasks can be identified. First, the Act provided for the transfer of British Telecom from the public to the private sector by means of the sale of 51% of its shares. Further share sales took place in 1991 and 1993. Second, the Act established the Office of Telecommunications to supervise the activities of players in the telecommunications sector. Third, the Act laid down the principle that it is unlawful to operate in the telecommunications sector except where an appropriate licence has been awarded. The scope of the licensing regime is such that even domestic users requires a licence in respect of their telephone equipment and connection to a public telecommunications network.

2.17 Licences fall into two categories, individual and class. Individual licences are awarded by the Secretary of State on the recommendation of the Director General of Telecommunications. Other than large scale operators, most parties operate under a class licence. No application need be made for such a licence, the requirement being only that parties conduct their activities within the scope of the relevant licence.

2.18 Although the licensing requirement remains, even where individual licences are required, there is a strong presumption in favour of grant. From a condition in the 1970s when one telephone operator held a monopoly, Oftel reported in 1999 that:

> The UK now has over 200 licensed operators which include 5 national carriers, 4 mobile operators and over 60 companies licensed to operate international facilities.

2.19 We have therefore varying control regimes over all forms of technology. An initial question concerns the location of the Internet within the various regulatory regimes. As users of the system will be aware, the Internet crosses many traditional boundaries. It can be used to publish text and visual materials. Many radio programmes can be listened to over the Internet and as bandwidth constraints lessen, a similar trend can be seen with television broadcasts. With the use of software packages such as MP3, the Internet is being used for the dissemination of audio works to the extent that some involved in the music industry have predicted the demise of CDs and high street record stores. The Internet is also being used increasingly as a channel for voice telephony. The nature of its structure means that calls to anywhere in the world will be charged on the same basis as local telephone calls. Although the quality of performance may still be a little inferior to that attainable using traditional telephone networks, the gap is closing whilst cost savings are very substantial.

2.20 For the first time, there now exists a global communications network which is in large measure outwith the control of national authorities and certainly does not fit into many existing regulatory schema. Whilst it is emphatically not the case that Internet-based activities are not subject to legal regulation, it is equally clear that no single state can exert control over the Internet as a whole. Although some states make considerable efforts to control Internet access and use, it is unclear also how effective such controls can be. That said, a considerable number of agencies can be identified as playing significant roles in determining the destiny of the Internet. The nature and legal status of these will be considered in the next chapter. What may be said at this stage is that the Internet is at an important stage in its organisational history. From its beginnings as an adjunct to US defence policy, it has expanded into the academic sphere and, increasingly, into the commercial world. Differing demands and expectations of users means that the notion of a set of shared and common values is no longer applicable. From a situation where all network nodes were located in the US, its tentacles have spread to the furthest corners of the world. Control mechanisms developed in an era of US hegemony may not be appropriate for application in other political and social cultures. It has been said (Bruce Sterling *A Brief History of The Internet*) that:

> In principle, any node can speak as a peer to any other node, as long as it obeys the rules of the TCP/IP protocols, which are strictly technical, not social or political.

2.21 The history of the Internet may suggest that predictions are dangerous but the Internet's move into the mainstream of world affairs makes social and political, economic and legal factors of nearly as much importance as the original technical specifications. The first telegraph message transmitted by Marconi across the Atlantic Ocean consisted of the text 'What hath God wrought?' The task of answering this question has occupied law makers ever since. The same will surely also apply to the Internet.

Regulation of the Internet

2.22 Depending on the perspective of the commentator, for most of its existence, the Internet could be described either as being governed on the basis of consensus amongst Internet users or directed by an unelected self-perpetuating clique. Regulatory structures have tended to evolve rather than being developed in any structured manner and a baffling range of organisations and acronyms need to be confronted in any attempt to understand the manner in which the Internet is controlled.

IP numbers and domain names

2.23   The TCP/IP protocols referred to above enable any user to connect to the Internet which operates in large part over the normal telecommunications network. There are no social or political controls over the making of such a connection and the cost implications are minimal. All computers linked to the Internet are allocated a unique identifier known as an IP number. At present these are 32 binary digits in length (normally in the region of eight or nine decimal numbers). Just as Oftel needed to insert an extra '1' into all UK telephone numbers in 1994 in order to secure what appears to be temporary relief from a shortage of available numbers, so the exponential rate of growth in Internet usage has led to the introduction of a new numbering system known as IP Next Generation (IPng). An increase in number length to 128 bit numbers is calculated to provide capacity for some 340 billion, billion, billion, billion computers. Even at the Internet's current rate of expansion, this should be sufficient for the foreseeable future!

2.24   The issuance of IP numbers is a relatively non-problematic task. As with phone numbers, although some combinations might be more memorable than others, this is a matter of limited importance. As the number of users increased, so pressure grew for a more memorable means of identification. In 1987 the system of domain names came into effect.

2.25   Two initial categories of domain name can be identified – generic and country code. There are currently three generic domain names:

- .com

- .net

- .org

These names carry no indication of country of origin. Although it is sometimes assumed that the names 'belong' to the US, this is not the case and many companies operating on an international basis see value in possessing a non-country specific identifier. British Airways, for example, have a web site at *http:/www.britishairways.com/*. Following prolonged and contentious discussions (described in more detail below) it is anticipated that the number of generic domain names will be expanded with discussion focusing on seven new categories:

- .firm for businesses, or firms;

- .shop for businesses offering goods to purchase;

- .web for entities emphasising activities related to the World Wide Web;

- .arts for entities emphasising cultural and entertainment activities;

- .rec for entities emphasising recreation/entertainment activities;

- .info for entities providing information services;

- .nom for those wishing individual or personal nomenclature, ie a personal nom de plume.

2.26 There exist also what are referred to as country code domain names. Based on ISO standard 3166, these consist of a two-letter denominator for every country in the world. The UK, for example, is referred to as .uk, France as .fr and Germany as .de. One country domain name with an interesting tale is that of Tuvalu. Tuvalu is a collection of nine small coral atolls in the Pacific ocean close to Fiji. It is classed as a 'Least Developed Country' with a population of around 10,000 and GDP of $11m. Its only export is copra. It has one computer connected to the Internet. It also 'possesses' the ISO code TV and in 1998 entered into a deal worth $50m with a Canadian company to licensing rights to the domain .tv. The company planned to sell domain names to television companies wishing to establish a web presence. Sadly for the Tuvaluans, the deal fell through when the company failed to make payments but it is hoped that it will enter into a similar agreement with another company. Another location which has proved a popular 'home' for web sites is Tonga, whose ISO code is .to.

2.27 In most countries, there is a further indicator of the nature of the business. In the UK domain names may be registered in the following categories:

Name	*Intended usage*
ac.uk	Academic
co.uk	Commercial
gov.uk	Governmental
ltd.uk	Limited liability companies
mod.uk	Ministry of Defence
net.uk	Internet networks

nhs.uk	National Health Service
plc.uk	Public limited companies
police.uk	Police
sch.uk	Schools

It should be emphasised that it is the system of IP numbers which is vital to the operation of the Internet. Typing an address such as *http://itlaw.strath.ac.uk* in a web browser initiates a process of trying to match the name with the appropriate IP number insert number. Initially, the attempt will be made by the Internet service provider's own equipment. If it fails to make a match, the query will be passed on to more comprehensive name servers, a process know as domain name resolution. The definitive tables of names and numbers are maintained on what are referred to as root servers. There are 13 of these machines. Ten are located in the US, with the remaining three in England, Japan and Sweden. The key root server is maintained by Network Solutions, with the other servers downloading information about new domains from this server on a daily basis. Although very many Internet service providers will maintain their own domain name server, the information on this will invariably have been copied, perhaps with a delay of a few days, from the root servers. In order to be accessible to the Internet world, therefore, it is imperative that a user be issued with an IP number and that the registered name and domain be accepted by the Network Solutions root server.

Administration of domain names

REGULATORY AGENCIES

2.28 The allocation of IP numbers was initially administered by an organisation, the Internet Assigned Numbers Authority, which is part of the Information Science Institute within the University of Southern California. Its web page proclaims that it is 'Dedicated to preserving the central co-ordinating functions of the global Internet for the public good'.

2.29 Initially, IANA also allocated domain names, but from 1993, although it has continued to play what has been described as a co-ordinating role, the task has been conducted by a range of domain name registries. In respect of most of the generic domain names, the United States National Science Foundation, which sponsored much of the pioneering development work on the Internet, entered into a five-year contract with a commercial organisation, Network Solutions Inc, for the management of most of the generic domains.

2.30 The operation of the system of domain names, and in particular the activities of Network Solutions Inc, has been the source of much controversy and some litigation in recent years. As indicated above, although we are all used to domain names such as strath.ac.uk, there is no technical reason why this is required, the name being merely an alias for the critical IP number. Some organisations have sought to set up alternative domain structures. One such company is Name.Space, which offers no fewer than 517 top level domains, including such delights as .beer and .president. The main problem that the company has faced has been the refusal of the keepers of the Internet root servers to include details of its users on their machines. Effectively, this limits significantly the range of persons with whom their users can communicate.

2.31 Faced with this refusal to include its details, a lawsuit was raised: *PGMedia, Inc D/B/A Name.Space v Network Solutions Inc and the National Science Foundation*. The basis for the complaint was that the defendants were in breach of US anti-trust law and, by preventing the plaintiff and its customers using such names as they wished, were in violation of the US Constitutions guarantee of free speech. The claims were dismissed by the US District Court in March 1999 and a subsequent appeal was also rejected.

2.32 Although the District Court upheld the role of Network Solutions and the NSF, changes have been occurring from other directions. Concern at the working of the system of Internet domain names had been arising, not least prompted by the limited number of domains creating scarcity of what were perceived as suitable domain names. To give an example, the domain name ABA.COM is registered to the American Bankers Association, ABA.ORG to the America Birding Association and ABA.NET to a company, Ansaback, which provides E-mail auto-respond services. All appear bona fide organisations, but there is no room left for the perhaps better known (at least to lawyers) American Bar Association, whose WWW site has to use the less intuitive domain name ABANET.NET. In order to address the future of the domain name system, the Internet Ad Hoc Committee was established by a number of agencies (see para 2.34 below).

NATIONAL DOMAIN NAMES

2.33 The situation with regard to the national domains is rather more complex, with a mix of public and private sector organisations playing the role of domain name registry. In the UK this role is played by a non-profit making company, Nominet. As with much of the Internet, the legal basis for its actions is unclear, it being stated that:

Nominet UK derives its authority from the Internet industry in the UK and is recognised as the UK registry by the Internet Assigned Numbers Authority (IANA) in the USA.

REFORM OF THE DOMAIN NAME SYSTEM

2.34 Following widely expressed concern at the manner in which the system of Internet domain names was being administered, especially in respect of the generic .com sector, the Internet International Ad Hoc Committee (IAHC) was established in 1996 'at the initiative of the Internet Society, and at the request of the Internet Assigned Numbers Authority' jointly by a number of organisations concerned with the development and administration of the Internet, with the remit to:

> resolve a difficult and long-standing set of challenges in the Domain Name System, namely enhancing its use while attempting to juggle such concerns as administrative fairness, operational robustness and protection of intellectual property.

2.35 The IAHC recommended that administration of the .com domain should be removed from the sole control of Network Solutions and made available to a number of competing registries. It recommended also, as described above, an expansion in the number of generic domains. At the conclusion of its work, the IAHC put forward for signature by the various interest groups a Generic Top Level Domain Memorandum of Understanding. This initiative was criticised, particularly in the US, where the Department of Commerce instituted its own consultation exercise within the Internet community. Following this, discussions (and disagreements) ensued between the US and the European Union, which expressed concern at what it perceived as an attempt by the US to maintain its dominant position in Internet matters. Eventually, agreement was reached that yet another new body, the Internet Corporation for Assigned Names and Numbers (ICANN), would be established in October 1998. It is described as:

> a non-profit, private sector corporation formed by a broad coalition of the Internet's business, technical, and academic communities. ICANN has been designated by the U.S. Government to serve as the global consensus entity to which the U.S. government is transferring the responsibility for coordinating four key functions for the Internet: the management of the domain name system, the allocation of IP address space, the assignment of protocol parameters, and the management of the root server system.

Effectively, ICANN has taken over the role of IANA and also removes the monopoly of Network Solutions. Whilst the first part of the process was carried out smoothly, negotiations with Network Solutions were more difficult, with legal action being threatened by Network Solutions on more than one occasion. Agreement was eventually reached in November 1999 and at the time of writing, 14 organisations were accredited to act as registries for the .com domain.

Conclusion

2.36 A number of features of the Internet might be identified as critical to the discussion of legal issues which will take place in the remainder of this book. First, perhaps, is the factor that a number of computers may be linked together in a network. This is not, of course, something which is unique to the Internet, which is merely the largest. Networking can achieve at least two significant results. First, the combination of the processing power of a large number of computers can turn a network of relatively low power personal computers into a rival to the largest 'super computer'. An excellent example can be seen in the field of encryption, where a test message encrypted using the US official encryption standard, DES, was decoded through the efforts of a network of personal computers connected over the Internet and running a decryption package during the night whilst their normal users slept. A second effect is very notable in the field of data protection. Where networks operate, the physical location of data becomes virtually irrelevant. It is no longer necessary for users to hold data on their own computers, so long as there is the assurance that it can be accessed when needed. The consequence is that it will become virtually impossible for individuals to discover what data a particular user may be in a position to use in matters concerning them. Subject access – one of the cornerstones of data protection legislation – may be rendered largely irrelevant.

2.37 It is not just individuals who face challenges because of the emergence of computer networks. Another term which will be used throughout this book might send a chill down the collective spines of national governments. The phenomenon of 'globalisation' challenges the continued effectiveness of national boundaries. Although some countries such as China are attempting to control the range of information which its citizens may access over the Internet, developments in communications technology, such as the use of mobile telephones as the means for Internet access may make attempts at censorship impracticable within the short- to medium-term future. The English poet John Donne wrote, famously, that 'no man is an island'. In today's world, the concept of an island state has a bleak future. We live in a global society and global solutions have to be found to global problems. The task will not be easy. Many of the headline issues – pornography, privacy, intellectual property, freedom of speech – involve matters of considerable social, political and religious significance.

2.38   Finally, and at the heart of this work, we inhabit, or are at least moving towards, an information society. For most of the developed world, the services sector overtook manufacturing as a major contributor towards gross national product some time ago. We are moving to a situation where information, rather than physical property will become the major measure of wealth and power. In many respects, traditional legal principles are ill equipped to deal with the new world. The bulk of the law has been concerned with allocating rights in respect of physical or tangible property. In this respect it has developed concepts of exclusive rights associated with ownership of property. Whilst the system of intellectual property law demonstrates that these can also be applied in an information context, the structures are creaking. When a car or a domestic appliance breaks down, its owner is faced with the choice whether to seek to have it repaired or to replace it with a new model. A similar dilemma faces today's law makers. In a number of significant areas, the introduction of information technology is exposing limitations in existing legal provisions. The question whether the response should involve repair or replacement is of critical importance.

Chapter 3

Privacy in the information society

Privacy and surveillance

3.0 Privacy is an elusive concept. It is a condition which is almost universally valued but once the attempt is made to turn debate from the most general and abstract level, discussion inevitably becomes lost in a quagmire of competing claims and expectations and differing social and cultural experiences.

3.1 At the general level the best accepted definition of privacy is that it consists of the right to be left alone. Put in terms perhaps more appropriate for the information society, this might be classed as the right not to be subject to surveillance. Surveillance can take a variety of forms. Physical surveillance is as old-established as society. At an official level it might involve placing individuals suspected or criminal conduct under surveillance, whilst at the private level reference can be made to the nosy neighbour looking at life through the corner of a set of lace curtains.

3.2 In some instances the success of surveillance may depend on its existence being unknown to its target. In other cases the fact that conduct may be watched is itself used as an instrument for social control. As George Orwell wrote in his novel *1984*:

> There was of course no way of knowing whether you were being watched at any given moment. How often, on what system, the Thought Police plugged in on any individual wire was guesswork. It was even conceivable that they watched everyone all the time. But at any rate they could plug in your wire whenever they wanted to. You had to live – did live, from habit that became instinct – in the assumption that every sound you made was overheard and, except in darkness, every movement scrutinised.

The development of infra-red camera technology might render George Orwell's vision almost too optimistic.

The automation of surveillance

3.3 Although some use was made of technology in George Orwell's work, spies and informers played a much greater role in the constitution of the surveillance society. Increasingly, technical devices are used to monitor every aspect of our lives. The numbers we call from our phones are recorded to produce itemised bills. Signals from mobile phones can be used to track the movements of individuals around the country. Every time money is withdrawn from a cash machine or a payment is made by credit card, information is recorded concerning the time, location and nature of the transaction. Increasing numbers of closed circuit television monitor movement in the streets, whilst countless thousands of cameras are operated by commercial operators to monitor our movements in shops and offices and car parks. 'Intelligent' cameras allow images of individuals to be compared with a database of suspected persons. A system is being tested in Newham in London where it has been reported that images from 150 cameras are compared:

> with a database of known criminals stored on computer at the council's headquarters. Information is then passed to police.
> The makers say the system is sophisticated enough to take into account light conditions, whether the suspect is wearing glasses, makeup or earrings, the expression and even the ageing process.
> Growing a beard or trying some other disguise will apparently not fool the camera because it can see through it.
> If the system, known as Mandrake, recognises a crook, it sounds the alarm and displays a code number. A council operator, who never knows the identity of the suspect, then phones police, who have their own screens.
> (*Daily Mail*, 15 October 1998)

Images of around 60–100 convicted criminals are maintained on the system which claims an accuracy rate of around 75%. The downside, of course, is that 25% of those targeted will be innocent of any offence but will become the object of suspicions.

3.4 Surveillance devices in the workplace allow employers to monitor the activities and efficiency of individuals. Most word processing packages maintain records of the time spent working on particular documents. Even the Internet and WWW, which are often touted as the last refuge of individualism, might equally accurately be described as a surveillance system *par excellence*. E-mail messages may be copied many times in the course of transmission and remain on a variety of servers. An individual browsing the Web leaves electronic trails wherever he or she passes. A software program known as a 'cookie' may be transmitted from a website to the user's computer and remain there until the site is next accessed, at which time details of the user and previous visits to the site will automatically be transmitted. Many readers may participate in Internet newsgroup discussions. Although messages will disappear from most sites after a few days, systems such as DejaNews archive copies of all postings and provide the facility for users to search postings by reference to criteria including the name of the poster. It is, therefore, a comparatively simple matter to obtain a complete list of all messages written by a particular individual. This information might have attractions for direct marketeers, prospective employers and even, given the nature and content of some newsgroups, potential blackmailers.

3.5 The list could go on and on. With almost all of these examples the point may fairly be made that application of technology is seen as desirable by a majority of the population. Television cameras are perceived as reducing crime, itemised phone bills allow customers to monitor usage of their equipment, whilst systems of 'caller id' deter the making of hoax or harassing calls. In the case of shopping, millions of consumers have applied to participate in 'loyalty schemes', thereby volunteering to supply store owners with extensive and individualised information about the nature of their spending patterns. An excellent illustration of the commercial value of personal data can be seen from schemes operating in the US whereby consumers can apply for a free computer. The machine may be free but the price paid is in terms of the personal information which is required to be supplied to the scheme's promoters. The information can be sold on to other commercial undertakings and is also used to set up the computers in such a way that whenever users access the Internet they are presented with adverts from a range of companies whose products or services, analysis of the data supplied suggests, are likely to prove attractive to consumers. Typically the value of the computers supplied will be in the region of £600, a figure which gives a good indication of the value personal data has acquired as a commodity.

Threats arising from the processing of personal data

3.6 Whilst some data such as medical records may be considered intrinsically sensitive, many items of data are relatively mundane. Two factors may give rise to concern. First, whilst individual items of data may be non-threatening, the combination of items may change the picture. As was suggested in a leading English case (*Marcel v Metropolitan Police Commissioner* [1992] Ch 225):

> ... if the information obtained by the police, the Inland Revenue, the social
> security offices, the health service and other agencies were to be gathered
> together in one file, the freedom of the individual would be gravely at risk.
> The dossier of private information is the badge of the totalitarian state.

3.7 In the early stages of computerisation the fear was sometimes expressed that a single large computer might hold all information about an individual. The proliferation of computers and the development of the Internet and WWW puts extensive communications capabilities into the hands of everyone. The notion of a single all-powerful computer is no longer relevant, but the ease with which data may be transferred from one computer network to another, a phenomenon epitomised in the Internet, is serving to break down boundaries between systems. Techniques such as data mining strive to extract the last ounce of value from raw data, whilst the practice of data matching enables linkages to be made between the contents of what were previously discrete data banks. Once again, the notion of convergence becomes apparent. It has been reported that the Greater Manchester Police makes use of credit reference agencies in order to identify the addresses of individuals. This source, it is claimed, is more current and detailed than the Police National Computer. Information held by credit reference agencies has also been accessed by insurance companies in determining whether to accept applications for motor vehicle insurance. Again, much of the administration of the tax system has been contracted out to private sector organisations.

3.8 In many respects the fact that information is collected about our actions and movements raises no new issues. It was perhaps only in the 1960s and 1970s that a number of factors combined to bring about a major increase in individual privacy. A growth in social mobility saw millions move away from close-knit communities, whether rural or urban, to more anonymous housing schemes, whilst the shift from public to private transport associated with expanding numbers of motor cars allowed individuals to make journeys without the need to interact with railway booking clerks, bus and train conductors and tens or hundreds of other passengers. Additionally, supermarkets started to replace the corner shop, whose owner possessed an encyclopaedic knowledge of her customers and their shopping preferences. It is a common complaint in modern society that the right to be let alone takes on almost a negative meaning, with an individual's suffering going unnoticed.

3.9 Every action that we take tells something about ourselves. The books we read, the journeys we made, the food and drink we consume all tell something of our opinions and lifestyles. In the past, our actions would have been known to a number of individuals. Life, however, has tended to be lived in a series of compartments. Again, 'knowledge' might be distinguished from 'recorded information'. Knowledge is essentially a human quality. It tends to comprise an amalgam of facts and opinions. In previous times an individual seeking a bank loan might approach the fearsome figure of the bank manager. Following an interview and scrutiny of the state of the customer's finances, a decision would be made whether to advance credit. Today, systems of credit scoring increasingly take elements of human interpretation out of the decision whether to grant credit. An applicant is asked to complete a form giving various items of information – address, marital status, employment history etc, etc. Point values are associated with each item, based upon an assessment of their relevance to the statistical likelihood that a debtor will default on an agreement, and the decision made on the basis of the risk that a particular creditor is willing to accept. Nothing need be known about the individual applicant. In that respect the technique can be seen as safeguarding individual privacy but in a further example of how confused and confusing the debate about privacy has become, the European Data Protection Directive, which proclaims itself as a measure to protect individual privacy, provides that decisions affecting individuals may be made on the basis of automated processing only when an adverse decision may be appealed to some human agency.

Misuse of data

3.10 In general it may be assumed that personal data is seldom obtained as an end in itself. The intention will be to put the data to some purpose. One obvious danger is that information may be sought for a purpose which is harmful to the individuals concerned. A classic example is concerned with the activities of a blackmailer. Fortunately, such instances are relatively rare. A further example of a situation where information is sought which will be used against individuals is concerned with law enforcement. This example introduces a further element into the equation requiring that the individual's right to anonymity should not extend to the commission of a crime. What may complicate matters further, of course, is that the investigation of crime may necessarily gather information about many other innocent purposes. As more and more reliance is placed upon systems of CCTV, DNA testing and the trawling of information on data bases – a practice referred to as data matching – so more and more data concerning law abiding citizens will be collected. In many respects we are witnessing a change in policing practices. Traditionally, much policing has been reactive, in that investigation has followed the commission of a crime. Systems of image and vehicle recognition are more proactive, in that they involve the monitoring of persons whose profile fits that of suspected offenders.

3.11 One of the factors which makes personal data such a valuable asset is its flexibility. Information originally obtained for one purpose may readily be used for other purposes. It is a little-known fact that purchasers of black ash furniture are 20 times more likely than the average citizen to respond positively to a subsequent direct marketing promotion. Corollations such as this form the basis for the success of the direct marketing industry but raise a second and more insidious problem, that information which may well have been supplied voluntarily by an individual for one purpose will subsequently be put to other, less welcome, ends. The direct marketing industry is one of the major users of personal data and attempts to control its activities have been integral to a number of recent European legislative initiatives.

The Distance Selling Directive

3.12 Direct marketing and the associated avalanche of junk mail (and increasingly telephone calls and e-mails) might be regarded as a nuisance rather than a threat to individual freedom. This has itself prompted legislative intervention. The European Distance Selling Directive makes special provision for the use of telephone and fax systems for marketing purposes. The directive was drafted in the early 1990s, before e-mail came into widespread use and, perhaps unsurprisingly, makes no special mention of this technology. It does, however, contain a general provision requiring that messages may not be sent to a consumer who has expressed the clear wish not to receive such communications. This will require the establishment of some system of e-mail preference service along the lines of the existing mail and telephone services. The draft Electronic Commerce Directive, a measure which will be discussed in more detail below, is more explicit providing in art 7 that:

> Member States shall lay down in their legislation that unsolicited commercial communication by electronic mail must be clearly and unequivocally identifiable as such as soon as it is received by the recipient.

3.13 In the case of e-mail, an indication in the header of a message would appear to be necessary, allowing the user to decide whether to read further. In many cases, however, such notification will not save the consumer on-line time and costs. Many e-mail packages will download all the text of waiting messages before presenting the results to the user, who may then choose to read messages and compose any replies off-line. The more effective remedy is undoubtedly to stop messages being sent in the first place. Here the draft directive in art 7(2) provides that:

... Member States shall take measures to ensure that service providers undertaking unsolicited commercial communications by e-mail consult regularly and respect the opt-out registers in which national persons not wanting to receive such commercial communications can register themselves.

3.14 Implementation of this provision would require the establishment of an e-mail preference system along the lines of the current telephone and mailing preference systems. Although this provision makes explicit reference to an 'opt-out' system, in its second consultation paper on implementation of the Distance Selling Directive, the Department of Trade and Industry suggests that the directive leaves it open to member states to adopt either an 'opt-out' or an 'opt-in' approach.

2.4 The Government appreciates that there are arguments for both opt-out and opt-in approaches to unsolicited e-mail, and we would welcome views on either option. There are two alternative draft implementing Regulations, which implements Art 10.2 in respect of e-mail by means of opt-in and opt-out.

The paper continues to identify a variety of approaches already adopted within the EU:

2.5 Some countries already ban unsolicited commercial e-mail (e.g. Austria). The draft EUE-commerce directive does not prevent this, and is neutral on opt-in or opt-out, leaving the Distance Selling Directive to regulate this. However, where Member States permit such e-mail, the draft E-commerce directive requires them to ensure that service providers established on their territory make unsolicited e-mail clearly identifiable as such as soon as it shows up in the recipient's in-tray, in recognition of the additional communication costs of the recipient and the need to promote responsible filtering initiatives by industry. We understand that a number of Member States (e.g. Austria, Italy, Germany and Sweden) either have or are likely to implement the e-mail provision of the Distance Selling Directive by opt-in, although others (e.g. Belgium) have gone for opt-out.

3.15 Significant UK precedents exist for the implementation of an opt-out scheme in the form of the mailing and telephone preference services. The latter operates on a statutory basis in accordance with the requirements of the European directive concerning the processing of personal data and protection of privacy in the telecommunications sector. Enforcement is in the hands of the Data Protection Commissioner. The Direct Marketing Association has indicated the intention to adopt a voluntary e-mail preference service based on a scheme operating in the US – generally considered to be the home of 'spam'. Implementation of the Directive, however, will again serve to establish a statutory scheme.

3.16 Although the DTI paper identifies benefits and disadvantages from both opt-in and opt-out schemes, the balance of the argument appears to lie in favour of an opt-in approach. Accompanying the paper is a set of draft regulations for implementing the directive. As presented, the opt-in approach is adopted in the body of the text, with an alternative, opt-out, provision included at the end of the measure. One point which may carry considerable weight is the suggestion that attempts to opt out of the receipt junk e-mail are sometimes misused by unscrupulous sellers. Sending a request not to receive e-mail indicates that the address used is accurate and in use, factors which make it valuable to the compilers and users of e-mail lists. Against this, it might be argued that existing requirements under the Data Protection Act recognise that the use of data for direct marketing purposes can be legitimised by giving the data subject the opportunity to opt out. Establishing a general prohibition against unsolicited communications might create potential for conflict and confusion. A consumer might, for example, have purchased goods from a direct marketing organisation and not have taken the opportunity to indicate an unwillingness to receive further mailings (either from the supplier or from third party organisations). The consumer may not, however, have opted in to the general e-mail preference scheme. The question may then arise whether future mailings from the original supplier will be permitted?

3.17 A further practical difficulty arises from the fact that many e-mail solicitations originate from outwith the EU. Although a breach of one or more national data protection or distance selling regimes may well have occurred, it is unlikely that jurisdiction can be effectively claimed unless the advertiser has an establishment or resources within the EU.

The emergence of data protection

3.18 The major form of legal regulation of the activities of data processors takes the form of data protection laws. Originally a western European concept, these are now being adopted across the world, although, as will be discussed, significant differences of approach exist between the EU and the US. As with other aspects of life, the emergence of the Internet and other global communications networks challenge the effectiveness of national laws and attempts to regulate international or transborder data flows are a prominent feature of the latest European legislation.

Background to data protection

3.19 The world's first data protection statute was enacted in the German state of Hesse in 1970. The first national statute was enacted in Sweden in 1973. The fact that data protection emerged in these two states may not be entirely a matter of chance but the reasons behind the legislation differ significantly. Germany acted in part out of the memory of the misuse of records under the Nazi regime and with the desire to place controls over those wishing to obtain and process personal data. The legislation can be considered somewhat defensive in tone. Sweden's background was very different. Freedom of information has been a tenet of Swedish life since the eighteenth century. Virtually every item of data held within the public sector can be accessed by any individual. Tax returns, for example, are a matter of public record. A perhaps apocryphal tale recounts that the Swedish tax system was brought to a virtual halt at the time the pop group 'Abba' were at the height of their fame. Thousands of fans discovered that they could obtain a (free) copy of their idols' tax returns, which included a photograph. The main purpose of the Swedish data protection law can be seen as extending rights of access to data held within the private sector.

3.20 Following the German and Swedish lead, data protection laws were adopted in a number of European countries during the 1970s. Although the topic was discussed in the UK and a Committee on Data Protection was appointed in 1975, legislation was slow in coming. If reference is made to the German and Swedish motives, a possible explanation for the UK's ambivalence emerges. Unlike Germany, there has been no recent experience of totalitarian regimes and few documented instances of the misuse of personal data. Unlike Sweden, there has been no tradition of freedom of information, with statutes such as the Official Secrets Act treating the most mundane items of information as highly confidential.

3.21 Ultimately, international pressure was required to persuade the UK to adopt data protection laws. As communications technologies developed, states which had adopted data protection became concerned that provisions of domestic law designed to protect the public could be circumvented by data processors sending data out of the country for processing. In 1980 the Council of Europe had adopted a convention 'for the protection of individuals with regard to the automatic processing of personal data'. This convention provides for the free flow of data between its signatory states. In order to sign the convention, states were required to have data protection laws which conformed to basic standards laid down in the convention.

3.22 Although not stated expressly, there was the implied threat that the attempt might be made to place non-signatory states into a form of data quarantine. Such a result would have been extremely damaging to the UK economy. If the example could be taken of a multinational company with subsidiaries in the UK, France, Germany, the Netherlands and Sweden, it would be possible that the computer systems of the UK subsidiary might not be able to be linked with those in the other countries. Even the possibility that such a situation might occur would deter companies from investing in the UK.

3.23 Faced with this situation, a Data Protection Bill was introduced in 1982 and became law in 1984. There was little governmental enthusiasm for the measure. In commending the Bill to the House of Commons, the then Home Secretary stated that the purpose of the legislation was to 'meet public concern, to bring us into step with Europe and to protect our international, commercial and trading interests'. All this was to be achieved at the minimum possible cost to data users. Time and again it was made clear that the measure set out to do the bare minimum to enable the UK to accede to the Council of Europe Convention.

3.24 During the 1980s a number of the pioneering countries adopted revised data protection laws. As the number of computers in use increased dramatically, so the notion of licensing individual users came to be seen as outdated, with more attention being paid to substantive provisions seeking to regulate forms of data processing. The process was taken to its most extreme lengths in Germany, which pioneered the notion commonly referred to as 'informational self-determination'.

3.25 Subject to the inevitable caveats and exceptions, this sought to give primacy to the subject's wishes, providing that consent should be a prerequisite to lawful processing. A further trend has been to require that those processing data demonstrate that reasonable security measures have been taken to guard against its wrongful disclosure or destruction. Essentially, the focus of the legislation has switched from seeking to repair damage arising from improper processing to emphasising the need to prevent the damage occurring.

European union activities

3.26 As reference to the work of the Council of Europe indicates, international bodies have been active in the data protection field from the earliest days. Prior to its convention, the Council adopted recommendations on the topic in 1973. Subsequently, a raft of recommendations have been adopted seeking to tailor general principles of data protection for the requirements of specific areas, eg Recommendation (87) 15, regulating the use of personal data in the police sector. In addition to the Council of Europe, both the OECD and the United Nations have promoted initiatives in the field in the form of guidelines. Even from the 1970s, the rationale has been that without such efforts, national laws could easily be bypassed by users transferring data outwith the jurisdiction for processing to take place in another state, often referred to as a 'data haven', which imposed few, if any, obligations upon data users. With developments in communications technology, this is becoming a still more important issue.

3.27 Initially, the EU took the view that the adherence of all Member States to the Council of Europe convention would remove the need for it to act in the field. A recommendation to this effect was addressed to the member states. By the end of the 1980s this view had changed. In spite of the Commission recommendation, only six of the member states had signed and ratified the Council of Europe Convention. Of equal importance was the fact that significant differences existed between national data protection statutes. Whilst legislation in states such as the UK contained the minimum provisions necessary to ratify the convention, other states, such as Germany and Sweden, had adopted much more extensive provisions. Variation in national approaches was seen as posing a threat to the Single Market and proposals for a harmonising directive were published in 1990.

3.28 The directive proved controversial throughout its passage through the EU's law making process, so much so that five years elapsed between publication of the first proposal in 1990 and adoption of the final text in 1995. Criticism came from both ends of the data protection spectrum. The UK objected to the measure as extending the scope and cost of legislation, and ultimately abstained on the final vote in the Council of Ministers. Criticism was also voiced from Germany on the basis that the protection afforded to its citizens might be weakened. The directive has also attracted controversy on a worldwide basis with its provisions regarding control of transborder data flows being criticised, especially within the US, as being driven by considerations of economic protectionism and constituting a thinly veiled attack on the US data processing industry.

3.29 These issues will be discussed more fully in subsequent sections. To conclude the story of the directive, it was finally adopted (the UK abstaining on the final vote in the Council of Ministers) in October 1995, with member states being required to implement its provisions by 24 October 1998. This timetable has proved difficult for a number of member states and, towards the end of 1999, the Commission commenced legal proceedings against a number of member states alleging breach of their obligation to implement the directive.

3.30 Assuming this target is met, a period of ten years will have elapsed from the date when the directive was proposed until its implementation in the UK. Whilst some of the basic tenets of data protection – for example that individuals should be entitled to access data held about them – are relatively timeless, it is a cause for concern that, in other structural and procedural matters, technical developments will have rendered the legislation outdated before it even enters into force.

Key features of data protection

3.31 Three elements can be identified as integral to the concept of data protection. First, there is the appointment of some supervisory agency to supervise those processing personal data and to act to protect the interests of individuals. Linked to this is the second feature which sees the establishment of a system whereby at least some of those engaged in the processing of personal data are required to notify or seek the permission of the supervisory agency to commence or continue their processing activities. Finally, substantive rules are laid down prescribing the conditions under and manner in which personal data may be processed.

3.32 These issues will be considered in more detail below. Initially, however, examination requires to be made of key definitions defining the scope of the legislation and indicating what categories of persons and actions are subject to regulation.

Scope of the Act

3.33 The data protection world consists of *data controllers*, *data processors* and *data subjects* engaged in some capacity in relation to the *processing* of *personal data*. Each of the terms italicised is subject to a specific definition in the Act.

Data controller

3.34 An individual or undertaking will be classed as a data controller when it:

> (either alone or jointly or in common with other persons) determines the purposes for which and the manner in which personal data are, or are to be processed. (s 1(1))

The question whether a person determines the manner in which data are processed is to be answered by reference both to practical and legal criteria. Clearly, a business which processes data on its customers will be classed as a data controller but it is quite possible that a person could be classed as a data controller without owning any form of computer. The example might be given of a business person who maintains all records relating to the business on paper. If these are passed on to an accountant who transfers the data into electronic form and subjects it to processing, the client will be regarded as a data controller. It is likely that the accountant will also be considered as a controller on the basis that he or she has control over the particular manner in which work is conducted.

Data processor

3.35 As in the example given above, some data controllers may seek to have processing carried out on their behalf by a third party. This was perhaps more prevalent in the early days of computing than is the case today, although one aspect which remains significant is where undertakings make arrangements as part of a disaster recovery plan to access external processing facilities in the event of some interruption to service. The term 'data processor' is defined to encompass:

> any person (other than an employee of the data controller) who processes the data on behalf of the data controller. (s 1(1))

One point that might be noted is that the definition of processing is sufficiently broad that persons collecting data, perhaps by canvassing shoppers in the street and recording answers on paper, will be classed as data processors if the intention is that the survey results will subsequently be processed by computer.

Data subject

3.36 A data subject is 'an individual who is the subject of personal data'. It would be a unique individual who is not to be classed as a data subject – many times over. In contrast to the situation with data controllers and processors, where the focus is very much on the obligations imposed under the legislation, for data subjects the purpose of the statute is to confer rights. The most important right for data subjects is undoubtedly that of obtaining access to data held by controllers and of securing the correction of any errors contained therein.

Processing

3.37 The Act defines the activity of processing as involving –

> obtaining, recording or holding the data or carrying out any operation or set of operations on the data, including—
> (a) organisation, adaptation or alteration of the data,

(b)   retrieval consultation or use of the data,
(c)   disclosure of the data by transmission, dissemination or otherwise making available, or
(d)   alignment, combination, blocking or erasure of the data. (s 1(1))

The new definition is extremely broad. It has been suggested that, whilst dreaming about data will not amount to processing, any other action will come within the scope of the definition. The Act, however, will apply only in relation to data which:

(a)   is being processed by means of equipment operating automatically in response to instructions given for that purpose,
(b)   is recorded with the intention that it should be processed by means of such equipment, or
(c)   is recorded as part of a relevant filing system or with the intention that it should form part of a relevant filing system.(s 1(1)

3.38 In common with many other statutes dealing with computer technology, the Act does not contain any definition of the word 'computer'. In fact, the word does not appear anywhere in the legislation. Traditionally, the reason given for the reluctance to use the term has been the fear that any definition adopted might quickly be overtaken by developments in technology. This concern is perhaps unwarranted but there is no doubt that the first two paragraphs in the definition are intended to apply to the situation where data is processed – or is intended to be processed – by computer. The final paragraph marks a new and controversial extension to the scope of the UK's data protection regime.

3.39 Under the 1984 Act manual data was totally excluded from control. The European directive, however, extends the scope of protection to certain forms of manual records and the term 'relevant filing system' seeks to give effect to this. The term is defined as:

> any set of information relating to individuals to the extent that, although the information is not processed by equipment operating automatically . . . the set is structured, either by reference to individuals or by reference to criteria relating to individuals, in such a way that particular information relating to a particular individual is readily accessible.

The key concept here is the notion of a structured set of data. Its meaning has been the subject of disagreement between the government and the Data Protection Registrar. In discussion in Parliament it was suggested that it would not be sufficient that information about an individual should be located in a single place, eg a manila folder containing all of an employee's work records. In order for the records to be covered, it would additionally be required that the information within the folder should be held in a structured format so that individual items might readily be extracted. The Data Protection Registrar, however, advocated a different and broader interpretation of the provision. Effectively, all that would be required would be for all manila folders to be stored in a systematic fashion.

3.40 The extension of the legislation to manual records was one of the most controversial aspects of the directive, with UK opponents estimating the compliance costs to industry at some £100m for the banking sector alone. These figures may well be exaggerated. Although new to data protection, at least two other UK statutes, the Consumer Credit Act 1974 and the Access to Health Records Act 1990, provide for access to records irrespective of the format in which these are stored. Even more extensively, a Freedom of Information Bill is currently before Parliament. This will establish a general right of access to all data held by a public authority. As the Data Protection Registrar has commented:

> Experience elsewhere indicates that in practice, in many cases, information provided in response to Freedom of Information requests will relate to the individual making the request.

3.41 The Freedom of Information Bill proposes to replace the present office of Data Protection Commissioner with a new post of Information Commissioner. The Information Commissioner will be responsible for overseeing the operation of both the data protection and freedom of information regimes.

Personal data

3.42 The premise underlying data protection legislation is that the processing of data relating to individuals constitutes a threat to the subject's rights and freedoms, most specifically the right to privacy. If an individual cannot be identified from the manner in which data is collected, processed or used, there can be no significant threat to privacy and no justification for the application of legislative controls. The question may arise, however, when an individual may be identified? The Act provides that personal data –

> means data which relates to a living individual who can be identified—
> (a) from those data, or
> (b) from those data and other information which is in the possession of, or is likely to come into the possession of, the data controller,
> and includes any expression of opinion about the individual and any indications of the intentions of the data controller or any other person in respect of the individual.

3.43 In the situation where data is held solely by one data controller, the question whether an individual is identifiable may readily be resolved. We live, however, in the age of the computer network. Distributive computing, epitomised at its most extensive by the Internet, renders the issue of physical possession of data secondary to the question of access. Practices such as data matching allow controllers to trawl across the contents of a wide range of computers.

3.44 An area where data matching has been applied has been in seeking to identify individuals making multiple applications for social or housing benefits. It is not just in the more formal instances of data matching that there might be a number of separate data controllers. In the case of the Internet, the proliferation of search tools such as 'Alta Vista' and 'Dejavu News' allows users to scan thousands of sites to develop profiles of individual's postings to newsgroup discussions. Anyone placing material on the Internet, an act which will constitute processing as defined in the Act, should be aware that third parties may engage in such forms of processing.

Sensitive data

3.45 The extent to which certain forms of data can be classed as especially sensitive and deserving of special protection has long been a contentious issue. In the case of personal data, the context in which data was held or used might be more important than the data itself. A list of names and addresses, for example, would not normally be considered sensitive but this view might change if it referred to details of prominent persons and was in the hands of a terrorist organisation. Whilst this view is not without merit, it seeks to transform the exceptional into the norm. Ultimately, it was accepted that there are certain categories of information which would generally be regarded as possessing a degree of sensitivity. As defined in the 1998 Act, data is sensitive if it relates to:

(a) the racial or ethnic origin of the data subject,
(b) his political opinions,
(c) his religious beliefs or other beliefs of a similar nature,
(d) whether he is a member of a trade union,
(e) his physical or mental health or condition,
(f) his sexual life,
(g) the commission or alleged commission by him of any offence, or
(h) any proceedings for any offence committed or alleged to have been committed by him, the disposal of such proceedings or the sentence of the court in such proceedings.

Sensitive data may be processed only if special conditions laid down in the Act are satisfied.

Supervisory authorities

3.46 The establishment of some form of independent supervisory agency has become a hallmark of European data protection regime. The approach adopted, however, has varied considerably between states. In some countries, separate agencies operate in respect of public and private sector data processing, in others responsibility is shared between federal and state agencies. Under the 1984 Act, the UK established the office of Data Protection Registrar. In the mid-1990s the Registrar indicated concern that the title of Registrar placed undue emphasis on one (rather bureaucratic) aspect of her role and, responding to this concern, the term Data Protection Commissioner is substituted in the 1998 Act.

3.47 Having appointed an agency, the question arises what it is to do? The directive requires that national supervisory agencies must be given powers to supervise data controllers, to monitor and enforce compliance with the legislation together with the duty to act in the interests of data subjects.

The Data Protection Register

3.48 A feature of many of the early data protection statutes was the imposition of a system of licensing of data users. Effectively, this required users to demonstrate fitness to be permitted to process personal data. With the massive increase in the number of computers, the impossibility of exercising effective control in this manner has been widely recognised. An initial step, which was implemented in the Data Protection Act 1984, saw the introduction of a system of registration of data users. Registration as applied in the Data Protection Act retains qualitative criteria but switches the onus to the supervisory agency to indicate cause why an application should be rejected.

3.49 The danger of such a half-way house, and something which has been criticised within the Data Protection Act, is that these regimes impose bureaucratic burdens and costs on data users whilst providing minimal benefit to the public. The Data Protection Register is a publicly available document which can now be accessed over the Internet (*http://www.open.gov.uk/dpr/register.htm*) and readers may wish to check on the entries of organisations with which they have had dealings. In many cases, it is suggested, the register entries will give little precise guidance concerning the forms of processing of personal data carried out by these parties.

3.50   More recent statutes, such as the German Data Protection Act of 1990 have moved away from the requirements of universal registration. The directive follows this model, although substituting the term 'notification' for that of 'registration'. Whilst providing initially that:

> Member States shall provide that the controller or his representative, if any, must notify the supervisory agency ... before carrying out (processing of personal data) (art 18(1))

it goes on to state that simplification or exemption from notification may be provided:

> for categories of processing operations which are unlikely, taking account of the data to be processed, to affect adversely the rights and freedoms of data subjects (art 18(2))

3.51   Initially, it was anticipated that wide use would be made of this power to exempt thousands of small-scale data controllers from the requirement to notify details of their activities. In the event, financial constraints and definitional difficulties have combined to make it unlikely that many data controllers will be exempted. The Data Protection Commissioner's office (which employs around 100 people) is required to be financially self-supporting. The only significant income is that received by way of fees from those wishing to register (notify) details of their processing activity. Under the 1984 Act, a fee of £75 was levied for a registration valid for three years. There are some 250,000 entries on the register, equating to an annual income of around £6.25m. If large numbers of data users were to be exempted, either fee income would be reduced or the fees payable by those remaining subject to the notification requirement would rise dramatically. Neither option was considered desirable. Although some limited exceptions are provided, the number of entries on the register is likely to remain as before.

Information to be supplied on notification

3.52   The Act specifies the information – the 'registrable particulars' – which must be supplied to the Commissioner (s 16(1)). This includes details of the identity to the identification of the data controller and the purposes for which the data is held, used and disclosed. Notice must also be given of the 'names or a description of, any countries outside the European Economic Area to which the data may be directly or indirectly transferred. A further item has proved more controversial. Controllers are required to give:

> a general description of measures to be taken for the purpose of complying with the seventh data protection principle.(S 18(2)(b))

3.53 The seventh principle relates to the requirement to maintain appropriate data security measures. Whilst the making of such a statement has been a feature of the German legislation for a number of years, opponents have suggested that to publish such information in a public document might give assistance to hackers and others seeking to obtain unauthorised access to the data. Emphasis may, however, reasonably be put on the phrase 'general description' and a statement that security complies with, for example, a relevant British or international information security standard should comply with the obligation.

Preliminary assessments

3.54 Although a data controller may not commence processing operations without notifying the Commissioner (or being covered by an exemption), certain forms of processing are subject to additional controls. The Secretary of State may determine categories of processing, referred to as 'assessable processing' which appear particularly likely:

(a) to cause substantial damage or substantial distress to data subjects, or
(b) otherwise significantly to prejudice the rights and freedoms of data subjects (s 22(1))

It has been indicated that few forms of processing will be covered by such regulations. In Parliament, specific reference was made to activities involving data matching, genetic data and private investigations (Standing Committee D, 19 May 1998).

3.55 Where processing comes within the ambit of such regulations, the controller may not commence activities until an assessment of its compliance with the data protection principles has been made by the Commissioner.

Enforcement of the Act

3.56 Having established a register of those processing personal data, the ongoing task for the supervisory agency is to seek to ensure that controllers remain within the scope of their entries on the register and that, in general, processing complies with the substantive requirements of the legislation. Failures on the part of controllers may constitute an offence and will also expose them to a range of sanctions made available to the Commissioner.

Enforcement notices

3.57 The Commissioner may serve an enforcement notice on a data controller where she is satisfied that a breach of one or more of the data protection principles has occurred. The notice will identify the act or omission complained of and specify the steps that require to be taken to put matters right. Failure to comply with an enforcement notice constitutes an offence. As with all other forms of notice served by the Commissioner, the recipient data controller may appeal to a further body established under the legislation, the Data Protection Tribunal. Save in exceptional circumstances, the lodging of an appeal will suspend the operation of the notice.

Information notices

3.58 Although the 1984 Act empowered the Registrar to seek and execute search warrants in the event a breach of the principles was suspected, that statute conferred no general investigative power and placed data users under no obligation to co-operate with any enquiries made by the Registrar. The 1998 Act stops short of providing a general investigative power but confers a new power on the Commissioner to serve an 'information notice' requiring the supply within a specified time of specified information relating to the matter under investigation. Failure to comply with an information notice will constitute an offence, as will the reckless or intentional provision of false information.

3.59 Although the information notice does constitute a new weapon in the Commissioner's armoury, it may be queried how useful the power will be in practice. The notice may be served when the Commissioner reasonably requires information to determine whether the principles are being observed rather than the requirement for service of an enforcement notice that the Commissioner be satisfied that a breach has occurred. Beyond this, however, the appeal procedures are identical. Whilst it may be expected that many controllers will be happy to respond to an information notice in order to clarify what might be a misunderstanding of the nature of their processing activities, the possibility for appeal may persuade less scrupulous controllers to prevaricate in their response. Even if the Data Protection Tribunal ultimately upholds the information notice and the Commissioner obtains information indicating that a breach of the principles has occurred, no action can be taken until an enforcement notice, with its own appeal procedures, has been served.

The data protection principles

3.60 At the core of any data protection statute is a set of rules prescribing the circumstances under, and manner in which, the processing of personal data may lawfully take place. In the UK legislation the approach adopted has been to specify a set of 'data protection principles', the 1998 Act requiring that:

1. Personal data shall be processed fairly and lawfully and, in particular, shall not be processed unless—
(a) at least one of the conditions in Schedule 2 is met, and
(b) in the case of sensitive personal data, at least one of the conditions in Schedule 3 is also met.
   2. Personal data shall be obtained only for one or more specified and lawful purposes, and shall not be further processed in any manner incompatible with that purpose or those purposes.
   3. Personal data shall be adequate, relevant and not excessive in relation to the purpose or purposes for which they are processed.
   4. Personal data shall be accurate and, where necessary, kept up to date.
   5. Personal data processed for any purpose or purposes shall not be kept for longer than is necessary for that purpose or those purposes.
   6. Personal data shall be processed in accordance with the rights of data subjects under this Act.
   7. Appropriate technical and organisational measures shall be taken against unauthorised or unlawful processing of personal data and against accidental loss or destruction of, or damage to, personal data.
   8. Personal data shall not be transferred to a country or territory outside the European Economic Area unless that country or territory ensures an adequate level of protection for the rights and freedoms of data subjects in relation to the processing of personal data.

3.61 The data protection principles can perhaps be analogised to the Ten Commandments. As with the commandments, few could disagree with the contents of the principles as a prescription for good data processing. It is difficult, for example, to object to a requirement that data be processed fairly. The determination of what is fair may be a more difficult task. Detailed guidance concerning the application of the principles can be taken from a variety of sources. No fewer than four Schedules to the Act expand upon the interpretation of the principles, whilst provisions in the body of the statute make additional provisions, often in the form of providing exceptions from their application. As with other statutes, further guidance on issues of interpretation will become available through decisions of the courts and Data Protection Tribunal resolving actual cases. Finally, a significant role is envisaged for sector specific codes of practice, although the legal status of these is rather obscure.

3.62 As stated in the first principle, in order for processing to be considered legitimate, the controller must meet at least one of the conditions specified in Schedule 2. For sensitive data, Schedule 3 lays down more restrictive conditions. Schedule 2 identifies six conditions which may make processing legitimate. These are that:

1. The data subject has given his consent to the processing.
2. The processing is necessary—
(a) for the performance of a contract to which the data subject is a party, or
(b) for the taking of steps at the request of the data subject with a view to entering into a contract.
3. The processing is necessary for compliance with any legal obligation to which the data controller is subject, other than an obligation imposed by contract.
4. The processing is necessary in order to protect the vital interests of the data subject.
5. The processing is necessary—
(a) for the administration of justice,
(b) for the exercise of any functions conferred on any person by or under any enactment,
(c) for the exercise of any functions of the Crown, a Minister of the Crown or a government department, or
(d) for the exercise of any other functions of a public nature exercised in the public interest by any person.
6. (1) The processing is necessary for the purposes of legitimate interests pursued by the data controller or by the third party or parties to whom the data are disclosed, except where the processing is unwarranted in any particular case by reason of prejudice to the rights and freedoms or legitimate interests of the data subject.
(2) The Secretary of State may by order specify particular circumstances in which this condition is, or is not, to be taken to be satisfied.

The subject has consented to processing

3.63 The Act does not define 'consent'. The directive refers to 'any freely given specific and informed indication of his wishes by which the data subject signifies his agreement to personal data relating to him being processed'. Where sensitive data is to be processed, the legislation requires the data subject's 'explicit consent'. It may be taken that the requirements for mere 'consent' will be somewhat less and that the system prevalent, with many forms of transaction where a customer is informed of the fact that data supplied may be used for specific purposes and given the opportunity to object to this (the opt-out) system, would be compatible with the requirements.

Necessary for concluding or performing a contract with the data subject

3.64 Processing may lawfully take place when this is necessary either for entering into or performing a contract with the subject. Some stress should be placed on the adjective 'necessary'. This appears frequently in instruments such as the European Convention on Human Rights, and the jurisprudence of the European Court of Human Rights, which has been approved by the European Court of Justice, has adopted an interpretation requiring that the practice in question be close to essential for the specified purpose. Clearly, information about a data subject's income may be necessary for a lender to determine whether to grant a loan, and information as to address will be vital for a mail order sale, but controllers should take care not to require more information than is strictly necessary for the purpose.

Necessary for the controller to comply with a legal obligation

3.65 Similar comments will apply to this requirement. A controller may, for example, require information to ensure that credit facilities are not extended to those under 18. It would be reasonable for such a controller to require applicants to give an indication that they are over 18.

Necessary to protect the vital interests of the data subject

3.66 It is easy to envisage situations where the interests of the data subject may require that data be processed in situations where it is not practicable to obtain consent. The limitation to the subject's 'vital interests' might mean in practice that the data is likely to be of a kind considered sensitive and so its processing will be governed by the provisions of Schedule 3 discussed in the previous chapter.

Necessary for the administration of justice etc

3.67 Data may be processed lawfully when this is necessary for a range of specified public sector purposes. In addition to the administration of justice, processing may be carried out when necessary for the exercise of statutory functions, eg compiling registers of data controllers, in the exercise of governmental functions or any other functions of a public nature exercised in the public interest. This might include, for example, the operation of systems of educational scholarships.

Necessary in the legitimate interests of the controller

3.68 This final justification for processing is perhaps the most controversial. An employer, for example, will need to process some data relating to employees and a supplier data relating to customers. An expansive definition of the provision could, however, largely negate the requirement for subject consent and the interaction between these two provisions is likely to be one of the most significant aspects of the new data protection law.

Accuracy and timeousness of data

3.69   The fourth data protection principle requires that 'personal data shall be accurate and, where necessary, kept up to date. Data is regarded as being inaccurate when it is 'incorrect or misleading as to any matter of fact'.

3.70   The question whether data is accurate will not always be susceptible of a straightforward answer. A statement may be in the format: 'Fred Smith informs us that Joe Bloggs has defaulted on three loan agreements.' If it is assumed that Joe Bloggs is in reality a person of the utmost financial probity, can it be said that the statement is false? In determining this issue the fourth data protection principle is interpreted:

> The fourth principle is not to be regarded as being contravened by reason of any inaccuracy in personal data which accurately record information obtained by the data controller from the data subject or a third party in a case where—
> (a) having regard to the purpose or purposes for which the data were obtained and further processed, the data controller has taken reasonable steps to ensure the accuracy of the data, and
> (b) if the data subject has notified the data controller of the data subject's view that the data are inaccurate, the data indicate that fact.

These requirements are cumulative and should oblige a controller to accept data only from sources which there is reason to believe are reliable and also to take such steps as are practicable to verify information prior to subjecting it to processing.

3.71   The second element of this principle requires that necessary updating of information shall be carried out. The Act does not expand on this requirement but it would appear that the question whether updating is required will be dependent upon the nature of the data and the purpose to which it will be put. If the data is merely a record of a transaction between the data user and the data subject, no updating would be either necessary or justified. Where the information is being used as the basis for continuing decisions and actions, regular updating may be essential. Thus, where information is to be used for assessing an employee's suitability for promotion, an indication of periods of absence would require to be supplemented by any explanations which might subsequently have been provided.

Duration of record keeping

3.72 Linked to the issue of the topicality of data are the provisions of the fifth principle which require that data should be retained for no longer than is necessary for the attainment of the purpose for which it is held. In many cases data users will be under an obligation to maintain data for a specified period of time, eg solicitor-client data. In more general terms there would appear justification for retaining data until the expiry of any limitation period for possible legal action. Save in the situation where data is maintained as a matter of historical record (Sch 8, Pt 4), the fifth data protection principle would appear to require that users operate some form of policy for monitoring their data holdings and removing items which are no longer of value or relevance to their activities.

Data security

3.73 Under the terms of the seventh data protection principle, data users and the operators of computer bureaux are obliged to ensure that:

> Appropriate technical and organisational measures shall be taken against unauthorised or unlawful processing of personal data and against accidental loss or destruction of, or damage to, personal data.

Additionally, controllers will be responsible for ensuring that any data processors contracted by them comply with the requirements of the principle.

3.74 The Registrar has identified a considerable number of matters which are relevant to data security. Account might be taken of the physical security of premises, of any security measures incorporated into computer systems, for example password requirements, and of the level of training and supervision of employees. Account can also be taken of the manner in which data and equipment are disposed of. A number of instances have been reported of the purchasers of second-hand computers discovering that data belonging to the original owner remained in the machine's memory. Such lapses might constitute a breach of the principle, as might any deficiency in respect of the disposal of print outs of computer-generated data.

3.75 In November 1997, the Registrar published a consultation paper on information security in the context of the need to comply with the relevant provisions of the Directive. This suggested that data controllers would be required to undertake a risk-based approach in determining the relevant standard of security. Specific reference was made to BS 7799, which contains both a Code of Practice and a Specification for Information

Security Management. In Parliament, however, the government rejected an amendment which would have recast the interpretative provisions attached to the principle to make specific reference to 'the risks associated with processing' on the basis that, as a –

> general principle of law . . . it is usually necessary to prove a degree of damage. The words 'damage' and 'harm' can be taken together. There are not many actions before the courts that are based simply on the prospect of their being a problem.

It might be considered, however, that such an approach smacks of 'closing the stable door after the horse has bolted'.

Unlawful obtaining of data

3.76 The seventh principle makes it clear that the data controller is responsible for maintaining data security. A successful attempt, whether by means of computer hacking or other techniques, to obtain access to the data may lead to the controller incurring the Commissioner's wrath, perhaps in the form of service of an enforcement notice, and possible claims for compensation brought by aggrieved data subjects. During the 1980s and 1990s considerable publicity attached to the activities of private investigators and investigative journalists who, through various forms of subterfuge or bribery, were able to secure access to personal information held by a data user. Stella Rimington, the former head of MI5, for example, has been quoted as saying:

> When I was first appointed DG, the Sunday Times employed a private investigator to find out everything it could about me. Without much difficulty through getting access to . . . (various databases) . . . it found where I lived, where I banked, how much I had in my account, where I regularly bought my food and on what days, my telephone number (even though I was ex-Directory) and who I regularly telephoned.

3.77 As the Data Protection Act was originally formulated, although the data controller might face sanctions, no offence would be committed by the investigator. The Criminal Justice and Public Order Act 1994 provided that an offence would be committed in such a case, an approach continued in the 1998 Act, which provides an offence will be committed by a person who 'knowingly or recklessly, without the consent of the data controller' seeks to obtain or disclose personal data or procure its disclosure to a third party. A further offence will be committed by any person who sells or offers to sell data obtained in contravention of this provision.

Individual rights and remedies

3.78 The Data Protection Act provides a variety of rights on data subjects and establishes a number of remedies which can be invoked in the event that data controller's either violate a subject's rights or, by virtue of some breach of the legislation, cause some form of damage to the data subject. As implemented in the 1984 Act, the subject's right was effectively limited to the obtaining of a copy of information held. The 1998 Act supplements this in a number of important respects, providing for enhanced rights to be informed as to the nature and purposes of processing and to object to the use of personal data for these ends.

Subject access

3.79 The right to obtain a copy of information held and concomitant rights to correct errors and obtain compensation constituted the most high-profile aspect of the data subject's rights as established under the Data Protection Act 1984. The 1998 Act extends significantly the range of information which requires to be supplied, to such extent that the term 'subject information' is used in preference to 'subject access'. If personal data is being processed, the data subject must be given a description of the nature of the data held, the purposes for which it is to be processed and the persons or categories of person to whom it may be disclosed. Finally, the 1998 Act provides that an enquiring subject must also be supplied with 'any information available to the data controller as to the source of those data'. Such information may prove useful in providing a form of audit trail allowing the subject to track down the source of any erroneous data. In addition, where decisions affecting the subject are likely to be taken solely on the basis of automated processing, a subject requesting access is also to be supplied with information regarding the 'logic involved in that decision taking'.

Access procedures

3.80 The basic features of the system can be stated shortly. Data subjects may approach a data controller with the request to be informed whether the data controller holds any personal data concerning them and, if so, require to be supplied with a copy (in intelligible form) of the data together with the other items of information referred to above. The controller is required to respond only to requests which are made in writing, which contain sufficient information to allow for identification of the data subject and which enclose any fee (up to a maximum of £10) which may be required.

3.81 Valid requests for access must be satisfied within 40 days. The information supplied must generally be that held at the date of receipt of the access request in order to avoid the possibility that the data controller may seek to 'sanitise' the data before disclosing it to the subject. Account may be taken, however, of any amendments or deletions made subsequently where these would been made 'regardless of the receipt of the request'. In the event, for example, that a subject request a copy of information held by a bank, account may be taken of any transactions which were processed between the date of receiving and of satisfying the request for access.

Exceptions to the subject information provisions

3.82 In certain situations, the individual's interest in obtaining access to personal data has to be restricted either in the subject's own interests or as a result of giving priority to other competing claims. Access to medical data provides an example of the first situation, whilst restrictions on access to data held for the purpose of crime prevention or detection illustrate how the subject's desire to know what information is held might reasonably be subjugated to the requirements of the data user or of third parties.

3.83 One difficulty which should be discussed at this stage concerns the nature of the reply which should be given to a data subject by a controller who considers that data is covered by one of the exceptions. In some cases it may be as revealing to inform the data subject that data is being withheld as it would be to supply a copy of the information. A data controller may therefore validly reply to the effect that 'I do not hold any relevant personal data'. Given that relevant personal data is data to which the subject is entitled to obtain access, the reply is factually correct but may well give a misleading impression.

3.84 It may be relatively rare that all of the data held by a controller is covered by an exception. In this case, the controller is obliged to supply such data as may be possible. This may require, for example, that a printout be supplied with excluded elements blanked out.

National security

3.85 Under the 1984 Act, information held for the purpose of national security was totally exempted from the legislation in the event a certificate to this effect was issued by a minister. Such a certificate could not be challenged in any way. Given the increasing involvement of national security agencies such as MI5 in crime-related functions such as operations against suspected drug dealers, the division between national security and criminal functions is frequently blurred. This has led the Registrar to express concern that exemptions have been claimed on an organisational rather than a task-related basis. Providing a partial response to these concerns, the 1998 Act provides that a ministerial certificate may be challenged before the Data Protection Tribunal by any person 'directly affected'. This may include a data subject who for the first and only time is given a right to initiate proceedings before the tribunal. Applying 'the principles applied by the court on an application for judicial review', the tribunal may quash the certificate if it considers that the minister did not have 'reasonable grounds' for issuing it.

Third party data

3.86 Whilst the grant of access to personal data is a key element of data protection law, many records may contain information relating to third parties. Whilst as a general proposition it is clear that a data subject should have no right of access to data relating to a third party, in many cases the data will be linked closely. An example concerns the situation where the third party has compiled a report on the data subject.

3.87 Under the 1984 Act, a data user was under no obligation to supply information relating to a third party – including the fact that the third party had been the source of information relating to the data subject. No obligation was imposed on the data user to enquire whether the third party would be willing for the information to be transmitted to the subject. Effectively, the data subject would be placed in an impossible situation. He would not be informed of data relating to a third party because the third party had not consented. The reason for lack of consent may well have been that the third party had not been asked. The subject could not ask the third party because his or her identity would not have been revealed.

3.88 A significant change to the extent of access rights has been introduced following the decision of the European Court of Human Rights in the case of *Gaskin v United Kingdom* (1989) 12 EHRR 36. In this case Mr Gaskin had spent much of his childhood in local authority care. In adulthood he claimed that he had been the subject of ill-treatment and instituted legal proceedings against the local authority. As part of these proceedings he sought discovery of all documents held by the authority relating to his case. Many of the documents had been compiled by third parties, such as doctors. The authority contacted the third parties seeking their approval to disclosure. A number of parties refused to consent to this and the authority took the view that this was determinative of the issue. The European Court of Human

Rights disagreed and held that, whilst the applicant did not have an unqualified right of access to data, the failure to provide an independent review constituted a breach of his rights under art 8 requiring respect for his private and family life.

3.89 In seeking to ensure conformity with the decision in *Gaskin*, the Act provides that a data controller will not be required to supply information relating to a third party unless that party has consented or:

> it is reasonable in all the circumstances to comply with the request without the consent of the other individual.

In determining the question of reasonableness, account is to be taken of a number of factors including any duty of confidentiality owed to the third party, the nature of the steps taken to secure consent, whether death or other incapacity might make it impossible for the third party to give consent and whether consent was expressly refused. An appeal may be made to the courts against any refusal to supply information.

3.90 A further issue concerns the question when a third party is to be considered identifiable. A controller is obliged to supply as much information as is possible without disclosing the third party's identity. In particular, it is stated, this might involve the omission of names or other identifying particulars. Account is to be taken of:

> ... any information which in the reasonable belief of the data controller, is likely to be in, or to come into, the possession of the data subject making the request.

This requirement may cause some difficulties for data controllers. In a case such as *Gaskin*, for example, it may be a very difficult task for controllers to assess whether the enquiring data subject would have, after the passage of many years, any recollection of the identity of particular doctors or social workers who had been responsible for submitting reports.

Data held for policing and revenue gathering purposes

3.91 The 1984 Act excluded data held for the purpose of:

(a) the prevention or detection of crime;
(b) the apprehension or prosecution of offenders; or
(c) the collection or assessment of any tax or duty

from the subject access provisions where this would be prejudicial to the attainment of the purpose in question. The determination whether access would be prejudicial requires to be made in the context of an individual request for access. In theory this might raise some difficult issues. A police force might have data on file indicating that a particular subject planned to stage a bank robbery at a certain date in the future. At that stage, the subject would not have committed a criminal offence. Planning a robbery only becomes criminal when positive steps are taken to put the plan into operation. This might only occur at the moment the subject entered the bank premises, gun in hand. In terms of the list of excluded subject matter, the data could only be regarded as held for the prevention of crime. If the subject requested access to his data, it might be argued that the purpose of preventing that particular crime would be facilitated rather than prejudiced by the grant of access. In practice, however, a distinction is drawn between factual data, such as details of criminal convictions, which are subject to the access regime and intelligence data which is not.

3.92 The 1998 Act retains these exclusions but, in the light of the increasing use of data matching techniques for detecting fraudulent benefit claims, provides that subject access will not be permitted where personal data is processed by a government department, local authority or other authority administering housing benefit or council tax benefit as part of a system of risk assessment relating to the assessment of collection of tax or duty, the prevention or detection of crime or the apprehension or prosecution of offenders and:

> ... where the offence concerned involves any unlawful claim for payment out of, or any unlawful application of, public funds

and where exemption is required in the interests of the operation of the system (s 29(4)).

Health and social work data

3.93 The 1984 Act established the general principle that access should be provided to medical and social work data. The Access to Personal Files Act 1987 and Access to Health Records Act 1990 extended these rights to manual files with procedures which are now gathered under the umbrella of the 1998 Act. Access might be denied where, in the opinion of a qualified person (defined in the legislation), this would be likely to cause serious harm to the data subject's physical or mental health (and in the case of social work data, emotional condition).

3.94 It would appear that limited use has been made of these provisions. In the case where a data controller relies on an exemption in order to refuse an access request whether in whole or in part, it is likely that the subject will be aware of the fact that a record is held and that access is being restricted. It is difficult to know what would be the worse outcome for data subjects. To be told information about health which will be so shattering as to cause serious illness or to be effectively told that 'we cannot tell you what is in your records because the knowledge will make you seriously ill'!

Regulatory activity

3.95 A broad range of statutory agencies engaged in regulatory tasks are provided with exemptions from the subject information provisions to the extent that compliance would these would prejudice the attainment of their purpose. A number of agencies are specifically identified in the Act, namely the Parliamentary, Health Service, Local Government and Northern Irish Assembly and Complaints Ombudsmen. Exemption is also offered to the Director General of Fair Trading in respect of the discharge of functions in the fields of consumer protection and competition policy. In addition to named agencies, exemption is also offered to those performing 'relevant functions' which are designed to protect against specified risks. The term 'relevant functions' is defined to encompass functions conferred by statute, performed by the Crown, ministers or government departments or 'any other function which is of a public nature and is exercised in the public interest'. The activities involved relate to protection against loss due to 'dishonesty, malpractice or other seriously improper conduct' within the financial services, corporate and professional sectors or through the conduct of discharged or undischarged bankrupts. Also exempted are functions concerned with the supervision of charities and the protection of health and safety both for workers and for third parties who might be affected by particular activities.

Research history and statistics

3.96 Where data are 'not processed to support measures or decisions with regard to particular individuals' and where the processing is not likely to cause substantial damage or distress to any data subject, exemption is offered from the subject access provisions subject to the further condition that the results of processing are not made available in a form permitting identification of data subjects.

Information required to be made available to the public

3.97 In many instances personal data will be contained in some document which is made available to the public. An example would be the electoral roll, copies of which may be supplied in electronic format. In the situation where the data made available is the only data held concerning the data subject, there would be little value for the subject in exercising a right of access.

Miscellaneous exceptions

3.98 Schedule 7 contains a substantial list of additional exceptions, which list may be supplemented by regulations made by the Secretary of State. The extent of the individual exemptions varies ranging from the application of modified access procedures, through exemption from access, to exemption from the fair processing requirement.

Confidential references

3.99 In many cases under the 1984 Act, such references would have been excluded from scrutiny under provisions referring to the processing of data purely in order to create the text of a document (the word processing exemption). This exemption is not retained in the 1998 Act and the expanded definition of processing in the 1998 Act will bring such documents within its scope. It is provided that the subject access provisions will not apply to references given in connection with the data subject's education, employment or appointment to any office, as well as to the provision of any services by the data subject.

Armed forces

3.100 The subject information provisions will not apply where their application would be likely to prejudice the combat effectiveness of the armed forces. This is a new provision and it is difficult to identify situations in which it is likely to apply.

Judicial appointments and honours

3.101 Under the 1984 Act, information held for the first of these purposes was exempted from the subject access provisions (s 31). The new Act extends the scope of the exemption to data processed in connection with the 'conferring by the Crown of any honour'. Such data are exempt from the subject information provisions regardless of any issue of prejudice.

Management forecasts

3.102 Personal data processed for this (undefined) purpose benefit from an exemption to the subject information provisions where compliance would prejudice the attainment of the purpose. Under the

1984 Act, a data user was not required to give access to information indicating intentions held towards the data subject. Such information might frequently be held in records maintained for career planning purposes and these may benefit from this provision.

Corporate finance

3.103 Extensive provisions are made for exemptions under this heading. The exemption will apply to data processed by 'relevant persons' concerned with the underwriting of share issues or the provision of advice on capital structure, industrial strategy and acquisitions and mergers and will apply when the application of the subject information provisions could affect the price of any shares or other instruments. In the situation in which this criterion is not satisfied, it is further provided that exemption may be granted 'for the purpose of safeguarding an important economic or financial interest of the United Kingdom'. The Secretary of State may specify in more detail the circumstances and situations in which this latter exemption is to apply.

Negotiations

3.104 Data processed in relation to negotiations between the controller and subject which record the intentions of the controller are exempt from the subject information provisions where compliance with these would be likely to prejudice those negotiations. This provision is likely to apply to many instances of career planning within forms and organisations.

Examination marks and examination scripts

3.105 The 1984 Act made special provision allowing examination authorities to delay responding to requests for access beyond the normal 40-day period. This was considered necessary for large-scale examinations such as the GCSE, where a period of months might elapse between examination and publication of the results. This approach continues in the 1998 Act. One point which should be noted is that where an examination authority relies upon the extended time limits upon receipt of an access request, its response must provide information as to the data held at the time of receipt of the request, at the time the request is complied with and any further data which was held at any intervening stage. An enquiring subject will, therefore, receive details of any changes made to exam marks during the various stages of the assessment process.

3.106 A novel exemption from the subject access provision relates to the materials produced by students during the examination process. Under the 1984 Act, it is unlikely that these would have been covered by the legislation. With the extension to some forms of manual records and the deletion of the text processing exemption the 1998 Act may well govern such materials as a collection of examination scripts held in alphabetical order or by reference to student number. It may be noted that although the Data Protection Act provides for exemption for such materials, there appears to be a trend to return scripts (with examiners comments) to students with trials being conducted in respect of A Level scripts.

Information about human embryos

3.107 The Act provides an exemption from the subject information provisions in respect of information indicating that an individual was born following IVF treatment. An alternative access procedure involving prior counselling is, however, provided under the Human Fertilisation and Embryology Act 1990.

Legal professional privilege

3.108 Data is exempt from the subject information provisions where it consists of information in respect of which a claim to legal professional privilege (or client-lawyer confidentiality in Scotland) could be maintained in legal proceedings. Effectively, this means that a party engaged in litigation cannot use the subject access provisions to obtain a copy of data relating to the case held by the other party's legal advisers.

Self-incrimination

3.109 Data controllers need not supply information in response to a request for access when the provision of the information would indicate that an offence might have been committed (other than under the Data Protection Act), thereby exposing them to the risk of criminal prosecution. Any information supplied pursuant to a request for access is not admissible in any proceedings for an offence under the 1998 Act.

Enforced subject access

3.110 Some 100,000 access requests are received each year by police forces and the DSS. Such a statistic might seem to indicate that subject access is a valuable right for the individual. In reality, however, it is estimated that the vast majority of requests are made at the behest of third parties. In a neat reversal of history, it is suggested that the Australian immigration authorities are major initiators of access requests, wishing to satisfy themselves that potential immigrants do not have criminal records. To achieve this, applicants are required to exercise their rights of access under the Data Protection Act and pass the results on to the authorities. Although employers and others are entitled to require information about criminal convictions and a false reply might be grounds for dismissal, the data obtained pursuant to an access request will include details of convictions which are regarded as 'spent' under the provisions of the Rehabilitation of Offenders Act 1974.

3.111 The situation where access rights imprison rather than empower the data subject has long been the subject of criticism, not least by the Data Protection Registrar. Devising an appropriate method of control has proved more difficult. The major difficulty facing any attempt to control the practice is the imbalance of power typically existing in such situations. If the subject is seeking employment, for example, a request that the information be supplied may carry as much weight as a demand. The initial drafts of the directive provided that data subjects should be entitled:

> to refuse any demand by a third party that he should exercise his right of access in order to communicate the data in question to that third party.

In the final text, the directive contained the somewhat enigmatic provision that data subjects should be guaranteed the right to exercise access 'without constraint' (art 11(a)). Other language versions of the directive make it clearer that the provision is intended to apply to enforced access, the German text, for example, requiring that access be provided 'frei und ungehindert'.

3.112 Although the government indicated the intention to act against enforced subject access from the earliest stages of the Act's parliamentary passage, finding an appropriate form of prohibition proved a difficult task. A variety of possibilities were considered. Subject access might, for example, be provided only in person rather than in writing. This would, of course, have made a dramatic change to the whole system of subject access and would have caused great inconvenience in the event, for example, a data subject was located in Glasgow and the data controller in London. An alternative suggestion canvassed was that all access requests should be filtered through the Commissioner. Again, practical constraints might make this solution unworkable. Ultimately, however, it was determined that the only feasible approach was to make the practice criminal. The prohibitions apply, however, only in respect of certain forms of records – criminal records, prison records and DSS records – and in respect of a limited range of situations. A person must not require the provision of information obtained following a request for access (a relevant record) in connection with the recruitment or continued employment of the data subject or with any contract under which the subject is to provide services. Similarly, when the person is concerned with the provision of goods, facilities or services to members of the public, it is prohibited to require the production of any relevant records as a condition for the provision of such goods, facilities or services. It is further provided that any contractual terms will be void in so far as they purport to require the production of any medical information obtained pursuant to an access request.

3.113 In this, as in other areas, the provisions of the Data Protection Act will not operate in isolation. Under the provisions of the Police Act 1997, new arrangements have been made for providing access to criminal records. Three categories of access are created. A basic certificate may be sought be any applicant and will reveal details of any convictions which are not spent under the Rehabilitation of Offenders Act 1974. A more extensive 'criminal record certificate', adding details of spent convictions, will be issued upon the joint application of the individual and an organisation which is exempted from the provisions of the 1974 Act. This will include professional organisations such as the Law Society in respect of their roles in determining whether individuals might be considered suitable for admission to the profession. The most extensive certificate, the 'enhanced criminal record certificate', will include police intelligence data and details of acquittals, will be reserved for situations where an individual is seeking to work with children or vulnerable adults (or other sensitive positions such as those related to gambling or judicial appointments).

3.114 Given the large numbers of requests for access relating to criminal records, there will clearly be a close relationship between the access provisions of the Police Act and those of the Data Protection Act. It was stated in Parliament that the Data Protection Act's provisions will not be implemented before those of the Police Act. Again, whilst a public interest defence will be available to parties charged with an offence under the 1998 Act's provisions, this will not be available in respect of data relating to the prevention or detection of crime.

Rights to object to processing

Direct marketing

3.115 Direct marketing is one of the fastest-growing sectors of the economy. Although it tends to be referred to under the epithet 'junk mail', each item delivered represents a not inconsiderable investment on the part of the sender. In many instances retailers will possess information linking an individual to a purchase and may use this in order to attempt to stimulate further sales. The purchaser of a motor vehicle, for example, is likely to receive a communication from the seller around the anniversary of the purchase in the hope that the buyer might be considering buying a new model. The increasing use of store-based credit cards, coupled with the utilisation of laser scanning cash points provides retailers with detailed information about their customers and their purchases. There are few technical barriers in the way of processing data so as to be able to 'talk to every customer in his or her own life style terms'. It has even been suggested that 'intelligent shopping trolleys' might guide customers towards promotions which analysis of their previous purchases suggests might prove alluring. Assuming that the data users involved have registered the fact that they intend to process personal data for sales and marketing purposes, the only legal barrier to such techniques might come from a determination that such processing is unfair.

3.116 The use of personal data for purposes of direct marketing has been the cause of some recent controversy. Reference has previously been made to the *Innovations* case and the data protection implications of list broking. Additionally, however, organisations are seeking to exploit their customer databases by entering into agreements to provide mailings on behalf of other companies. This may take a variety of forms. Analysis of, for example, purchases made with a credit card, may indicate that an individual frequently stays in hotels. The credit card company may then enter into an agreement with a hotel chain to include a promotional leaflet with its statement of account. In this example, no personal data will be transferred between the companies.

3.117 Treatment of data obtained and used for the purposes of direct marketing constituted one of the most controversial aspects of the directive. As originally drafted, the legislation would have imposed strict obligations on data controllers to inform subjects whenever data was to be used for such a purpose. The proposals were weakened in subsequent drafts and as enacted, the directive offers member states a choice of control regimes. It may be provided that data subjects be given the right to object to a controller's intention to process or to disclose data for the purposes of direct marketing. As an alternative, the directive provides that controllers might be required to give specific notice to data subjects before data is used by or on behalf of third parties for direct marketing purposes.

3.118 Effectively the two options offered relate to 'opt-out' and 'opt-in' systems. A voluntary preference system has been operated for some time by the direct marketing industry. Under this individuals can contact the Mailing Preference Service with the request that they should not be sent any promotional mail. The 1998 Act continues with an 'opt-out' model providing that a data subject may serve notice on the controller at any time objecting to this form of processing and requiring its cessation. In the event the controller fails to act on the notice, an application may be made to the court which may make such order as it thinks fit to secure compliance with the subject's wishes.

3.119 Although the Act is silent concerning the role of the Mailing Preference Service, which operates on a voluntary basis, it is arguable that a data controller who does not screen a list of names and addresses against those held by the service could be considered to be engaging in unfair processing of personal data.

Other forms of processing

3.120 In the case of direct marketing data, the subject's wishes are absolute. In the case of other forms of processing, the subject may serve notice requiring the cessation of processing on the basis that this is likely to cause substantial and unwarranted damage or distress This right will not apply:

> where the subject has previously consented to the processing;
> where the processing is necessary to conclude or perform a contract with the data subject;
> where it is necessary to comply with any legal obligation on the data controller; or
> where the processing is necessary to protect the vital interests of the data subject.

The Secretary of State may specify other situations in which the right to object is to be withdrawn.

3.121 Upon receipt of such a notice, the controller must respond in writing within 21 days, indicating either that the subject's request will be granted or giving reasons why or to what extent this should not be the case (s 10(3)). A negative response may be appealed to the courts which may make such order for ensuring compliance as it thinks fit (s 10(4)).

Automated decision making

3.122 Tales abound of computers sending out bills for the sum of £0.00p, followed by reminders and final demands for payment.

Many of these tales may be apocryphal, but many individuals have encountered difficulty in persuading some human to intervene in data processing operations when computers are acting with remorseless logic but basing actions on original data containing errors. As the maxim has it, 'Garbage In, Garbage Out'.

3.123 Adopting provisions originally found in the French legislation, the directive seeks to address the problem by providing that decisions adverse to an individual are not to be made purely on the basis of automated data processing. As implemented in the Act it is provided that a data subject may give notice in writing to a data controller requiring that:

> no decision which significantly affects that individual is based solely on the processing by automatic means of personal data in respect of which that individual is the data subject for the purpose of evaluating matters relating to him such as, for example, his performance at work, his creditworthiness, his reliability or his conduct.

3.124 Such a prohibition clearly cannot be absolute. The act of obtaining money from a cash dispensing machine, for example, would be prohibited in the situation where the bank's computer system makes a check on the state of the customer's account before allowing the withdrawal to proceed. It would be a uniquely altruistic bank that would accept restriction on its rights in this situation. The Act provides that, as exceptions to the general rule, automated decisions may be made in the course of entering into or performing a contract with the data subject or under statutory authority where the decision is either favourable or where 'steps have been taken to safeguard the legitimate interests of the data subject (for example by allowing him to make representations)'. Additional exceptions may be made by order of the Secretary of State.

3.125 In the event a data controller is found to have breached the prohibition against automated decision making, the data subject may seek a court order that the controller either reconsider the decision or take a new decision other than on the basis of the automatic process. It might be also that such conduct might be considered to constitute a breach of the first data protection principle (fair processing) and might form the subject of an enforcement notice.

3.126 In cases where no notice is served on a data controller and where decisions are made solely on the basis of automated processing it is provided that the controller must, as soon as reasonably practicable, give notice to the subject of the fact that the decision was made on such a basis. The subject may, within 21 days serve notice requiring the controller 'to reconsider the decision or take a new decision otherwise than on that basis'.

Data subject remedies
Rectification of inaccurate data

3.127 Data will be considered inaccurate if they are false or misleading as to any matter of fact. In such an event, the data subject may request the court to order the controller to 'rectify, block, erase or destroy' the data in question. These remedies may also be invoked when the data controller has acted in such a fashion as would give the subject an entitlement to claim compensation under the Act. Additionally, the controller may be ordered to amend any statement of opinion which appears to be based on the inaccurate data. Where data constitutes an accurate transcription of information received from a third party, the court may make one of the above orders; alternatively, it may permit the data to be retained but be supplemented by a further statement of the true facts as determined by the court.

3.128 The above remedies are effectively identical to those operating under the 1984 Act. The 1998 Act introduces one potentially significant extension. Where the court determines that data is inaccurate and requires that it be rectified, blocked, erased or destroyed, it may, where this is considered reasonably practical, order that the controller notify details of the changes to any third party to whom the data has previously been disclosed. Such a remedy may provide a valuable audit trail allowing the detrimental consequences of inaccurate data to be minimised.

Compensation

3.129 Under the 1984 Act, data subjects were entitled to claim compensation for damage and distress resulting from inaccuracy in data or from their unauthorised destruction or disclosure. These rights were seldom utilised, the requirement in particular to demonstrate both damage and distress proving a substantial hurdle.

3.130 The 1998 Act adopts a more extensive approach. An individual who suffers damage by reason of any breach of the Act will be entitled to compensation from the data controller concerned. Where damage in the form of quantifiable financial loss can be demonstrated, further compensation may be claimed for any related distress. Where data is processed for media related purposes (the 'special purposes') an aggrieved may seek compensation for distress alone. In all cases, the controller will have a defence if it can be shown that reasonable care was taken to avoid the breach.

Data protection and the media

3.131 The application of data protection provisions in respect of media activities raises a number of complex issues. Investigative journalism may involve the use of tactics and techniques which might normally be stigmatised as unfair (if not unlawful). Again, where the text of published articles is maintained in electronic format, the attempt by a featured data subject to invoke rights to have errors of fact rectified, together with changing any related opinion, calls to mind the operation of George Orwell's Ministry of Truth.

3.132 The Data Protection Act 1984 made no special provision for the media. In large measure this approach was justified by the limited use of computer equipment for journalistic purposes, the existence of the text processing exemption and the limited nature of the definition of processing. Time and technology have moved on. A study produced for the Council of Europe in 1992 identified a range of practices within member states regarding the treatment of media activities within data protection legislation. Some countries, such as the Netherlands and Sweden, provided a total exemption from data protection laws, others provided partial exemption, in the case of Germany, for example, requiring only that media users comply with requirements relating to data security. Other regimes, including that of the UK, provided no form of special treatment. The study identified a potential conflict between the provisions of the European Convention on Human Rights relating to freedom of expression and the right to seek out and impart information and those concerned with the right to privacy. Providing solutions is a difficult task and the Council of Europe contented itself with a recommendation that the potential conflict should be borne in mind in framing legislation.

3.133 Media issues are covered in the European directive which, in its Preamble, states that:

> Whereas the processing of personal data for purposes of journalism or for purposes of literary of artistic expression, in particular in the audio-visual field, should qualify for exemption from the requirements of certain provisions of this Directive in so far as this is necessary to reconcile the fundamental rights of individuals with freedom of information and notably the right to receive and impart information, as guaranteed in particular in Article 10 of the European Convention for the Protection of Human Rights and Fundamental Freedoms. (Recital 37)

Article 9 of the directive provides that:

> Member States shall provide for exemptions or derogations from the provisions of this Chapter, Chapter IV and Chapter VI for the processing of personal data carried out solely for journalistic purposes or the purpose of artistic or literary expression only if they are necessary to reconcile the right to privacy with the rules governing freedom of expression.

3.134 This formula empowers rather than requires member states to act but for the UK, the decision was taken to include special provisions for these activities, described as the 'special purposes' in the 1998 Act. Section 3 of the Act defines the concept of 'special purposes'. These relate to the processing of personal data:

(a) for the purposes of journalism,
(b) artistic purposes, and
(c) literary purposes.

3.135 It was stressed in Parliament that no qualitative criteria would be applied to determine whether a work could be classed as artistic, journalistic or literary. Although much of the debate in Parliament focused on the activities of the media, this definition recognises that literary and artistic works also raise issues of freedom of expression. The prime purpose of the Act's exceptional provisions is to place limits on the ability of data subjects to invoke statutory rights to impede publication of a work. Similar restrictions are placed upon the powers of the Data Protection Commissioner, with modified provisions for the service of information and enforcement notices. Once the work is in the public domain, the provisions of the general law will apply, including the law of defamation, although, as indicated in the previous chapter, the 1998 Act does provide new rights of compensation for distress caused as a result of processing carried out in connection with one of the special purposes.

Activities covered

3.136 The Act applies a three-stage test to determine whether processing for a special purpose should benefit from exemption. Personal data must be subject to processing:

(a) . . . with a view to the publication by any person of any journalistic, literary or artistic material,

(b) the data controller reasonably believes that, having regard in particular to the special importance of the public interest in freedom of expression, publication would be in the public interest, and

(c) the data controller reasonably believes that, in all the circumstances, compliance with [statutory provisions] is incompatible with the special purposes.

3.137 In determining whether belief that publication is in the public interest is reasonable, it is specifically provided that account is to be taken of any relevant code of practice. Such codes are to be designated by the Secretary of State. Examples given in the House of Lords included codes prepared by statutory bodies such as the Independent Television Commission, the Broadcasting Standards Commission and non-statutory bodies such as the Press Complaints Commission. It was suggested that:

> We have deliberately placed on the face of the Bill, I believe for the first time in an Act of Parliament in this country, that the public interest is not the narrow question of whether this is a public interest story in itself but that it relates to the wider public interest, which is an infinitely subtle and more complicated concept.

Scope of the exemption

3.138 The Act defines a range of provisions which will not apply where processing is carried out for the special purposes. With the exception of the seventh principle relating to data security, the data protection principles will not operate, neither will the subject access provisions nor those enabling a data subject to object to data being processed. Also excluded are the provisions of section 12 relating to subject rights in respect of automated decision making and the general provisions of section 14 relating to the subject's rights to compensation. These latter provisions are substituted, however, by special and more extensive rights.

3.139 These exceptions are wide ranging. One consequence will be that even the unlawful obtaining of personal data will not expose the controller to action under the Data Protection Act – although other criminal sanctions such as, for example, a charge of theft, may be imposed in respect of the offending conduct. It should be stressed that these exceptions apply only to the period of time prior to publication of material. A data subject, for example, will not be able to exercise access rights to discover material which a newspaper has obtained about, for example, financial dealings and which will form the core of a report on the subject's activities. Once the story has appeared the subject access provisions will apply subject only to the normal exceptions.

Procedural aspects

3.140 The question whether processing is covered by one of the special purpose exemptions is likely to arise in the course of legal proceedings. In this regard it is provided that proceedings must be stayed when the data controller claims, or it appears to the court, that the data are being processed for a special purpose and:

> With a view to publication by any person of any journalistic, literary or artistic material which, at the time twenty four hours immediately before the relevant time, had not previously been published by the data controller.

The relevant time will be the moment at which the controller makes the claim for protection or the court determines that the processing is for a special purpose.

3.141 It will be recognised that there is no requirement that the controller's claim that processing is covered by the special purpose should have any merit. As discussed below, procedures for the lifting of such a stay are complex and the Registrar has criticised the situation whereby an unscrupulous party could delay proceedings for a period of months, if not years, with little justification.

3.142 Once a court has determined that procedures should be stayed, the focus of attention switches to the Commissioner, who will be required to make a written determination as to whether the processing is being conducted only in connection with one of the special purposes or with a view to the publication of material not previously published by the data controller. In obtaining evidence necessary to reach such a view, the Registrar may require to exercise powers conferred under the legislation to serve a special information notice. Service of such notice may itself be the subject of an appeal to the Data Protection Tribunal. If the Registrar determines that the processing is not exempt, this finding may itself be appealed to the tribunal. It will only be when appeal procedures have been exhausted that the determination will come into effect and the court will be in a position to lift the stay. Although reference was made to the possibility of a 'fast track' procedure for resolving appeals to the tribunal, the Registrar has been markedly less optimistic than the government as to the possibility that disputes can be resolved speedily.

Codes of practice

3.143 Provision relating to codes of practice was inserted into the 1984 Act at a late stage during its parliamentary passage by a somewhat reluctant government, which pointed to the nebulous legal status of these documents. Under the 1984 regime, the Registrar's role is limited to encouraging 'trade associations or other bodies' to prepare and disseminate codes of practice'. Such codes had no formal legal status –

a fact confirmed by the Data Protection Tribunal in the case of *DPR v Innovations* (unreported), in which it held Innovations to be breach of the data protection principle relating to the fair obtaining of data, even though its conduct complied with a relevant industry code of practice.

3.144 In spite of doubts concerning their legal status, a considerable number of codes have been adopted under the Act. The directive also envisages a substantial role for both national and Community codes, art 27 providing:

> 1. The Member States and the Commission shall encourage the drawing up of codes of conduct intended to contribute to the proper implementation of the national provisions adopted by the Member States pursuant to this Directive, taking account of the specific features of the various sectors.
>
> 2. Member States shall make provision for trade associations and other bodies representing other categories of controllers which have drawn up draft national codes or which have the intention of amending or extending existing national codes to be able to submit them to the opinion of the national authority.
>
> Member States shall make provision for this authority to ascertain, among other things, whether the drafts submitted to it are in accordance with the national provisions adopted pursuant to this Directive. If it sees fit, the authority shall seek the views of data subjects or their representatives.

3.145 The major novelty for the UK is the directive's provision that supervisory agencies should take a view on the conformity of a draft code with statutory requirements. This is coming close to giving an unelected agency law making powers, a practice which traditionally has been resisted in the UK.

3.146 The Data Protection Act establishes two roles for the Commissioner in respect of codes of practice. Acting either on her own initiative or under the direction of the Secretary of State, and after consulting with relevant trade associations and representatives of data subjects, the Commissioner may 'prepare and disseminate codes of practice for guidance as to good practice'. Any code of practice prepared following directions from the Secretary of State is to be laid before Parliament either in its own right or as part of another report by the Commissioner to Parliament.

Transborder data flows

3.147 Transborder data flows do not constitute a new phenomenon. During the nineteenth century the development of telegraph networks provided a medium for the speedy transfer of data both nationally and internationally. The possibility that messages might be sent into or out of the jurisdiction without the possibility of control caused concern to many governments. A response was to require a physical break in the telegraph network at the national border and to require that messages be decoded and carried across the border in paper format before being retransmitted. The delays involved in the process when, for example, a message was to be sent from Madrid to Berlin, coupled with the potential for transcription errors to be introduced, threatened the viability of the international telegraph system. The International Telegraph Union (now the International Telecommunications Union) was established in 1865, in large measure to promote governmental confidence in the integrity of the system and to avoid such artificial barriers to the use of communications technology.

3.148 In keeping with history's tendency to repeat itself, concerns at the implications of transborder data flows have been evolved paralleling the development of national data protection statutes. Typically, the fear is expressed that an absence of control may result in evasion of national controls. Controls over transborder data flows have been a feature of almost all national data protection statutes with restrictions being justified on the basis of safeguarding the position of individuals. Whilst there may be concerns at the implications of transfers, however, transborder data flows are essential for commercial activities. Many thousands of messages must be transmitted prior to an aircraft flying from London to New York. This will include passenger details. In this context transborder data flows constitute no mere esoteric topic. If the data cannot flow, planes cannot fly.

International initiatives

3.149 As concern at the impact of national controls over telegraphic and then voice traffic led to the establishment of the ITU, so international initiatives have sought to establish what are effectively free trade zones in respect of personal data. In 1980 the OECD adopted Guidelines on the Protection of Privacy and Transborder Flows of Personal Data. These guidelines, which have no legal effect, were supplemented by a Declaration on Transborder Data Flows adopted in 1995. This declared its signatories' intention to 'avoid the creation of unjustified barriers to the international exchange of data and information'. The UN has also adopted 'Guidelines Concerning Computerised Personal Data Files', whilst the most extensive and effective form of international action has been taken by the Council of Europe. Beginning with sets of recommendations directed at public and private sector data processing adopted in 1973, the Convention for the Protection of Individuals with regard to the Automatic Processing of Personal Data was adopted in 1981 and ratified by the

UK following the enactment of the Data Protection Act 1984. The convention prescribed minimum standards which were to be provided in national data protection statutes and provided that no barriers were to be imposed on grounds of protection of privacy in respect of data flows between those states which had signed and ratified the convention.

3.150 The Council of Europe Convention has been shaped by the experiences and practices of western European states which have adopted data protection legislation. Such legislation has three major features. First, it applies to all sectors of automated data processing; second, it contains substantive provisions regulating the forms of processing which can take place and the rights and remedies available to individuals; finally, it provides for the establishment of some form of supervisory agency. A different approach has prevailed in other countries, notably the US.

Transatlantic differences

3.151 The US approach can be characterised as one of privacy protection with laws generally being introduced on a sectoral basis – often in response to publicised instances of informational misuse. To give one example, the Video Records Privacy Act was introduced following disclosure of details of videos (revealing a penchant for pornographic material) rented by a US judge, the information being disclosed at the time his nomination for appointment to the Supreme Court was being considered in Congress. The result of this approach is that, whilst some areas are well protected, others, especially in the private sector, are less so. It has been suggested for example, that records of a person's video preferences are better protected than medical records. A further point of distinction relates to the US reluctance to establish supervisory agencies along the lines of the Data Protection Commissioner. Such agencies are seen as excessively bureaucratic with the US preference being for individuals to pursue their own complaints regarding data processing before the courts.

3.152 To date, the discrepancies in approach between Europe and the rest of the world have been of limited practical significance. Whilst the Council of Europe and the Data Protection Act of 1984 left it open to national authorities to prohibit a transfer of data to a third country where it was considered that the result would be a breach of one or more of the data protection principles, this power was seldom invoked. In the 16 years since the 1984 Act was enacted, only one case has been reported from the UK of a proposed data transfer being blocked. This prohibited the transfer of personal data in the form of names and addresses to a variety of US organisations bearing such titles as the 'Astrology Society of America', 'Lourdes Water Cross Incorporated' and 'Win With Palmer Incorporated'. These companies, which had been involved in the promotion of horoscopes, religious trinkets and other products in the UK, were the subject of investigations by the US postal authorities alleging wire fraud and a variety of other unsavoury trading practices

3.153 With the implementation of the EU Directive containing stringent provisions regulating transborder data flows this may change, the Directive's provisions in this respect being the cause of considerable and continuing transatlantic controversy. The provisions will be of particular significance to the operation of multinational companies as well as to undertakings such as airlines which operate on a worldwide basis.

Requirement for an adequate level of protection

3.154 Major decisions concerning the operation of the new system will be made at a Community level. To this extent, the provisions of the directive are more important in the field than those of the 1998 Act. The directive's preamble recognises the dilemmas arising in this area:

> Whereas cross-border flows of personal data are necessary to the expansion of international trade; whereas the protection of individuals, guaranteed in the Community by this Directive does not stand in the way of transfers of personal data to third countries which ensure an adequate level of protection.

The critical questions are, of course, what might be considered an adequate lack of protection and whether any perceived inadequacies in general legal provisions might be overcome by other sources of rights and remedies?

3.155 In implementing this principle the directive requires member states to ensure that:

> the transfer to a third country of data which are undergoing processing or which are intended for processing take place only if . . . the third country ensures an adequate level of protection.

Effect is given to this provision by the Act's eighth data protection principle, which provides that:

> Personal data shall not be transferred to a country or territory outside the European Economic Area unless that country or territory ensures an adequate level of protection for the rights and freedoms of data subjects in relation to the processing of personal data.

Procedures for determining adequacy

3.156 The determination what might be considered an adequate level of protection has been the cause of considerable and continuing controversy and uncertainty. It would appear that the determination is to be made by reference to both substantive and structural provisions in the third country. Given that the notion of having omnibus data protection statutes is largely limited to Europe, the effect might be to cut the continent off from data links with the rest of the world. Even where a third country accepted a right of privacy and the notion of subject access, its regime might be stigmatised for lack of any supervisory agency along the lines of the Data Protection Commissioner.

3.157 Mirroring provisions in the directive, the Data Protection Act states that the issue of adequacy is to be assessed by reference to a range of factors, including the nature of the data and of the proposed transfer, the legal position in the recipient country, including any international obligations, together with any relevant codes of practice and any provisions relating to data security.

3.158 Use of the phrase 'adequate level of protection' clearly does not carry the requirement that the laws of the recipient state conform in every respect with the provisions of the directive. It would appear unlikely, however, that a total absence of data protection legislation could be regarded as providing adequate protection. As has been discussed earlier, the US has followed a very different model of privacy protection from that adopted in Europe. Although proposals have been brought forward for the introduction of a data protection statute, there appears little prospect that this situation will change in the near future.

The Commission Working Party

3.159 The uniform application of the directive would clearly be threatened if the decision whether third countries offered an adequate level of protection was to be made by each member state. It is provided therefore that the member states and the Commission are to inform each other of any cases where they feel that a third country does not provide an adequate level of protection. In practice, general decisions regarding adequacy will be made at a Community level. Article 29 of the directive establishes a Working Party on the Protection of Individuals with regard to the Processing of Personal Data. This Working Party is to be:

> composed of a representative of the supervisory authority or authorities designated by each Member State and of a representative of the authority

or authorities established for the Community institutions and bodies, and of a representative of the Commission.

3.160 If the Working Party determines that a third country does not provide an adequate level of protection, a report is to be made to a committee established under art 31. Consisting of representatives of the member states and chaired by the Commission, the Committee will consider a proposal from the Commission for action on the basis of the Working Party's findings and deliver an opinion. The Commission may then adopt legal measures. Member states are obliged to take any additional measures necessary to prevent data transfers to the country involved.

3.161 Utilisation of this procedure may have the result of establishing a 'black list' of countries to which data transfers will be prohibited. The directive also provides for the procedures described to be used to identify countries which the Commission considers does provide an adequate level of protection. Given the reference in the directive to the role of 'sectoral rules' and 'professional rules and security measures', it is perhaps unlikely that there will be many 'black listings' affecting all data processing activities in a particular jurisdiction.

Transfers where an adequate level of protection is not provided

3.162 As originally drafted, the directive's prohibition of data transfers to a country which did not guarantee an adequate level of protection was not offered was absolute. Even allowing for the provisions relating to acceptance of sectoral and professional rules, such an approach would have posed major problems for transborder data flows. As adopted, the directive modifies this provision to a considerable extent, it now being provided that national implementing statutes may authorise transfers, notwithstanding the absence of adequate protection in the recipient state where:

(a) the data subject has given his consent unambiguously to the proposed transfer; or

(b) the transfer is necessary for the performance of a contract between the data subject and the controller or the implementation of pre-contractual measures taken in response to the data subject's request; or

(c) the transfer is necessary for the conclusion or performance of a contract concluded in the interest of the data subject between the controller and a third party; or

(d) the transfer is necessary or legally required on important public interest grounds, or for the establishment, exercise or defence of legal claims; or

(e) the transfer is necessary in order to protect the vital interests of the data subject; or

(f) the transfer is made from a register which according to laws or regulations is intended to provide information to the public and which is open to consultation either by the public in general or by any person who can demonstrate legitimate interest to the extent that the conditions laid down in law for consultation are fulfilled in the particular case. (art 26(1))

3.163 The 1998 Act makes full use of these provisions. Transfers coming under these headings may take place, subject to their being in conformity with any entry on the Data Protection Register without the need for any further permissions. The directive provides additionally that:

> a Member State may authorize a transfer or a set of transfers or personal data to a third country which does not ensure an adequate level of protection . . . where the controller adduces adequate safeguards with respect to the protection of the privacy and fundamental rights and freedoms of individuals and as regards the exercise of the corresponding rights; such safeguards may in particular result from appropriate contractual clauses.

Any exercise of this power must be reported to the Commission and the other member states.

Contractual solutions

3.164 In recent years considerable attention has been paid to the possible role of contract in ensuring equivalency of protection in respect of transborder data flows. The Council of Europe, in co-operation with the Commission of the European Communities and the International Chamber of Commerce, has produced a model contract which might be used by data users for this purpose.

3.165 The objectives of the model contract are stated as being:

a. to provide an example of one way of resolving the complex problems which arise following the transfer of personal data subjected to different data protection regimes;

b. to facilitate the free circulation of personal data in the respect of privacy;

c. to allow the transfer of data in the interest of international commerce;

d. to promote a climate of security and certainty of international transactions involving the transfer of personal data.

The contract terms are divided into five sections. The first two concern the obligations of the party initiating the transfer, the licensor, and those of the recipient, the licensee. The licensor is obliged to ensure that all domestic data protection requirements have been satisfied, whilst the licensee undertakes to ensure that these are complied with in the course of his or her activities. The contract also proposes a number of more detailed obligations which should be accepted by the licensee. Thus, the purpose for which the data will be used should be specified, there should generally be a prohibition on processing of sensitive data, the data shall be used only for the licensee's own purposes and any errors subsequently notified by the licensor will be rectified immediately upon receipt.

3.166 Further provisions would hold the licensee liable for any use which may be made of the data and require that the licensor be indemnified in the event of liability arising through the licensee's breach of contract or negligent act. In the event of any dispute between the parties, the model contract contains provisions for dispute resolution. Reference is made to the possibility that disputes may be submitted to arbitration under the rules established by the International Chamber of Commerce (ICC) or the United Nations Commission on International Trade Law (UNCITRAL). Finally, provision is suggested for the termination of the contract in the event of a failure by the licensee to demonstrate good faith or to observe the terms of the agreement. Any personal data held by the licensee must be destroyed in such an eventuality.

3.167 The Commission Working Party produced a report in April 1998, outlining its 'preliminary views on the use of contractual terms in the context of transfers of personal data to third countries'. This document identified a number of elements that must be found in any relevant contract. The contract must provide for observance of the data protection principles. Whilst it was recognised that no system could provide a total assurance of compliance, it would be required that the provisions should provide a reasonable level of assurance, should provide support and assistance for data subjects and appropriate forms of redress.

3.168 The utilisation of contractual techniques may provide what has been described as 'a sort of palliative or complement to the legal framework for data protection and transborder data flow'. There remain, however, a number of objections to their widespread utilisation. A major problem concerns the enforceability of contracts at the suit of an aggrieved data subject. Under the doctrine of privity of contract, only those who are party to the instrument can generally rely on it in the course of legal proceedings. It might be, for example, that a data user in the UK would enter into a contract with a user in the US under which it is agreed that data will be transferred to the US with the recipient agreeing to observe all aspects of the data protection principles. In the event the US party were subsequently to deny a request for subject access in breach of the principles, although an action for breach of contract may be available to the exporting data user, there would not appear to be any remedy for the data subject. A possible approach suggested by the Working Party was that the UK controller would enter into a contractual agreement with the data subject undertaking to compensate for any damage or distress suffered as a result of the data being transferred to a third country.

The 'safe harbor' negotiations

3.169 Almost since the enactment of the directive, negotiations have been taking place between the EU and US with a view to achieving a satisfactory mechanism to ensure that data flows between the two jurisdictions are not adversely affected. The key approach has been to seek to devise a set of so-called 'safe harbor' principles. US-based data processors could indicate to its Department of Commerce to observe these principles, which are designed to replicate the substantive requirements of the directive regarding the conditions under which personal data might lawfully be processed. The principles also require mechanisms to ensure that disputes regarding the validity of processing activities may be adjudicated by an independent agency. To date, however, the 'safe harbor' principles have not been accepted by the Commission Working Party as providing an adequate level of protection with particular concern focusing on the lack of a public sector enforcement mechanism. Discussion remains ongoing.

Conclusion

3.170 Given the nature of the Internet and its manner of operation, it may be questioned how far there is today any realistic prospect of exercising control over transborder data flows. If consideration is given to the nature of computer networks, concepts such as transfer take a secondary place to the issue of access. Where information is provided on a WWW site, it may be a matter of semantics whether the data is accessed by browsers or is transferred to them. Whilst the motives of the EU in attempting to safeguard the interests of its citizens should be applauded, the contrast may be made between the UK's overt reference to the fear of being placed in a form of data quarantine as a reason for the enactment of the Data Protection Act 1984 and the facility with which countries in the Caribbean and Far East proclaim their status as data havens in seeking to secure inward investment. If true progress is to be made, the task for the EU will be to secure the minds of third countries, persuading them of the need to introduce data protection legislation. It will only be when the subject moves beyond its Western European fiefdom that there will be the realistic prospect of control over global computer networks.

Chapter 4

Computer fraud, hacking and viruses

The emergence of the problem

4.0 It appears an inevitable feature of technological developments that criminal applications follow legitimate uses with very little time lag. The computer has proved no exception to the rule. The first instances of computer-related crime date back to the 1960s, with the topic beginning to attract the attention of academic and industrial commentators from the early 1970s. Today, if credence is given to popular myth, the Internet and financial institutions are the constant target of fraudsters, computer viruses constantly threaten the survival of computer networks, whilst the most secret information held on computer systems is at the mercy of the computer hacker

4.1 As computer applications have developed and expanded, so the focus of legal and popular debate has tended to shift over the years. In the early stages much attention focused on the involvement of computers in fraudulent schemes. Given the state of technology and the fact that the financial sector were early users of computer technology areas, this was perhaps inevitable.

4.2 The issues concerned with computer fraud differ from those relating to other aspects of the topic. In a situation where someone takes money or other property belonging to another person, there is little doubt that a criminal offence will be committed. The more significant issues concern the questions when and where such an offence is committed and which courts will have jurisdiction to hear any case. With the development of global communications networks, computer fraud – as with other forms of computer-related crime – is increasingly adopting an international dimension. In one recent case, banking computers located in the US were penetrated by hackers in St Petersburg, accounts belonging to customers in a range of South American countries were fraudulently debited and the proceeds diverted through other accounts in Finland, Germany, Israel, the Netherlands and the US. One of the individuals suspected of

96

involvement in the scheme was subsequently arrested at Stansted Airport in England. Although, ultimately, the individual was extradited to the US where he pled guilty to various charges of fraud, extradition proceedings were prolonged and complex.

4.3 As technology developed, other forms of conduct became feasible. Telephone companies were early users of computer systems and the practice referred to as 'phone phreaking' revolved around attempts by users to manipulate telephone networks and their controlling computers in such a way as to obtain free telephone calls. Developing from extremely basic origins, when it was discovered that a toy whistle supplied as a free gift with packets of breakfast cereal mimicked exactly the frequency used by telephone network codes used to bypass charging mechanisms, practitioners developed more elaborate electronic techniques.

4.4 Once again, the activities involved could be characterised as a species of fraud and a number of individuals were prosecuted and convicted on this basis. As the number of computer systems increased, new forms of conduct became possible. By the early 1980s communications between geographically separate computer systems was possible and with it the possibility of external access to computer systems. Although the terms 'hacking' and 'hacker' have a lengthy pedigree in computer technology, they have now become synonymous with the act of obtaining unauthorised access to a computer system and, more specifically, obtaining this access by means of a telecommunications connection from another computer.

4.5 Often linked in the public mind with the activity of hacking is the promulgation of computer viruses. The dictionary defines the word virus as:

> the transmitted cause of infection: a pathogenic agent, usually a protein-coated particle of RNA or DNA, capable of increasing rapidly inside a living cell.

For its computer equivalent, a simple definition refers to 'malicious software which replicates itself'. Although some viruses can be relatively harmless, and indeed it has been suggested that the programming techniques incorporated in some forms of virus could usefully be used for purposes such as copying documents, there is no doubt that the concept has entered into popular demonology. Like human viruses, computer viruses can readily be transmitted from one computer to another either by the exchange of an infected disk or, as is increasingly the case, may be transmitted over the Internet when a user downloads information from a remote site.

4.6 In addition to the use of the Internet as a means for disseminating viruses, much concern is currently centred on what the European Commission have referred to as 'illegal and harmful content on the Internet'. Here the focus is more on the activities of computer users with the key issue concerning the application and, more problematically, the enforcement of statutes relating to matters such as pornography or the dissemination of racially inflammatory material in the context of the operations of worldwide computer networks. This aspect of the topic will be considered in the following chapter.

The legal response

4.7 In considering the application of the criminal law to instances of computer-related conduct a variety of issues arise. One of the most critical is whether computer-related conduct should be regarded as requiring technology specific legislation or whether it might satisfactorily be regulated through the application of more general criminal law provisions. Although a trend can be identified throughout Europe and the US to enact computer crime statutes, experience in the UK with the Computer Misuse Act 1990 suggests that such an approach is not without its pitfalls. The debate preceding the enactment of this statute was notable for a difference of opinion between the Law Commissions for Scotland and England concerning the scope of such legislation, the Scottish Law Commission being considerably more sanguine about the effectiveness of general provisions of the criminal law.

4.8 Although the enactment of the Computer Misuse Act in 1990 followed the deliberations of the Law Commissions, it must be stressed that no attempt was made to develop a comprehensive computer crime statute. To this extent, the provisions of the Computer Misuse Act, albeit of considerable significance, should not distract attention from the role played by other aspects of the criminal law. In most respects, the provisions of this statute supplement rather than substitute for the provisions of the general criminal law.

4.9 Another issue which is sometimes neglected in the debate on the role of the criminal law concerns the availability of other legal remedies. In the case of *Denco v Joinson* [1992] 1 All ER 463, for example, the Employment Appeals Tribunal ruled that the act of an employee in seeking to obtain access to information held on the employer's computer for purposes unconnected with his employment constituted serious industrial misconduct justifying summary dismissal. Again, a university or school student making use of computer equipment for an unauthorised purpose may face disciplinary sanctions. As will be discussed below, the Computer Misuse Act criminalises the act of unauthorised access to data rather than its unauthorised use. Where an employee or student has access rights it may be unlikely that a criminal offence has been committed. The fact, however, that dismissal or expulsion results might be seen as sufficient punishment.

4.10 Regardless of the form of the legal response two propositions may be put forward for consideration:

- In the event conduct is criminal when it is conducted other than on or by means of a computer, the same result should apply when the technology is utilised.

- In the event that conduct is not generally regarded as criminal, it should not become so when it occurs in a computer context.

4.11 The topics of computer fraud and of damage to data provide the main examples of conduct which would generally attract criminal sanctions in a non-computer context. The relatively uncontroversial element of recent law reform has concerned the attempt to remove lacunae created by the inappropriateness of traditional formulations and concepts within the context of information technology applications. As will be discussed below, these efforts have not always been successful and it appears a feature of case law that modern statutes, drafted to take account of the features of computer technology, have not fared notably better before the courts than more venerable enactments

4.12 The second proposition is more contentious and debate has been especially heated on the issue whether the act of obtaining unauthorised access to information held on a computer (commonly referred to as hacking) should be criminalised in the situation where the act of obtaining access does not serve as the precursor to further aggravating conduct, such as the deletion of data or the evasion of access charges. Apologists for hackers would argue that activities are driven by the challenge of identifying weaknesses in security measures. On this analysis, hacking becomes a intellectual pursuit similar in concept, perhaps, to solving crossword puzzles. In terms of the legal response, the act of obtaining unauthorised access to information might be analogised with conduct which is invasive of individual privacy. As has been discussed previously, neither English nor Scots law currently recognises any general right to privacy and it may be queried whether the notion of informational privacy should be defined in the sense of conferring rights of privacy on information (and information holders).

Computer hacking

4.13 In strictly computing terms, a hack is a quick fix or clever solution to a restriction. A 'hack' is a temporary if ingenious fix or 'make do', rather than an attack on a system. Tricking a machine into performing an unintended task is the predominant characteristic of a 'hack'; even well-known simple tricks such as sticking sellotape over pre-recorded audio or video tapes to enable reuse as a 'blank' tape can be described as 'hacks'. In the popular – and in the legal – mind, however, hacking has become unequivocally associated with the act of obtaining unauthorised access to programs or data held on a computer system. This initial act if often followed by attempts to modify or delete the contents of a computer system. When, for example, the Communications Decency Act, which sought to impose controls over the content on Internet sites, was being debated in the US legislature, hackers secured access to the Department of Justice's WWW pages and replaced the department's logo with a pornographic picture. More recently it has been reported that hackers accessed a web page associated with the Stephen Spielberg film *Jurassic Park – The Lost World*, changing the title to *Jurassic Duck – The Lost Pond* and images of snarling dinosaurs into less threatening water fowl. Incidents such as these lend some weight to the notion that hacking is a relatively harmless phenomenon. Unfortunately, other forms of conduct can be far more damaging.

4.14 Consideration of the legal response to hacking prompted some of the most intense debates during the second half of the 1980s, when the Law Commissions' deliberations were leading towards the enactment of the Computer Misuse Act. There is little dispute that where the act of obtaining unauthorised access to the contents of a computer system is accompanied by further aggravating conduct, such as deletion or amendment of data, criminal sanctions should follow. The more controversial issue concerns the question whether the act of obtaining access to computer systems should, of itself, constitute a criminal offence. In a number of countries, it is provided that, in order for an offence to be committed, there has to be some element of overcoming security measures, thereby placing some onus on computer users to safeguard their own interests. Given the manner in which some of the more noted UK incidents of hacking have occurred, this might not seem an unreasonable requirement. In the leading case of *R v Gold* [1988] AC 1063, which involved unauthorised access to British Telecom's Prestel system, the perpetrators visited a computer exhibition where the system was being demonstrated by a BT engineer. By engaging in the practice known as 'shoulder surfing' they watched as he typed in his (own) password details. The password itself consisted of the number 2 repeated eight times, whilst the user identification number was the sequence 1234.

4.15 Although the Scottish Law Commission argued in favour of a requirement that a hacker should overcome security or cause some form of damage to the system, the Law Commission for England and Wales was swayed by reports of a number of cases where knowledge of the fact that unauthorised access had occurred led computer owners to expend significant amounts of time and labour in checking or even rebuilding a system in order to be certain that no damage had occurred. On this basis it was argued that the mere fact of obtaining unauthorised access should suffice as the basis of liability and this approach is adopted in the Computer Misuse Act, which provides that:

> (1) A person is guilty of an offence if—
> (a) he causes a computer to perform any function with intent to secure access to any program or data held in any computer;
> (b) the access he intends to secure is unauthorised; and
> (c) he knows at the time when he causes the computer to perform the function that that is the case.

Breach of the provision can be punished by a six-month term of imprisonment and a fine of up to £500.

4.16 In common with other statutory interventions in the computer field, no attempt is made to define any of the more technical terms. In order for the unauthorised access offence to be committed, a variety of conditions have to be satisfied. Access must be attempted or obtained, the access must be unauthorised and the person charged must know that this is the case. Application of these requirements has proved somewhat complex and a number of perhaps surprising court decisions have robbed the statute of at least some of its impact.

The concept of access

4.17 The first stage in the commission of the offence will consist of causing a computer 'to perform any function with intent to secure access to any program or data held in any computer'. This definition is exceptionally broad. Access will be secured to a program or data when the user, by causing the computer to operate in any manner:

(a) alters or erases the program or data;
(b) copies or moves it to any storage medium other than that in which it is held or to a different location in the storage medium in which it is held;
(c) uses it; or

(d) has it output from the computer in which it is held (whether by having it displayed or in any other manner)

4.18 Although the above provisions are somewhat tortuous, it is clear that any action whereby a user makes contact with a computer system and causes that system to display or to transmit information will come within its ambit. The simple act of switching on a computer will cause various messages to be displayed on the screen, whilst the act of making contact with some external system will cause some form of 'log in' screen to be displayed.

To a program or data held in any computer

4.19 The basic offence requires that access be sought to any program or data held in any computer. In order to commit the offence, it is not necessary that the unauthorised user should direct their attention at any particular computer system or seek to inspect any specific programs or data held in the system. The effect of this provision is to render liable to prosecution those hackers who, perhaps by dialling telephone numbers at random, seek to discover those which serve as the gateway to a computer system.

4.20 One further point deserves consideration as relevant to all of the offences established under the Act. No attempt is made to define the words 'computer', 'program' or 'data'. This is very much in line with the approach adopted in other statutes (such as the Data Protection Act) operating in the area. The offences, it will be recalled, relate to dealings in respect of programs or data and may be triggered by an act causing a program to perform its function. Many modern appliances make extensive use of simple computers, often consisting of a single microprocessor chip, to control their functioning. A washing machine may, for example, have its operation controlled by such chips, whose circuitry will contain the programs necessary for the performance of their dedicated tasks. Motor vehicles also are increasingly computerised, to the extent that it has been estimated that the value of the microprocessors used exceeds the cost of the metal used in manufacturing the car. In such a situation, it might be argued that an unauthorised person using the washing machine or car might be guilty of the unauthorised access offence. Especially in respect of the first scenario, this might appear an extreme and unwarranted consequence, but it does serve to illustrate the problem of framing special laws to deal with computers. Typically, the legal assumption appears to remain that computers are stand-alone pieces of equipment, when the reality is that they are inextricably integrated with a vast range of other products and systems.

The access is unauthorised

4.21 The question whether access is authorised can be determined only by reference to the intentions of a party entitled to determine such matters. Thus, access is held to be unauthorised when the user:

(a) is not himself entitled to control access of the kind in question to the program or data; and
(b) he does not have the consent to access of the kind in question to the program or data from any person who is so entitled.

4.22 In many cases, the person entitled to control access will be the owner of the computer system itself. In other cases, a computer system may serve as a 'host', providing storage space and access facilities for programs or data controlled by other parties. In this situation, the question who has the right to consent to access may be more complex. Most university computer systems provide illustrations of this form of activity. Here, the fact that a student is granted rights of access does not confer any entitlement to transfer these on to a third party.

4.23 In order to commit the offence, it is necessary that the unauthorised party should know that their presence is unwanted. In most cases, the initial act of making contact with a computer system will not suffice. Even though a hacker dialling telephone numbers at random (or making use of a number supplied by a fellow enthusiast) may well suspect that their attentions may not be welcome, and be reckless whether this would be the case, it may be very difficult to establish that they had actual knowledge that access was unauthorised.

4.24 The dividing line between reckless and intentional conduct may well be crossed at the time access is obtained to a computer system. A user accessing the main computer system at the author's university is presented with the message 'Unauthorised access to this system is ILLEGAL: Computer Misuse Act 1990'. The appearance of such a notice might be sufficient to support the argument that any further attempt to operate or access the contents of the system will be conducted in the knowledge that this is unauthorised. The installation of a security system, typically allocating authorised users with passwords and requiring these to be entered in order to proceed beyond the stage of initial contact, would undoubtedly reinforce this position.

4.25 More difficult situations will arise where the user has limited access rights. Typically, this may arise within an employment relationship or where computing facilities are made available to students. Here establishing that the user was aware of the fact that their access rights had been exceeded will require that the limitations be specified unambiguously. The Law Commission refer to the distinction between conduct which constitutes 'a deliberate act of disobedience, and indeed of defiance of the law' and that which amounts to 'merely carelessness, stupidity or inattention'. Only the former, it was recommended, should face prosecution under the Computer Misuse Act.

Unauthorised use by authorised users

4.26 A further distinction should also be made at this point. The legislation prohibits unauthorised access. It does not strike at the situation where access is authorised but the use to which it is put is unauthorised. As the Law Commission pointed out, the use of an office typewriter to type a private letter will not expose a typist to criminal sanctions and it would be most inequitable to alter that situation merely because a word processor was used. There may, however, be situations where such an approach may limit the effectiveness of the legislation. In the case of *R v Bignall* (unreported) a police officer obtained access to data held on the police national computer in order to identify the owner of a motor vehicle. The information was sought for the owner's personal interest and was not connected with his duties as a police officer. The conduct being discovered, he was charged with an offence under s 1 of the Computer Misuse Act. Although it was not contended that the use to which the data was put was authorised, the Divisional Court accepted submissions by counsel for the respondent to the effect that:

> the primary purpose of the Computer Misuse Act was to protect the integrity of computer systems rather that the integrity of information stored on the computers . . . a person who causes a computer to perform a function to secure access to information held at a level to which the person was entitled to gain access does not commit an offence under S.1 even if he intends to secure access for an unauthorised purpose because it is only where the level of unauthorised access has been knowingly and intentionally exceeded that an offence is committed, provided the person knows of that unauthorised level of access.

and held that no offence had been committed under the Computer Misuse Act. In a case such as *Bignall* there would be little doubt that the individual concerned might face disciplinary sanctions at work. It is also likely that an offence would have been committed under the Data Protection Act. As will be discussed below, however, the approach places a substantial obstacle in the path of prosecutions for certain forms of computer fraud.

Computer fraud

4.27 As suggested above, in the case where an individual pursues some fraudulent scheme to completion, there is no doubt that a criminal offence will have been committed. One problem may be to determine when the offence is committed. The case of *R v Thompson* [1984] 3 All ER 565 provides a useful illustration. Thompson was employed as a computer programmer by a bank in Kuwait. Whilst so employed, he devised a plan to defraud the bank. Details of customers' accounts were maintained on computer and, in the course of his work, Thompson was able to obtain information about these and, in particular, to identify five dormant accounts. These possessed substantial credit balances but had not been the subject of any debits or credits over a substantial period of time. This might well have been caused by the fact that the account holder had forgotten about the account's existence or had died. The chances of fraud being identified by the account holder would thus be minimised.

4.28 Having identified the target accounts, Thompson opened five accounts in his own name at various branches of the bank. He then compiled a program which instructed the computer to transfer sums from the dormant accounts to the accounts which he had opened. In an effort to reduce further the risks of detection, the program did not come into effect until Thompson had left the bank's employ and was quite literally seated in an aircraft returning to England. The program was also intended to erase itself and all records of the transactions once this task had been accomplished. Although the law report does not go into detail on this matter, the fact that Thompson stood trial for his actions might indicate that this part of the scheme was not completely successful.

4.29 On his return to England, Thompson opened a number of accounts with English banks and wrote to the manager of the Kuwaiti bank instructing him to arrange for the transfer of the balances from his Kuwaiti accounts. This was done. Subsequently, his conduct was discovered and Thompson was detained by the police. Charges of obtaining property by deception were brought against him and a conviction secured. An appeal was lodged on the basis that the English courts had no jurisdiction in the matter as any offence would have been committed in Kuwait.

4.30 Dismissing Thompson's appeal, the Court of Appeal ruled that the offence was committed only at the time when a message was sent from England to Kuwait instructing the transfer of funds from the Kuwaiti back accounts. At that time Thompson was in England and therefore the English courts had jurisdiction.

4.31 Given that Thompson was convicted of an offence, the case might be seen as an instance of the criminal law working effectively. The problem lies in the fact that a criminal offence was committed at a relatively late stage in the proceedings. In most areas of criminal law, the attempt to commit an offence is regarded as seriously as its completion. It might be argued that, whilst in Kuwait, Thompson was attempting to commit the offence. The criminal law, however, draws a distinction between conduct which is preparatory to and conduct which forms part of the perpetration of the offence. Although the distinction is not clear-cut, it is the case that a person can plan to commit an offence without fear of criminal sanctions. It will only be at the stage that the plan is put into operation that the conduct becomes a matter for the criminal courts. In the case of Thompson, the Court of Appeal held that his actions in altering data on the Kuwaiti bank's computer was equivalent to someone forging a cheque. Here the act of writing on the paper would not be unlawful. The paper would be of no value to the forger until the attempt was made to cash the cheque.

4.32 Such an approach is reasonable in the case of cheques. Literally billions of pounds are transferred every day between banks making use of computerised payment and electronic funds transfer systems. Some 85% by value of all money transactions in the UK are handled by some form of electronic fund transfer (EFT). Not only do the transactions represent vast amounts of money, their speed is also significant. It has, for example, been estimated that all of the UK's foreign currency reserves could be transferred abroad within 15 minutes. Under international protocols agreed between the participating banks, such transfers are regarded as irrevocable. To this extent, therefore, an electronic signal transferring funds from one account to another represents more than just evidence of the payee's entitlement to the specified assets. The ex-head of Scotland Yard's Computer Crime Unit has commented:

> The prevention of crime here is important. No, it's not important, it's vital. These days money is not the pound in your pocket; it's the $234 billion worth of transactions which go out from the City of London and back every day. All that money really amounts to is electronic digits travelling down wires. That's real money

4.33 In an effort to address these difficulties, s 2 of the Computer Misuse Act establishes what is referred to as the ulterior intent offence providing that:

> (1) A person is guilty of an offence under this section if he commits an offence under section 1 above ('the unauthorised access offence') with intent—
> (a) to commit an offence to which this section applies; or
> (b) to facilitate the commission of such an offence (whether by himself or by any other person);
> and the offence he intends to commit or facilitate is referred to below in this section as the further offence.

4.33 The key word in the section is, perhaps, 'facilitate'. Essentially, the intention is to bring forward in time the moment at which a serious criminal offence is committed. The maximum penalty for breach of the section is a five-year term of imprisonment and a fine of an unlimited amount.

4.34 Subsequent events have shown the limitations of the approach. Most studies of computer fraud have indicated that the offence is typically committed by or with the connivance of employees. The *Thompson* case can be seen as typical in involving a person who has a right to access the computer systems involved. The case of *DPP v Bignall* [1998] 1 Cr App R 1 has been referred to above as indicating that use of access for an unauthorised purpose does not constitute a s 1 offence. Commission of such an offence is, of course, a pre-requisite for committing a s 2 offence. A further and very relevant case illustrating this point is that of *Re Allison* [1999] 4 All ER 1. This involved the attempt to defraud the American Express Corporation. Allison who was employed by the American Express corporation in a capacity which required her to have access to customer account details held on its computer systems. Allison, it was alleged, in conjunction with a number of other persons, used her access to obtain data relating to accounts, the data being used to facilitate the issuing and use of false credit cards. Allison was subsequently arrested in England and the US authorities sought his extradition. In order for a person to be extradited from the UK, it is necessary that the conduct complained of should constitute an offence under UK law. In the present case it was argued that a s 2 offence would have been committed. This contention was rejected by the courts. As in the *Bignall* case, the American Express employee was authorised to access the computer system. Although access rights were misused, this did not constitute an offence under s 2.

4.35 The result in these cases might appear somewhat strange. It should not be taken to give a green light for computer fraud. In the

Allison case, extradition was authorised on other grounds relating to the making of an unauthorised modification to the contents of the American Express computer. This offence will be discussed below. In a sense, the result is in line with the status of the Computer Misuse Act as an 'anti-hacking' measure. Almost by definition, hackers are outsiders, seeking to obtain access to the contents of a computer system. By focusing on external parties, the statute ignores the unfortunate fact that most instances of computer misuse are committed by insiders. Whilst it may well be debated whether the availability of other sanctions may serve to deter employees and other insiders from misuse of computer systems, the fact that s 2 of the Computer Misuse Act has never been successfully invoked in a domestic case may cast doubt on its utility.

Computer viruses and unauthorised modification of data

4.36 Anyone possessing a degree of familiarity with computers and their method of operation will be only too well aware how fragile is the hold on electronic life of any piece of data. The accidental depression of a key or the placing of a computer disk in undue proximity to a magnetic field as produced by electrical motors or even telephones, can speedily consign data to electronic oblivion. To the risks of accidental damage have to be added those of deliberate sabotage.

4.37 The vulnerability of computer users to such events is not questioned. Once again, our concern must be with the legal consequences which may follow such behaviour. The basic scenario involves a party altering or deleting data held on a computer system, such action taking place without the consent of the system owner. Within this a wide range of activities can be identified. At the most basic level, the perpetrator may use 'delete' or 'reformat' commands or even bring a magnet into close proximity to a computer storage device. Other actions may be driven by the intent to cause disruption to the computer owner's activities. This might involve manipulation of computer programs through, for example, the insertion of logic bombs, whilst an ever expanding range of computer viruses present a continual threat to the well-being of computer owners. Finally, data held on a computer may be modified through the use of keyboard commands so as to impair its reliability or accuracy as in the cases of *Thompson* and *Allison* discussed above.

4.38 Prior to the 1990 Act, a number of successful prosecutions were brought under the Criminal Damage Act 1971. This Act provides that:

A person who without lawful excuse destroys or damages any property belonging to another intending to destroy or damage any such property . . . shall be guilty of an offence.

The most important computer-related case brought under this Act was perhaps that of *R v Whiteley* [1991] 93 Cr App Rep 25 which, rather ironically, was decided by the Court of Appeal after the Computer Misuse Act had entered into force. The case concerned the activities of Whitely who, operating under the pseudonym 'The Mad Hacker', exploited security loopholes made extensive (and expensive) use of the UK's academic computer network, JANET. Using his computing skills he was able steadily to extend his user rights eventually obtaining the status of the controller of particular computers. This allowed him to delete the files 'Accounts Journal' and 'Systems Journal', which would otherwise have recorded details of his activity.

4.39 After some time, the computer operators became aware of unusual activities on their machines. Efforts were made to detect the intruder and for some considerable time a game of 'cat and mouse' was played between the appellant and the operators. On one occasion, the appellant was reported as having been sufficiently 'astute to detect a special programme [sic], inserted by the legitimate operator to trap him and deleted it'. On a further occasion, the appellant succeeded in 'locking' legitimate users out of the computer systems. On occasion also, the appellant's activities caused computer systems to 'crash' and increasingly insulting messages were left in files. Ultimately, British Telecom instituted monitoring of telephone calls into computers frequently attacked by the appellant. Detecting a suspicious call, this was traced back to the appellant's home. He was arrested and charges of criminal damage were brought.

4.40 As with many incidents recounted previously, no damage was caused to any physical components but operations were seriously impaired and considerable staff time was expended in restoring the systems to full operation and in tracking down the perpetrator. The prosecution's contention, which was accepted both by the jury and the Court of Appeal, was that the changes made to the information held on the system would constitute criminal damage. Delivering the judgment of the court, Lord Lane CJ ruled:

What the Act requires to be proved is that tangible property has been damaged, not necessarily that the damage itself is tangible. There can be no doubt that the magnetic particles upon the metal discs were a part of the discs and if the appellant was proved to have intentionally and without lawful excuse altered the particles in such a way as to cause an impairment of the value or usefulness of the disc to the owner, there would be damage within the meaning of s 1.

4.41   Although the prosecution in *Whiteley* was successful, the view was taken that a computer specific offence should be introduced. Section 3 of the Computer Misuse Act now provides that:

(1) A person is guilty of an offence if—
 (a) he does any act which causes an unauthorised modification of the contents of any computer; and
 (b) at the time when he does the act he has the requisite intent and the requisite knowledge.

The Computer Misuse Act also modifies the provisions of the Criminal Damage Act in order to make it clear that in order to constitute the offence of criminal damage there must be damage to physical property.

What constitutes an unauthorised modification?

4.42   The concept of modification encompasses the addition of data or its alteration or erasure. A modification will be regarded as unauthorised if the person causing it is not authorised so to act or does not possess the consent of a person who is so entitled. Again, the possibility of different categories of rights and privileges attaching to different users must be borne in mind. Typically, an employee or a student may be entitled to use the facilities of a computer system but will not be entitled to delete any portions or to add any programs.

4.43   The effect of the modification must be:

(a) to impair the operation of any computer;
(b) to prevent or hinder access to any program or data held in any computer; or
(c) to impair the operation of any such program or the reliability of any such data.

It is immaterial whether the modification or its effects are intended to be permanent or merely temporary. There is also no requirement that the degree of impairment or restriction on access should be substantial. In theory, changing one letter in the text of a word processed document held on a computer without the authority of the computer owner would constitute the offence.

4.44   In the first prosecution brought under this provision of the Act, the accused had installed a security package on a computer belonging to a firm which he claimed owed some £2,000 in fees. The effect of the installation was to prevent the computer being used unless a password was entered. As this was not disclosed, the computer was effectively rendered unusable for several days with resultant losses estimated at some £36,000. The accused was convicted and fined £1,650. Amendments to data may also produce adverse effects. In one reported case, a nurse altered prescription details and other records on a hospital computer. The possible consequences of such activities do not need to be described and a conviction was secured under the Act.

4.45 An offence may also be committed when data is added to a computer system. One instance of this, which will be discussed below, occurs when a computer is infected with a virus. The offence will also be committed where logic bombs or other programs are added to the computer system with the intent that these will operate so as to cause inconvenience to the computer user. In one instance an IT manager added a program to his employers' system which had the effect of encrypting incoming data. The data would automatically be decrypted when it was subsequently accessed. The manager left his employment following a disagreement and some time later the decryption function ceased to operate. Once again, the effect was to render the computer unusable. Despite claims that the encryption function was intended as a security device and that the failure of the decryption facility was an unforeseen error, the manager was convicted of an offence under the Act.

4.46 A more interesting case, brought under the legislation, concerned a contract for the supply of bespoke software. The customer was late in making payment for the software and shortly afterwards the software stopped working. It transpired that the supplier, anticipating possible problems with payment, had inserted a time lock function. Unless removed by the supplier upon receipt of payment the software would stop working from a specified date. This conduct resulted in prosecution and conviction under the unauthorised modification offence.

4.47 In addition to proscribing acts impairing the operation of a computer, the unauthorised modification offence may be committed when data held on a computer is modified in a fashion which may affect its reliability. A possible scenario might involve an individual giving false information with a view to causing the modification of an unfavourable entry on a credit reference agency's files. This might render unreliable the data held on the computer and, as such, may constitute an offence under s 3.

Viruses and the unauthorised modification offence

4.48 Taking the concept of an unauthorised modification as a whole it would seem clear that the offence might be committed by a person who creates a computer virus and sends it out into the world with the intention that it will infect other computers. The Computer Misuse Act provides in this respect that:

> (3) The intent need not be directed at—
> (a) any particular computer;
> (b) any particular program or data or a program or data of any particular kind; or
> (c) any particular modification or a modification of any particular kind.

The originator will cause the modification of any computer which is infected even though they may not be directly responsible for the infection of any particular machine, this being brought about by an unsuspecting (or even reckless) authorised user. To this extent the phrase 'to cause' must be interpreted in two senses: in respect of the act which causes the effect and also of the act which is proximately responsible for its occurrence.

4.49 One of the most publicised cases brought under the Computer Misuse Act involved the prosecution of Christopher Pile. Using the pseudonym 'Black Baron', the accused was reported as having told detectives that 'he had wanted to create a British virus which would match the worst of those from overseas'. A number of viruses were created by Pile and concealed in seemingly innocuous programs which he published on the Internet. From there they would infect any computer onto which they were downloaded. It was estimated that the effects of the virus cost companies in the region of £500,000 and Pile secured the dubious distinction of being the first virus writer convicted under the Act being sentenced to a term of 18 months' imprisonment

4.50 In addition to being used against those who create a virus, the Act could also be used against those who deliberately cause a computer to be infected. Once again, the requirement that the prosecution establish intent may prove difficult to satisfy. In many cases viruses are spread through users bringing infected disks into offices or educational establishments. Many users now have policies either prohibiting the practice or requiring that disks be checked on a dedicated virus checking machine prior to being used. If an individual ignores these requirements and causes a viral infestation, the conduct might reasonably be characterised as reckless, but this would still fall some way short of the statutory standard.

Conclusions

4.51 The Computer Misuse Act is now some ten years old. It is difficult to argue that it has been a complete success. In the first case brought under the Act, *Attorney-General's Reference (No 1 of 1991)*

[1992] 3 WLR 432 wholesale locksmith. He left their employ but subsequently returned to the premises, indicating the intention to purchase an item of equipment. Details of sales transactions were entered into a computer terminal. The defendant was familiar with the use of the system and, taking advantage of a moment when the terminal was left unattended, entered a code into the system. The effect of this was to instruct the computer to give a 70% discount on the sale. Upon these facts coming to light, the defendant was arrested and charged with an offence under the Computer Misuse Act. At trial, the judge dismissed the charge, holding that the phrase in s 1(1)(a) referring to obtaining access to 'any program or data held in any computer' required that one computer should be used to obtain access to a program or data held on another computer.

4.52 This interpretation was speedily corrected by the Court of Appeal, the Lord Chief Justice stating that there were:

> no grounds whatsoever for implying or importing the word 'other' between 'any' and 'computer', or excepting the computer which is actually used by the offender from the phrase 'any computer'.

Any statute is vulnerable to strange interpretations. In another case a jury acquitted a defendant who had admitted to obtaining unauthorised access to numerous computer systems. Although no reasons are given why any jury reaches a particular verdict, it would appear that they may have accepted a claim that the accused was addicted to hacking and therefore acted under a form of compulsion rather than with intent.

4.53 When decisions such as these are coupled with others such as *R v Bignall*, there may be legitimate debate whether the Computer Misuse Act has proved an effective response to the undoubted problems of computer misuse. Whilst the notion of a technology specific statute might have represented an attractive option in the time when computers were fairly isolated items, we are at least moving towards an information society. The need is for the regulation of information and information technology to form an integral part of the criminal law.

Chapter 5

Criminal liability for content

Introduction

5.0 In 1995, at the meeting of the British Association for the Advancement of Science, estimates were put forward to the effect that almost half of all searches made using Internet search engines were seeking pornographic material. More recently, it has been suggested that searches using the term 'MP3' have taken the numerical lead. There remains, however, widespread concern at the extent to which the Internet may be used for the dissemination of material, especially pornographic in nature or which is intended to promote racial hatred.

5.1 In most instances it is questionable whether the involvement of the computer adds a new dimension to the question whether conduct may be classed as criminal. Behaviour which is unlawful in the real world is likely to be so regarded when conducted over the Internet. The Telecommunications Act 1984 provides that an offence will be committed by a person who:

> ... sends by means of a public telecommunications system, a message or other matter that is grossly offensive or of an indecent, obscene or menacing character.

Virtually every on-line services will involve use of a public telecommunications system at some stage and users will be exposed to the risk of prosecution should they transmit messages of this nature. A number of instances of successful prosecutions will be described below. Problems may, however, arise in two areas. First, there is the problem of defining or categorising the Internet. Different forms of regulation have tended to apply to different storage media and means of delivery. In part this has been dictated by the accessibility of material. A television broadcast, for example, is more accessible than a film in a cinema and is subject to more stringent regulation. Likewise, a greater degree of tolerance has tended to be given to printed works than to photographic materials. As has and will be

114

discussed, the Internet does not fall easily into existing categories of communications media. A second problem may prove even less soluble. The Internet is a global network. Material may be placed on a server anywhere in the world and accessed anywhere else. In theory, this means that the Internet is perhaps the most heavily regulated sphere of activity in existence, as any country may claim jurisdiction in respect of material accessible from its territory. Claiming jurisdiction is very different from being able to enforce it in any meaningful manner. If material is lawful in the country from which it originates, there may be little that any other jurisdiction can do to regulate it. In a report on the work of the UK's Internet Watch Foundation, it was suggested that of 453 reports made concerning the presence of pornographic material, in only 67 cases was the material held on a UK-based server. The bulk of the material was held in the US with, rather more surprisingly, Japan constituting the second largest host country.

5.2 Faced with the undoubted limits of legal control, considerable attention has been paid to what might be classed as self-help measures. In January 1999 the European Commission adopted an 'Action Plan on Promoting Safe Use of the Internet'. This claims as its objective:

> promoting safer use of the Internet and of encouraging, at European level, an environment favourable to the development of the Internet industry.

and indicates the Commission's intention to assist member states to develop systems of industry self-regulation, develop filtering tools allowing responsible persons to control the range of materials which may be accessed from a computer and encourage international co-operation.

5.3 A number of industry initiatives operate in the UK. UKERNA, which is the agency responsible for the operation of the academic network JANET, maintains a list of newsgroups which may not be accessed over its facilities. More generally, the Internet Watch Foundation was established by a number of the largest Internet service providers in 1996. In part this was a response by the industry to suggestions made by the Metropolitan Police that prosecutions might be brought against Internet service providers unless the industry took steps to regulate material accessible through its servers. As a number of recent cases have demonstrated, possession of material classed as child pornography is unlawful whilst Internet service providers could also be classed as publishers and subject to prosecution under statutes such as the Obscene Publications Act.

5.4 The Internet Watch Foundation's activities can be divided into two categories. It seeks to encourage the use of systems of content rating. A number of system exist such as PICS (Platform for Internet Content Selection) and RSACi, devised by the Recreational Software Advisory Council. The foundation also acts to report instances of potentially illegal material to the appropriate Internet service provider and law enforcement agencies. To date its efforts in seeking to prevent prosecutions being brought against service providers appear to have been successful, although it has been stressed by law enforcement agencies that no guarantee of immunity has been given. Implementation of the EU's draft directive on electronic commerce might reduce the liabilities of Internet service providers as a matter of law. Discussed in more detail in Chapters 14 and 15 below, this provides in art 12 that service providers will not be liable (other than to an injunction regarding future behaviour) where the provider:

(a) does not initiate the transmission;
(b) does not select the receiver of the transmission; and
(c) does not select or modify the information contained in the transmission.

5.5 In such cases, the service provider is considered to provide a 'mere conduit' through which information will flow. Article 15 goes on to provide that service providers are to be under no obligation:

> To monitor the information which they transmit or store, nor a general obligation actively to seek facts or circumstances indicating illegal activity.

If implemented in the UK, the effect of this provision would be to provide immunity to service providers save whether they had actual knowledge of the illegal nature of materials.

Computer pornography before the courts

5.6 As indicated above, in the vast majority of cases, the fact that images or text are recorded and transmitted on digital media rather than on paper or video tape will not affect the determination whether contents are obscene or pornographic. In similar manner to the topic of computer fraud, the use of computers and computer communications networks such as the Internet to disseminate material considered to contravene criminal statutes relating to obscene or pornographic material, raise comparatively few substantive legal issues. If material is considered to be illegal, this conclusion will generally not be affected by the medium in which it is displayed or disseminated. A number of issues have, however, arisen in recent years which provide useful illustrations of the problems encountered in trying to fit forms of computer related conduct into regulatory schema devised in the light of previous forms of technology.

Pseudo photographs

5.7 In the Criminal Justice and Public Order Act 1994 provisions were included to extend the ambit of the Criminal Justice Act 1988 and the Protection of Children Act 1978 to prohibit the possession or distribution what are referred to as 'pseudo-photographs'. The essence of a pseudo-photograph is that what appears to be an indecent image of a child is made up of a collage of images, modified by the use of computer painting packages, none of the elements of which is indecent in itself. Typically, the original photograph will have been of an adult but processed to alter the size of body parts to make the image appear to be one of a child. It is now provided that an offence will be committed where:

> If the impression created by a pseudo-photograph is that the person shown is a child, the pseudo-photograph shall be treated for all the purposes of this Act as showing a child and so shall a pseudo-photograph where the predominant image conveyed is that the person shown is a child notwithstanding that some of the physical characteristics shown are those of an adult.

The definition of a photograph extends to 'data stored on a computer disc or by other electronic means'.

5.8 Under the terms of the Act, an offence is committed by a person who distributes such a photograph or who has 'in his possession such photographs or pseudo-photographs with a view to their being distributed or shown by others'. The fact that possession may be a basis for conviction should give service providers cause for concern. A defence is provided that an accused 'had not himself seen the photographs or pseudo-photographs and did not know, nor had any cause to suspect, them to be indecent'. In the situation where users of a service are responsible for loading images, the service provider may be able to make use of this defence.

5.9 The Protection of Children Act, thanks to its amendment in 1994, is a relatively modern statute with its definition of photograph specifically formulated to include computer data. In many other cases, cases will require to be brought under older statutes with definitions dating back to the days when films were stored on paper or celluloid. An example of such a situation can be seen in the case of *R v Fellows* [1997] 2 All ER 548. This appears to have been the first case in which the word 'Internet' appears in the judgment of an English court. The appellant, who was at the time employed by the University of Birmingham, had, without its knowledge or consent, compiled a large database of pornographic images of children. The database was maintained on an Internet-linked computer belonging to the university. The conduct in question occurred before the entry into force of the 1994 Act's provisions and therefore the prosecution had to be brought under the older definition of photograph. The question before the Court of Appeal was whether images stored on a computer disk could be classed as photographs. Although outdated in respect of the application of the particular law, the case provides a useful indication of judicial response to the situation where new technology enables forms of behaviour which could not have been foreseen when statutory provisions were enacted.

5.10 Answering the question in the affirmative, two issues addressed by the Court of Appeal call for comment. First, whether graphical files held on a computer fell within the statutory definition of a copy of a photograph for the purposes of the 1978 Act and, second, whether a computer hard disk containing these files could be classed as an 'article' for the purposes of the Obscene Publications Act 1959.

5.11 Although aspects of the noun 'photograph' are defined in the 1978 Act, there is no general definition. In the Copyright Act 1956 'photograph' was defined as 'any product of photography or of any process akin to photography'. The trial judge and Court of Appeal both made reference to dictionary definitions of the term as 'a picture or other image obtained by the chemical action of light or other radiation on specially sensitised material such as film or glass'. On this basis the data stored on the computer's hard disk could not be classed as a photograph. The statutory prohibitions, however, extended to 'a copy of a photograph'. The computerised images had been produced by scanning 'conventional' photographs and it was held that nothing in the 1978 Act required that the copy of a photograph should itself be a photograph. Given the copyright status of a photograph as an artistic work and the broad definitions of copying applying to such works, there can be little ground to challenge such a finding.

5.12 Although this approach sufficed in the particular case, many cameras now record images directly onto disk rather than film. The contents of the disk may then be transferred directly to a computer and the image viewed on screen. There need never be any 'traditional' photograph to act as an original. In such a situation it may be doubted whether even the most purposive interpretation of the 1978 statute could have sustained a conviction.

5.13 Both the 1959 and 1978 Acts were enacted before the impact of computers had permeated the legislature's consciousness. The Court of Appeal's judgment indicates that, providing basic concepts are robust, a purposive interpretation can maintain the relevance of statutory formulations so long as electronic activities retain a connection with tangible acts or items. More substantial problems occur when electronic signals constitute the original record rather than a reproduction of a physical object. Here law reform will often be required. It is somewhat ironic, however, that in a number of cases concerned with computer-oriented statutes, the purposive interpretative techniques adopted in the present case appear to have been replaced by a much more literal and restrictive approach.

Multimedia products

5.14 A further case concerned with the application of obscenity law to computer related material is that of *Meechie v Multi-Media Marketing* [1995] 94 LGR 474. The defendant company established a club, 'The Interactive Girls Club', described as being an 'organisation dedicated to the production of erotic computer entertainment for broad-minded adults'. One product presented users with a short game. Successful completion of this would cause the display of a series of erotic images. A knowledgeable user would have been able to isolate the game element, moving directly to the erotic display.

5.15 Under the provisions of the Video Recordings Act 1984, introduced to control the distribution of so-called 'video nasties', it is an offence to supply video recordings which have not been issued with a classification certificate. No certificate had been sought or issued for the particular game and charges were brought under ss 9 and 10 of the Act alleging respectively supply and possession with a view to the supply of infringing recordings.

5.16 These charges were dismissed before the magistrates, who held that the product in question did not come within the scope of the legislation. Section 1 of the statute defines a 'video work' as:

> any series of visual images (with or without sound)—
> (a) produced electronically by the use of information contained on any disc or magnetic tape; and
> (b) shown as a moving picture.

Although it was accepted that the disc in question satisfied the requirements of s 1(a), it was held that the images did not constitute a 'moving picture' by reason both of their brevity and of the staccato nature of the presentation, which appeared more akin to a series of still images. It was further held by the magistrates that the work in question was excluded from the legislation by the provisions of s 2, which provides that a video game is not to be subject to the classification requirements.

5.17 Both of these findings were reversed by the Divisional Court. In respect of the argument that the display lasted for a short period of time, it was held that the short duration of the images in no way prevented their being regarded as a 'moving picture'. A significant development arising from advent of fast and powerful personal computers has been the linkage between text, sound and graphics. In the present case this relates to a computer game and picture sequences but the same could be said of most multimedia products. It would appear arguable, following the decision of the Divisional Court, that many multimedia products could also be classed as video recordings and hence be required to seek classification under the regulatory schema. Although there may be an argument in favour of such an approach, it would be difficult to explain to average computer users that their multimedia encyclopaedias are in reality video recordings.

5.18 The exemptions from the requirement to submit a video recording for classification under the legislation apply to computer games and to works 'designed to inform, educate or instruct'. In the present case, the court was able to separate the picture sequences from the game-playing element and so remove the former from the scope of the exemption. It must be likely that in the future there will be instances where video images are integrated more fully with the elements of a game, thereby making the classification more difficult. This will almost inevitably be the case with multimedia products. The court's dicta, which must be seen as affording a very restricted scope to the exemption, may make this of limited significance, and it would be arguable that many examples of multimedia products dealing with medical or artistic topics would be taken outside its scope.

5.19 A further point which may be a cause for future difficulty concerns the definition of a moving picture. Although the finding of the court was to the effect that the duration of a recording is of minimal significance in determining whether it is to be classed as a 'moving picture', there cannot have been many traditional recordings with a running time of less than 30 seconds. In the present case the images could be analogised to a more traditional cinematographic recording. In other computer-related products, the duration of individual picture sequences may be very much shorter. Even more problematically, a user may be afforded the opportunity to select particular aspects of an image for expansion or perhaps to manipulate the form of the still image. Such activities may present the impression of movement but it is not clear how they should be regarded for the purpose of the legislation.

5.20 The cases described above indicate clearly that traditional definitions can be applied in the context of digital technology. As indicated, however, although the results may seem desirable and justifiable in the context of particular cases, the decisions may raise more questions than they answer. Digitally recorded information is an extremely pliable commodity and one which does not fit easily into existing models. Images stored and transmitted over the Internet can be viewed by large numbers of people simultaneously making them appear akin to a broadcast. So called, 'webcasts' are an increasingly popular component of the Internet. Again, with the Internet, there is less and less need for individuals to maintain their own copies of works. If information can be accessed when required there is little need to maintain a permanent recording. Statutes such as the Video Recordings Act may be bypassed. These points will be considered in more detail below.

Applying legal provisions to the Internet

5.21 The development of the Internet and of systems such as the World Wide Web pose greater problems for the application of the legislation. In order for an offence to be committed under the Video Recordings Act 1984 a disc or magnetic tape must be supplied (or possessed with a view to supply). In the event that materials is made available over the Internet no tangible items will be supplied. As in the case of *R v Gold* [1998] AC 1063, where it was held that electronic impulses transmitted in the form of a user password could not class as an 'instrument' for the purpose of the Forgery and Counterfeiting Act 1981, such a transmission would not appear to class as a recording. It may be considered an unsatisfactory situation where material supplied on disk will face prosecution under the Video Recordings Act, whilst the same material transmitted over the Internet will escape sanction save, perhaps, under the more stringent criteria of the obscene publications legislation.

5.22 In part, the problem for the law and for law enforcement agencies is that the pace of technological development is so rapid that even comparatively modern statutes such as the Video Recordings Act and the Forgery and Counterfeiting Act can be applied only with considerable difficulty. Perhaps more fundamentally, developments such as multi-media and the World Wide Web straddle existing categories of works and defy precise categorisation. Text, which has hitherto been subject to minimal legal regulation, becomes inextricably linked with visual images, which have traditionally been subject to a much more rigorous system of regulation and control. When, as with the US Communications Decency Act, discussed below, legislation seeks to extend to cover textual material transmitted or stored in electronic form, the spectre of censorship is raised by civil libertarian lobbyists. The dilemma for the law maker is that be that the alternative to the extension of regulation may be to allow a de facto reduction in the controls previously exerted in respect of visual materials on the somewhat dubious basis that these are stored or transmitted in electronic format. There is no doubt that material such as that at issue in *Meechie* can and should be treated in the same manner as equivalent information held on a video tape. What is more questionable is whether a multimedia encyclopaedia should be treated differently by the law than its printed predecessor.

The Communications Decency Act

5.23 One of the most publicised attempts to control the content of material made available over the Internet occurred in the US with the passage of the Communications Decency Act 1996. This sought to control the dissemination of 'indecent' material over computer networks and indicates that attempts to introduce legislative controls over aspects of computer-related conduct are likely to prove controversial in the extreme. The Communications Decency Act created a number of offences providing that:

> (a) Whoever—
> (1) in interstate or foreign communications—
>> (B) by means of a telecommunications device knowingly—
>>> (i) makes, creates, or solicits, and
>>> (ii) initiates the transmission of,
> any comment, request, suggestion, proposal, image, or other communication which is obscene or indecent, knowing that the recipient of the communication is under 18 years of age, regardless of whether the maker of such communication placed the call or initiated the communication.

A second provision, prohibits the knowing sending or displaying of 'patently offensive messages in a manner that is available to a person under 18 years of age'.

5.24 A defence was, however, provided where it could be established that a person:

> (A) has taken, in good faith, reasonable, effective, and appropriate actions under the circumstances to restrict or prevent access by minors to a communication specified in such subsections, which may involve any appropriate measures to restrict minors from such communications, including any method which is feasible under available technology; or
> (B) has restricted access to such communication by requiring use of a verified credit card, debit account, adult access code, or adult personal identification number.

5.25 Immediately following the Act's entry into force, legal challenges were raised by a number of organisations challenging its constitutionality. This complaint was upheld by the Supreme Court, which held that the statute contravened the First Amendment to the Constitution of the United States, which guaranteed freedom of speech. To this extent the case is of little relevance outwith the US, although the provisions in the legislation providing a defence in the event technical measures are used to facilitate control over access is echoed in much recent European work in the area.

Jurisdictional issues

5.26 A further and perhaps more significant issue concerns the difficulty of applying localised concepts of obscenity, which are dictated by cultural, religious and societal values, in the global environment of the Internet. The attempts by Nottingham County Council to prevent publication on the Internet of a copy of a summary of a report into the handling by social work officials of a case of alleged Satanic abuse illustrate graphically the near impossibility of such an endeavour. Following publication of a copy of the report on a UK-based web site, the council obtained a High Court injunction preventing publication of the report on the basis that its reproduction infringed their copyright. It was stated that the order extended to any hypertext links to other sites maintaining copies of the report. Although the order was observed within the UK, by the time it was issued, copies of the report were also to be found on a number of other web sites around the world. A letter from Nottinghamshire's County Solicitor to the operator of a US Web site threatening legal proceedings unless its copy was removed drew a somewhat stinging response. Admitting to the presence of a copy of a report it was pointed out that the council –

> ignore the fact that I and my web site are located in Cleveland, Ohio, in the United States of America, a locus where the writs of the courts of the United Kingdom have never run.

5.27 As for the threat of legal action:

> My first reaction was simply to ignore this bit of silliness, grounded as it was on the misconception that the 'Copyright, Designs and Patents Act 1988' of the United Kingdom applies to actions taken in the United States when, as I trust you know, that Act specifically provides that copyright holders' exclusive rights apply only to 'acts in the United Kingdom' . . .
>
> But I confess that I found your threats irritating enough that I began to think that I should comply with your demand—publicly. I have little difficulty in imagining the headlines that would have resulted had I taken such a course of action: 'English Prosecutor Forces U.S. Law Professor to

Suppress Report on Satanic Social Workers' or 'Satanic Coverup Spreads to US.'

After all, no one would have mirrored the Broxtowe report at their sites on the World Wide Web had you not sought to enjoin its original publication. One would have thought that you would have learned that lesson by now. There are at least a dozen web sites where the report is mirrored, not one of which would have existed if you had not sought to suppress its original publication on the web. And at my site alone the report has already been retrieved more than 2,500 times. For those of us who are opposed to governmental censorship of information on the World Wide Web, this reaction is gratifying. I doubt that it is so for your client.

5.28 Numerous other instances could be cited of the failure of attempts to impose national controls. In the so-called *Homulka* case in Canada, a husband and wife were accused of committing a horrendous double murder and were to be the subject of separate trials – the wife tendering a plea of 'guilty' to the charge of manslaughter. An order was made prohibiting the publication in Canada of any report of the hearings involving the wife until the husband's trial had been concluded. Once again, the ban was of some effect where traditional media were concerned but served to prompt the establishment of a number of 'Usenet' newsgroups which carried full details of the case.

5.29 Other developments in the US raise a further issue which is of wider significance. The individual states retain power to determine what constitutes obscene material. This has raised questions whether the operators of on-line services may be subjected to the most restrictive laws of the range of jurisdictions where the service is made available. Whilst this may be the case in the situation where a service provider has a physical point of presence in a particular locality, in other instances:

> We may see a 'race to the bottom' of the type that created Delaware corporate law. Local jurisdictions may compete to provide a regulatory framework that rewards local placement of a hard disk. In a world of cheap bandwidth, users won't care where data is stored, any more than they care about where the corporate charter is filed . . . Even if we don't see a rise of 'data havens', there will be a natural selection of regulatory regimes that favor the net.

5.30 Against this, however, the case of *US v Thomas* (1997) US App LEXIS 12998 illustrates that parties located within one jurisdiction but offering services or facilities over the Internet may find themselves subject to the most restrictive legal regime reached by their activities. In this case the defendants operated a computer bulletin board allowing subscribers to download pornographic images (which appear to have been placed on the system in breach of copyright in the original pictures). Subscribers, who were required to submit a written application giving details of name and address, could also order videos, which would be delivered by post. Under US law, a federal statute provides that an offence is committed by a person who:

> knowingly transports in interstate or foreign commerce for the purpose of sale or distribution, or knowingly travels in interstate commerce, or uses a facility or means of interstate commerce for the purpose of transporting obscene material in interstate or foreign commerce, any obscene, lewd, lascivious, or filthy book, pamphlet, picture, film, paper, letter, writing, print, silhouette, drawing, figure, image, cast, photograph, recording, electrical transcription or other article capable of producing sound or any other matter of indecent or immoral character.

5.31 The interpretation of this provision may vary between states, the Supreme Court having accepted that the determination whether material is obscene is to be made having regard to 'contemporary community standards'. The material in question was considered lawful in California.

5.32 Following a number of complaints, a postal inspector in Tennessee subscribed to the board under an assumed name. In return for a fee of $55, he was able to download a number of images. The defendants were charged and convicted before the Tennessee courts of breach of the federal statute cited above. Appealing against conviction, it was argued that material had not been transported by the defendants. Alternatively, it was contended that that the trial court had erred in applying Tennessee standards of morality. Both arguments are clearly significant in the context of WWW activities.

5.33 The argument against transportation is essentially a simple one. The material in question remained on the defendants' bulletin board. All that was transmitted was a series of intangible electrical impulses, whilst the terms of the statute related to tangible objects. This argument was rejected by the Court of Appeals:

> Defendants focus on the means by which the GIF files were transferred rather than the fact that the transmissions began with computer-generated images in California and ended with computer-generated images in Tennessee. The manner in which the images moved does not affect their ability to be viewed on a computer screen in Tennessee or their ability to be printed in hard copy in that distant location.

5.34 This decision involves a robust interpretation of the statutory provision. Although it may appear in accord with the intention of the statute, it may be queried whether a UK court would adopt a similar approach. In the case of *R v Gold*, for example, it was accepted that the electrical impulses caused to be transmitted by the respondents could not themselves constitute an 'instrument'. If followed, however, the US reasoning might resolve the potential anomaly whereby sale of computer software in the form of a disk might be regarded as sale of goods, whereas electronic delivery of the same software could not.

5.35 The second ground of appeal is perhaps more relevant for the present discussion. The defendants, whose case was supported by a range of organisations including the American Civil Liberties Union and the Electronic Frontier Foundation, argued that:

> the computer technology used here requires a new definition of community, i.e. one that is based on the broad-ranging connections among people in cyberspace rather than the geographic locale of the federal judicial district of the criminal trial.

Although there is evidence to suggest that users of the Internet may consider themselves more intimately connected with fellow 'netizens' than with their physical neighbours, it would appear both extreme and undesirable to allow such an opt-out from national legal provisions.

5.36 In the particular case it would have been open to the appellants to have refused subscription requests from users in jurisdictions such as Tennessee. Although it might be argued that this would require detailed knowledge of 'contemporary community standards' throughout the US the possibility of controlling access by reference to geographic location was present. Where, as is typically the case with WWW sites, all registration activities take place on-line, it is much more difficult to restrict access. It would be arguable whether the display of a notice limiting access to a WWW site to users within a particular jurisdiction would suffice to defend a prosecution of the kind brought in *Thomas*.

5.37 The case provides useful evidence that the 'lowest common denominator' standard will not always prevail. The prosecution, however, could only succeed because US federal law provided for state courts to have jurisdiction in such cases and, more importantly, for mechanisms allowing the defendants to be brought to trial. Where service provider and user are located in different jurisdictions enforcement will become much more problematic. Invariably, extradition will only be sanctioned by national authorities where the conduct complained of would constitute an offence if committed on its own territory. If the bulletin board had been located in, for example, Denmark, and the material been lawful there, short of visiting the US, the service providers would have no cause to fear the application of Tennessee law.

Conclusion

5.38 The extensive reference to US cases in the preceding paragraphs should serve to indicate the global nature of the problems arising from conduct taking place on the Internet. That said, there is no doubt that cyberspace is regulated by law at present, albeit enforcement is difficult. Cyberspace will continue to be regulated by law and we can expect that the level of enforcement will increase. For this to happen, there is need for a massive effort to secure international consensus and harmonisation. This will be no easy task. Whilst there is general agreement that theft is wrong, the question where the legal balance should be struck between the claims of freedom of expression and the imposition of controls over content exposes massive political, social, religious and cultural differences.

Chapter 6

Intellectual property law

What is intellectual property law and why does it matter?

6.0 Until recently, few lawyers felt themselves impoverished because they knew little of the somewhat esoteric subject of intellectual property law. Given that we lived in what was generally referred to as an industrial society, such an approach was not unreasonable. The bulk of legal education and of professional legal practice was concerned with what is sometimes referred to as 'real property'. The word 'property' can be used in two legal contexts. First, it refers to an object in itself. A motor car, for example, is a piece of property. More significantly, the word refers to rights over objects. The classic form of property right is that of ownership. Subject to the inevitable exceptions, ownership confers an exclusive right to use or dispose of the property as the owner wishes. The owner of a house may reside in it, let it to a tenant, sell it, leave it to a relative in a will or burn it to the ground.

6.1 As this book has sought to describe, times are changing and the needs of the information society differ from those of its industrial predecessor. As the examples of many Internet shares has shown, the value of a company may well lie less in its physical property than in the information and expertise associated with the exercise of its business. An early example of the phenomenon concerned American Airlines, which developed one of the first computerised reservation systems. When it decided to sell the system, the value placed on it exceeded that of all the planes in the airline's fleet.

Forms of intellectual property law

6.2 When we talk about knowledge and expertise, we refer to 'intellectual property'. The term is a somewhat nebulous one which encompasses any intellectual output coming directly or indirectly from a human brain. The definition is broad enough to include the output from computer systems. Intellectual property law defines

128

certain forms of output which are considered as deserving of a measure of legal protection. The extent of protection differs according to the nature of the information at issue. Three main categories of right can be identified:

- copyright

- patents

- trademarks

6.3 At the outset it may be stated that the role of intellectual property rights is to confer rights on the person responsible for conceiving ideas and reducing these to some usable format. In some situations, most notably concerned with the patent system, the right is close to the monopoly entitlement associated with items of real property. In the case of copyright, however, the right is much more limited in its scope and has been described as a 'specialised and limited form of property'. The difference between the two regimes might be illustrated by reference to the story of Alexander Graham Bell and Elisha Grey. Both men invented the telephone. Alexander Graham Bell reached the United States Patent Office slightly ahead of Grey. The patent system works in large measure on the principle 'first come, first served'. Bell was awarded a patent and the exclusive right to exploit the technology described therein. Even though Grey had worked totally independently, he was unable to exploit his own work as this would have conflicted with Bell's patent. In the event that the case should have centred on a copyright claim, Bell's protection would have been limited to preventing the copying of his work. Grey would not have infringed Bell's copyright and would, indeed, have obtained his own copyright in his own work. Patents, it might be concluded, confer a monopoly, whereas copyright can only be invoked to prevent copying or certain other forms of unfair exploitation of the work.

Intellectual property and information technology

6.4 Until recent times, the law of copyright was seen as having the most relevance to information-related products and activities. The reason for this can be traced to the origins of the system as providing a means for the protection of the interests of those responsible for authoring and publishing literary works. At the time when software development was widely seen as an art or craft rather than an industrial process, this view was not unreasonable. It was a relatively simple step to class computer programs as a form of literary work. The patent system has always been seen as applying to the industrial sector. It used to be commonplace to refer to patent law as a form of 'industrial property right'. This approach was relatively easy to support and apply in the days when computers were large, stand-alone machines used mainly for the making of mathematical calculations. With the spread of computers and the introduction of microprocessors it is a rare industrial process which is not influenced by some form of computer program. We invariably talk in terms of 'the software industry', and the software company Microsoft is now the world's most valuable company. The exclusion of software from the patent system has become increasingly difficult to defend. Decisions by the patent authorities and courts in a range of countries have indicated increasing willingness to allow patents to be granted for what are frequently referred to as 'software-related inventions'. Whilst the criteria for the grant of a patent are considerably more demanding than those relating to the acquisition of copyright, the greater legal strength of this form of protection is making the patent route increasingly the preferred option for software developers.

6.5 If copyright and patents can be seen as overlapping to some extent, the role of trademark law is significantly different. If this book had been written, perhaps, no more than five years ago, it is unlikely that the topic would have received any attention. The role of a trademark is to serve to distinguish the goods or services offered by one party from those of anyone else. The current UK law concerning trademarks is to be found in the Trademarks Act 1994, which itself seeks to implement the European Trademark Directive. Also relevant is the common law doctrine of 'passing off'. As the name suggests, this operates to prevent a party using names or other indicators which are likely to mislead third parties as to the true identity of the person with whom they are dealing. Typically the impression will be given that a person is connected with some well-known and well-regarded organisation.

6.6 A trademark may consist of anything which may be recorded in graphical format. Traditionally, marks have tended to take the forms of names or logos, but the scope is increasing, with sounds and even smells forming the subject matter of trademark applications. For the present purpose, attention can be restricted to the use of names. Given the increasing commercialisation of the Internet, organisations frequently seek the registration of a domain name which creates an obvious link with their real-life activities. The software company Microsoft, for example, can be found at *http://microsoft.com*. In many cases indeed, firms have obtained trademark registration for their domain name as such. 'Amazon.com', for example, is a registered trademark in the US.

New forms of protection

6.7 As will be discussed in the following chapters, the task of fitting software and software-related applications into traditional forms of intellectual property law has not been a simple one. In some areas the attempt has been made to develop new, specialised forms of protection. The main area in which this has been attempted has been in the field of databases, where a European directive established a new form of right – the database right. More generally, concerns have been raised at the continuing relevance of the more traditional forms of protection, with the question being raised whether, given the pivotal role of information in modern society, any one person should be permitted to enjoy exclusive rights concerning its exploitation.

Chapter 7

Copyright and software

The concept of copyright

7.0 Until the invention of the printing press in the sixteenth century, the task of copying any work was a substantial one, only a little less demanding than that of creating an original work. Some of the major cultural inheritances from the first millennium are the decorated Bibles produced by teams of monks labouring in monastery scriboreums. The printing press provided for the first time a relatively cheap and easy mechanism for the making of multiple copies of a work. Within 50 years of Gutenburg's invention around nine million books were in circulation in Europe. An increase in the number of books prompted increased demand for education. Increasing numbers of literate persons created increased demand for books to the extent that by the end of the eighteenthth century some 6,000 new titles were published annually in the UK alone.

7.1 Initially, the response of governments was to regard the new technology as a threat to social order and to seek to impose restrictions upon its use. Typically, possession of a printing press required governmental approval, whilst each work published required the grant of an official licence or *imprimatur*. By the end of the seventeenth century, in large part prompted by social and political changes, controls over the use of printing were relaxed. At this point, however, new problems emerged. Publishing had become a significant revenue earner. The authors and publishers of popular works increasingly expressed concerns that their income was threatened by the activities of what we might now refer to as pirate publishers, who would produce competing editions of successful works. In the seventeenth century the English courts developed notions of common law copyright. Scots law did not, however, recognise such a system. When the Act of Union created the United Kingdom in 1707, Scotland retained its own legal system. English-based publishers became concerned that Scots publishers could continue to produce pirate editions. In 1709 the UK Parliament stepped in and enacted the world's first copyright Act, the so-called Statute of Anne.

7.2 This Act established principles of copyright law which remain valid today. The essence of copyright is contained in the word itself. The owner of copyright possesses an exclusive right to copy or to authorise the making of copies of a protected work. Under the Statute of Anne, protection lasted for a period of 14 years. Subsequent statutes have increased the length of protection, which now subsists during the lifetime of the first owner of copyright and continues for a further 70 years after that party's death. At the end of this period the works fall into the public domain and can be published or amended by anyone. One notable illustration of this phenomenon was the appearance of a number of 'corrected' editions of James Joyce's epic but complex novel *Ulysses* shortly after the original work came out of copyright. Less contentiously, several series of low-cost editions of classic works consist of collections of out of copyright works.

7.3 As with other forms of intellectual property right, copyright can be disposed of as its owner thinks fit. Save in the case where a work is created in the course of employment – in which case copyright will belong to the employer – an author is first owner of copyright. Special rules apply where a work has joint authors. If it is possible to identify individual responsibility for particular elements, for example a song where one party is responsible for the lyrics and another for the musical notation, each party will own copyright in that component. In other cases there will be joint copyright.

7.4 In practice, an author's copyright is often transferred to the publisher of the work in return for some financial settlement. In the case of the present work, for example, study of the title page will reveal that copyright belongs to Reed Elsevier. Problems may arise where copyright remains with the original creator in respect of work commissioned by another party. Examples might concern a photographer commissioned to take wedding photographs or a computer programmer engaged (other than as an employee) to develop a software package for a customer. In both these cases, unless a different result is agreed by contract, copyright will remain with the photographer or programmer. In the event extra copies of photographs are required or the software package requires to be modified, the consent of the original creators will be required.

Modern-day copyright law

7.5 The current UK law relating to copyright is to be found in the Copyright, Designs and Patents Act 1988. This Act has been amended on numerous occasions, largely in order to implement European directives. Given the increasing economic significance of the intellectual property sector, the European Commission has promoted numerous initiatives designed to harmonise national laws in this area. Notable instruments include a Directive on the Legal Protection of Computer Programs adopted in 1991 and the 1996 Directive on the Legal Protection of Databases. A further and more ambitious proposal for a directive is currently being discussed under the heading 'Copyright in the Information Society'.

7.6 In addition to European initiatives, considerable international harmonisation of copyright law has been accomplished under the auspices of the Berne Convention. First negotiated in 1886, this has been amended on a number of occasions, most recently in 1979. Until recently, the major weakness of the Berne Convention has been the absence of the US from its list of signatories. This was due to the fact that the US, almost uniquely, required that a copy of a work be registered with its Copyright Office as a condition for the grant of protection. No such requirement was mandated by the convention and it was only with the modification of this requirement that the US was able to sign the Berne Convention. With its adherence, the convention has now virtually worldwide coverage with the principle benefit being that the copyright of an author resident in one signatory state will be enforced in any other state.

7.7 Although Berne establishes a requirement for recognition of third party copyright, the task of enforcing legal rights has proved difficult in many developing countries. As a consequence, the topic of intellectual property law has been raised in the context of the international trade negotiations, now conducted under the auspices of the World Trade Organization, connected with the General Agreement on Tariffs and Trade (GATT). The most recent round of agreements included a protocol on Trade Related Aspects of Intellectual Property Services (TRIPS), which obliges signatories to recognise concepts of intellectual property law and provide adequate means for their enforcement. This has proved to be a controversial point although more in respect of the patent than the copyright system.

Forms of protected work

7.8 The 1709 Act provided for protection in respect of original literary works. Subsequent statutes, often reacting to developments in technology, have extended the scope of protection. The invention of the gramophone produced a capability to make recordings of audio performances. Copyright law was soon amended to extend to such works. Similar results can be seen in respect of films, TV broadcasts and computer programs. All forms of work, however, can be placed into three basic categories:

• artistic;

• literary;

• musical and dramatic works.

7.9 In all recent national, European and international agreements it is provided that computer programs are to be protected by copyright as a literary work. Such an approach is consistent with previous developments in UK law, which has protected items such as tide and mathematical tables as literary works. The current UK copyright statute is the Copyright, Designs and Patents Act 1988. This statute, as amended on a number of occasions, states clearly that:

> 'literary work' means any work, other than a dramatic or musical work, which is written, spoken or sung, and accordingly includes—
> (a) a table or compilation,
> (b) a computer program, and
> (c) preparatory design material for a computer program.

7.10 That the 1988 Act makes specific provision for this should be seen more as avoiding any element of doubt than as introducing a new approach. In a number of cases brought under the previous Copyright Act of 1956, which, not surprisingly, made no mention of computer programs, courts had no hesitation in protecting software on this basis. The same would apply to 'preparatory design material', a heading which would include material such as flow and structure charts depicting the organisation of a program.

7.11 The elements of the program which justify protection as a literary work are the lines of code which cause it to operate in a particular manner. Especially at the level of source code, these will be written in a form which approximates to English. In the early days of computer programs the code was effectively everything. Many early computers, indeed, did not possess any form of visual display unit and even when these began to become commonplace, the graphical displays were very limited and basic. Today the situation has changed. The development of graphical user interfaces has meant that form becomes almost as important as function, whilst a massive increase in processing power has made possible the development of computer games, including extremely sophisticated sound and motion effects. To class a modern computer game as a literary work appears somewhat unrealistic.

7.12 Many works will benefit from a range of copyrights. In the case of a film, for example, in addition to the copyright subsisting in the finished work, any songs or music included will gain separate copyright, whilst the original scripts will be protected as literary works. In saying that computer programs are to be protected as literary works, copyright law is not to be taken as excluding the applicability of other forms of protection. Indeed, given developments in computer technology for the use of special effects, it is becoming increasingly difficult to determine where the category of computer program should end and that of film or television programme begin. The movie *Toy Story 2* is the first 'film' which exists only in digital format. Not only were most of the images computer-generated but, at the cinema, the images are projected from a computer rather than a roll of celluloid.

The requirement of originality

7.13 In order to be protected, a work must be original. The interpretation of the requirement of originality has been the source of considerable problems. In the UK system, the requirement is effectively that the work has not been copied from elsewhere. No qualitative criteria are applied. The juxtaposition of the names of a group of football teams to produce a fixture list has been held to be protected by copyright. The Football League earns substantial income from football pools companies in return for the right to use fixture lists on their coupons. Other countries tend to impose higher standards of originality, and reconciliation between the UK and continental systems has proved difficult in the context of EU attempts to harmonise copyright law. Particular difficulties have arisen in the context of computer programs and electronic databases.

How does copyright come into existence?

7.14 The establishment of copyright is a simple matter of recording a work in some material form. The Statute of Anne required that a work be registered with Stationers' Hall in order to be protected. This requirement was quickly removed from UK law, although provisions relating to registration of a work remain a feature of US copyright law. Writing text on a page or recording a song on a tape recorder will suffice. Likewise, the contents of an e-mail or newsgroup posting will be protected by copyright, a rule which is more often honoured in the breach than in the observance.

What acts constitute infringement of copyright?

7.15 The protection conferred by the copyright system extends against certain forms of unauthorised treatment of a protected work. The infringing acts constitute the making of a –

* reproduction,

* translation, or

* adaptation.

of all or a substantial part of the work. It will also constitute infringement of copyright to cause a work to be performed in public.

7.16 Reproducing a work can be equated with the making of a copy. The activity of translation would encompass producing a version of a work written in English into French. In both of these cases there will be a clear and direct link between the original text and the infringing version. Matters become somewhat more complex in respect of the making of an adaptation of the work. An obvious example might be the use of a historical work as the basis for producing a script for a play or film relating to the events described in the book. Here, comparison between the book and the script may indicate few literal similarities. In particular, a narrative will have to be replaced by dialogue and screen or stage directions.

7.17 As with many aspects of law, the question what is a substantial part of a work does not admit of an easy or certain answer. The determination will have both qualitative and quantitative elements. It would clearly not be open to an alleged infringer to claim that as only 99,999 words from a 100,000 word text had been copied, there was no breach of copyright. Equally, copying ten words from the text would be unlikely to constitute infringement. Copying a 1,000 word section of text might be legitimate, but not if those 1,000 words constituted an executive summary of the whole piece.

7.18 In the case of traditional works, the application of these provisions is generally non-contentious. Matters take on a very different appearance when copyright law is applied to software or, indeed, to other works recorded in digital format. The key problem is undoubtedly rooted in the fact that whilst a book can be read or audio cassette played without any requirement that the contents be copied, use of a computer program or audio CD requires that the contents be copied from their normal storage location into the processing elements of the computer or CD player.

Scope of copyright protection

7.19 A popular saying is to the effect that if enough monkeys are given enough typewriters, eventually one monkey will hit the keys in such an order as to reproduce the works of Shakespeare. Discounting the inconvenient fact that the works of Shakespeare are out of copyright and considerable uncertainty whether a monkey could own copyright, the end product would not infringe copyright for the reason that it represents an independent composition.

7.20 The question whether one work infringes copyright in an earlier work is determined on the basis of objective criteria. It is not necessary that the act should have been deliberate. A number of cases have been brought in which the allegation has been made (and sometimes established) that a musical work was derived from an earlier composition which might well have been heard by the second composer, who retained a subconscious memory of the melody. The fact that the copying or plagiarism was unintentional will not serve as a defence. The key factors which will have to be established by a party alleging copyright infringement is that the alleged copyist would have had access to the work and that there are substantial similarities between the works which are not explicable by factors other than copying.

7.21 In situations where two or more people are working on the same topic, for example a history of the Second World War, it is likely that similarities will exist between the finished works. In a non-fictional work, the ending must be the same and there is likely to be consensus regarding the key events of the conflict. Greater levels of similarity may raise suspicions that one author has relied too heavily on the work of the other.

7.22 In the US copyright system a distinction is drawn between ideas – which are not protected by copyright – and particular forms of expression. The so-called idea/expression dichotomy features prominently in many cases concerned with copyright infringement in software. Generally, however, although providing a useful soundbite, the idea/expression dichotomy can offer only limited assistance in determining whether copyright infringement has occurred.

Applying copyright principles to software

7.23 In the early days of computers, little attention was paid to the topic of intellectual property law. Computers were rare creatures. Generally, the machines would not be sold to a user but rather supplied under the terms of a rental agreement which would also make extensive provision for the manufacturer to supply technical support staff to minister to the needs of the sensitive machines. The software to run on a particular computer could be obtained only from the manufacturer of the hardware and therefore the possibilities for copyright infringement were limited. A US anti-trust decision in the 1960s which compelled the computer giant IBM to separate its hardware and software divisions marked a change in the situation, and the emergence of the PC has totally transformed the position. Although in many cases computers may come with a range of software packages pre-installed, a vast range of independent software developers provide application packages capable of running on PCs and, to a lesser extent, other computers such as Apple Macs.

7.24 In discussing the extent to which activities relating to software might fall foul of copyright law, three categories of potential infringement can be considered. The first two relate to what is called 'literal' copying of software. Here, the program code is directly copied. In the first instance, this may be done for commercial gain and will be discussed under the heading of software piracy. As indicated above, the act of using software necessitates the making of a copy of the work. This creates problems for the relationship between copyright owner and user and has led in part to the emergence of software licences. These documents, which are an almost inevitable companion to mass-produced software packages, typically confer user rights but at the expense of seeking to oblige the user to accept other provisions limiting or excluding liabilities in the event the software fails to operate in a satisfactory manner and thereby causes some form of injury or damage to the user.

7.25 The third category of infringement raises the most interesting legal issues. It concerns the situation where two programs exhibit similarities at the level of screen displays but not at the level of code. Although the phrase has rather fallen out of legal favour, the argument might be put in terms that one program has copied the 'look and feel' of another. This topic might also be considered at two levels. In the first, and more common, case the alleged infringer will have had some access to the original program's code. Typically, a programmer will have worked on the development of one package, moved to another employer and been involved with the development of a competing program. In the second category, the parties will act much more at arms' length, with the only access obtained by the alleged infringer being to the working copy of the program.

Software piracy

7.26 Various studies have been conducted, largely by or on behalf of organisations set up by software producers to fight instances of piracy. The most prominent global organisation is the Business Software Alliance (BSA) whilst at the UK level much work is done under the auspices of the Federation Against Software Theft (FAST). Surveys published by the BSA have indicated that in some countries up to 98% of software in circulation is pirated, with annual losses to software producers running into billions of pounds. Clearly such figures can be no more than estimates and many of the calculations appear to be based on the perhaps unlikely premise that, in the absence of pirate copies of software, users would pay the full price for legitimate programs.

7.27 From a legal perspective, there is no doubt that the making of unauthorised copies of software is unlawful. When carried out on a commercial basis, such copying will attract criminal sanctions extending to a two-year term of imprisonment. For consumers making copies of programs for domestic purposes there is the remote prospect of civil action. A more difficult scenario has recently emerged in the US where a university student placed copies of software packages on a WWW site from where they could freely be downloaded by users. Such conduct could clearly cause substantial losses to copyright owners but the lack of a commercial motive behind the activity prevented criminal prosecution. US law has subsequently been amended to introduce criminal sanctions in such a situation, but it would not appear that a similarly 'philanthropic' UK-based infringer would commit an offence.

7.28 Whilst any work may be subject to infringement, there are a number of features relating to software and other forms of digital information which increase the exposure of copyright owners. Most libraries and many shops offer photocopying facilities. It would be a rare person who has not infringed copyright at some stage through over zealous use of a photocopier. Most readers will be familiar with the limitations of the copying technology. A photocopy of an article in a journal or a chapter of a book will invariably be of lower quality than the original. Slight movement of the page as the copy is being made will cause blurring of lines; the size of the book being copied and the paper being used in the photocopier may differ, again with adverse consequences for the appearance of the copy. Problems will be exacerbated if a photocopy is itself copied, and by the time the process is repeated over a few generations of copies the final version will be virtually indecipherable. Similar factors will apply when a cassette copy is made of a musical recording or television or film production.

7.29 Photocopying and cassette recording can be classed as forms of analogue technologies. Where information is recorded in digital format, the task of the copier is very much easier. A copy of a digital work will be identical in terms of quality with the original and the same result will apply no matter how many generations of copies are produced. The speed with which copies may be made is also generally increased, whilst the emergence of the Internet makes it possible for a program to be placed on a website and copied by tens or even hundreds of thousands of users around the world. The popular encryption program PGP was released to the world in this manner in order to pre-empt attempts by the United States authorities to prevent its distribution. Not even the might of the US could put the technological genie back in that particular bottle.

7.30 In the early days of PC software, many developers attempted to incorporate copy protection devices into their products. Virtually without exception these attempts failed. The use of copy protection techniques inevitably made a product more difficult to use and, given that other developers were willing to make their products available on an unprotected basis, the market spoke with a near unanimous voice. For some time, the emergence of the CD as a storage device offered a measure of protection against domestic copying. Whilst most CDs would be capable of reading the contents of a CD, the technology required to copy onto such a disc was much more sophisticated and expensive. The technology is moving on and although systems such as DVD which provides digital copies of films and other works on CD are again attempting to utilise copy protection devices, history would suggest that these will also be doomed to failure.

Use as copying – software licences

7.31 If the ease with which software may be copied makes copyright owners vulnerable to acts of copyright infringement, the lot of the user of software is not a significantly happier one. The purchaser of a book or audio or video cassette can use the object for its intended purpose without need to consider further the implications of intellectual property law. Reading a book or playing a cassette does not require that any form of copy be made of the contents of the work. Matters are different with software and, indeed, with any other form of digitised information such as a musical CD. In order to operate a software program, it is necessary that a copy be taken of the relevant data. At the simplest level this might see the contents of a disk being copied into a computer's internal memory. Every time a piece of software is used or a CD is played, therefore, a potentially infringing act occurs.

7.32 Such a result appears more than a little bizarre and yet is an inescapable consequence of the nature of the exclusive rights conferred on a copyright owner. In some cases a solution might be found with the notion of an implied contractual term. Where software is offered for sale with the consent of the copyright owner, it must be assumed that the owner is giving consent to its being used. In the case where a purchaser intends to use legitimately acquired software on a single computer, it is the author's view that this will be sanctioned by an implied term. Matters become more difficult when the user possesses two computers, one at home and the other at work. Could the same software lawfully be installed and used on both machines. Arguing in favour, the analogy might be made with a book. A purchaser can carry the book from place to place and read it as and when is convenient. There will remain, however, only one copy of the book, whilst the relatively simple scenario described will involve two permanent copies of the software and further transitional copies whenever the package is used. Possibly an implied term might suffice if it could be guaranteed that the two computers would never be used simultaneously, but it will be seen that the situation is becoming more complex.

7.33 The typical response of software producers to this situation has been to supply software accompanied by a licence. In the early days of consumer software the typical storage device was an audio cassette. The cassette was sealed in cellophane and the terms of a, necessarily brief, licence were printed on the packaging – hence the term 'shrinkwrap licence'. Although technology has moved on to the extent that licences may be contained in booklets of 40–50 pages found inside substantial boxes, reference is still made to shrinkwrap licences. These documents contain both good and bad news for software users. The positive element is that the licence will describe the level of use which is permitted to be made of the software. Clarification of the extent of legitimate use rights is not unwelcome. Less fortunate is the fact that the licence will normally contain extensive provisions seeking to limit or exclude the producer's liability in the event that the improper operation of the software causes some form of injury or damage to the user. The extent to which such exclusion clauses are valid is a matter of considerable controversy. In most of the software-related cases where exclusion clauses have been at issue, the courts have found them to be unreasonable under the terms of the Unfair Contract Terms Act 1977. Their presence may, however, serve to deter users from making complaint regarding the level of performance of software.

7.34 In the European Software Protection Directive provision was made to the effect that:

> In the absence of specific contractual provisions, the acts referred to in Article 4(a) and (b) (the making of a temporary copy of software) shall not require authorisation by the rightholder where they are necessary for the use of the computer program by the lawful acquirer in accordance with its intended purpose ...

This provision was widely interpreted as conferring a use right in respect of software acquired from or with the consent of the producer or copyright owner. The UK implementing regulations adopted a slightly different format sanctioning that the making of a temporary copy by a 'lawful user'. This term is defined to encompass a person who '(whether under a licence to do any acts restricted by the copyright in the program or otherwise) . . . has a right to use the program'. This formulation is somewhat unclear and some commentators have argued that a licence remains necessary for lawful use of software. The UK, however, is obliged to give effect to the terms of the European Directive and it is argued that the terms of this are much clearer. So long as software is obtained through a supply chain emanating from the copyright owner, ie that the copy of the software was first placed on the market by or with the consent of the copyright owner, a use right will be implied.

The rise and fall of look and feel protection

7.35 With the emergence of the PC, the possibilities for copyright infringement increased dramatically. As has been discussed above, in the situation where one party makes a complete or literal copy of a program, there is no doubt that infringement has occurred. A more difficult issue arises where there is an element of independent creative activity on the part of the second producer.

7.36 Starting in the late 1970s, a number of cases of this nature were raised in the UK and US courts. The disputes can reasonably be placed into two categories. In the first, a person would have been employed to work on the development of a particular computer program. The employment would come to an end and the individual, either in his or her own right or as an employee of another company, would be involved in the development of a similar program. The program might well be written in a different computer language, making evidence of literal similarities limited, and would often incorporate additional features or refinements not found in the original. The contention on the part of the original copyright owner would be that a substantial part of the original program had been copied into the new version.

7.37 A second category of case would see parties acting very much at arm's length. The alleged infringer will have had the opportunity to see a copy of the original program in operation and will have set out to create from scratch a competing product which will replicate all or parts of the on-screen appearance of the original. Such practice is quite commonplace in the industrial sector, where it is referred to as 'reverse engineering'.

Employment mobility

7.38 In the first category of disputes there is no doubt that the individual responsible for the development of the allegedly infringing product will have had access to all significant elements of the original program. The English case of *Richardson v Flanders* [1993] FSR 497 might be considered as a typical example of the species.

7.39 At issue in this case was a computer program designed for use by chemists. The program, which was developed to run on the then popular BBC micro-computers performed a number of tasks. Principally, when the computer was attached to a printer it would automate and simplify the task of preparing dosage instructions to be supplied with medicines. The program's other major function was to assist in stock-keeping by keeping a record of the drugs dispensed. The program was marketed by the plaintiff, who had also performed a significant amount of work on the original program. Subsequently, the first defendant was employed to work on the project. It was accepted that all relevant copyrights in the work belonged to the plaintiff.

7.40 The program achieved considerable commercial success. Relationships between the plaintiff and the defendant were not so fortunate. The defendant resigned from his position, although he continued to perform some work for the plaintiff as an independent contractor for a further period of time. With the advent of the IBM personal computer one of the plaintiff's major customers expressed interest in a version of the program capable of running on this machine and which could be sold on the Irish market. Following discussions the plaintiff decided not to proceed with the project but suggested that the defendant might be willing to perform the work. The program was completed and was sold in Ireland. The defendant subsequently contacted the plaintiff offering him the rights to market the product in the UK. These discussions proved fruitless and the defendant proceeded to market a modified version of the program in the UK. At that stage the plaintiff initiated proceedings alleging that the new product infringed copyright in his original program.

7.41 Because of the fact that the programs had been developed to run on different computers, examination of the code used would have revealed few evidences of similarities. The programs did perform the same functions and had very similar appearances when operating on their respective hardware.

7.42 The *Richardson* case was the first UK dispute to reach the stage of a full High Court action. In the absence of any relevant UK precedent the judge placed considerable reliance on US authority, notably the case of *Computer Associates Inc v Altai* 982 F 2d 693 (1992). This approach is widely used in the field of IT law where the dominant position of the US information technology industry has produced a much greater volume of case law than is available in the rest of the world. An English court, it was held, should, rather than attempting to identify the program's levels of abstraction with a view to discovering the 'core of protectable expression', conduct a four-stage test designed to answer the questions. This would seek to answer the following questions:

1. Is the plaintiff's work protected by copyright . . .
2. Do similarities exist between the plaintiff's and the defendant's programs
3. Were these caused by copying or were other explanations possible?
4. In the event that copying was established, did the elements copied constitute a significant part of the original work?

Given what has been said above regarding the willingness of UK courts to confer copyright protection on a work, it is not at all surprising that the first question could be answered quickly and definitively in the affirmative. Consideration of the other issues was a more difficult task.

7.43 Examining the operation of the original program, the judge identified 13 aspects of the functioning of the original program leading to the printing of the label for a drug container. This program also offered a stock-control function and some 17 other features allowing a pharmacist to customise the program in accordance with any particular requirements. When the same analysis was applied to the revised program, 17 points of similarity were identified between the two programs which would require further investigation to determine whether they were the product of copying.

7.44   These similarities were identified from an examination of the screen displays and key sequences. The judge did not attempt to compare the underlying codes. Although an expert witness for the plaintiff had presented an analysis of alleged similarities between the source codes of the two programs, the judge indicated that he found this 'extremely difficult to understand'. Counsel for the plaintiff failed to pursue an invitation to attempt further explanation and the analysis formed no part of the final decision.

7.45   One obvious cause of similarities, that of deliberate copying, was rejected by the judge. It was accepted, however, that the defendant must have retained considerable knowledge of the plaintiff's program and that, if similarities resulted from the unconscious use of this material, infringement might be established.

7.46   Examining the similarities between the two programs, most were considered explicable by reasons other than copying. The two programs, for example, presented dates in a similar format. Conventions for the presentations of dates are well established and the fact that two works utilise a similar format is more likely to be caused through adherence to such conventions than by copying.

7.47   In a second aspect, the original program had presented the pharmacist with the option of placing a date other than the current date on a label. This feature was reproduced in the revised program. Although the judge held that it was likely that this had been copied from the original, he also held that, given the very limited number of ways in which the idea could be expressed, the fact that the two programs utilised very similar approaches did not establish infringement.

7.48   In total, six of the 17 similarities identified by the judge were considered explicable by reasons other than copying. The remaining 11 items, it was considered, with varying degrees of conviction, might have been copied from the original program. Eight of these, however, referred to matters which in the opinion of the judge did not amount to a substantial part of the program. One element found in both programs gave users an indication that their instructions had been accepted. In both programs, the message 'operation successful' would appear on the screen and the computer would emanate a double-beep sound. This aspect of the original program, it was held, 'lacks originality and cannot have required any significant skill or effort to devise it'.

7.49   Ultimately, infringement was established in respect of only three of the points of similarity, comprising editing and amendment functions and the use of dose codes. The similarities in respect of the editing function were perhaps especially noticeable as it operated in the same idiosyncratic (and probably erroneous) manner in both programs. The dose code facility allowed the user to abbreviate certain instructions regarding the dosage and the manner in which the medication was to be taken. Thus in both programs, use of the abbreviation AC (ante cibum) would cause the instruction 'before food' to be printed on the label. Although a number of the abbreviations were held to be obvious, the fact that 84 out of 91 codes found in the original program were reproduced in an identical format in the later version with only minor changes in another five was held to raise an inference of copying.

7.50 Although copyright infringement was ultimately established, the plaintiff's victory was heavily qualified. The copying was described as constituting 'a fairly minor infringement in a few limited respects and certainly not . . . slavish copying'. Although some of the processes adopted clearly differ from those in *Computer Associates*, the effect of the judgment is similar in recognising that, for functional works, external forces may well be the cause of similarities, thereby excusing conduct that might otherwise appear to constitute a breach of copyright.

7.51 Allegations of copyright were again before the High Court in the case of *Ibcos Computers v Barclays Mercantile Highland Finance* [1994] FSR 274. Again, there was a background of the major defendant having worked for the plaintiff on the development of a software product intended for use by agricultural dealers which was marketed under the name ADS. On leaving its employment, he developed a further and competing product which was marketed under the name of Unicorn. The plaintiff alleged that sufficient features of this were copied from the original to constitute an infringement of copyright.

7.52 In determining the criteria which would be applied in determining the question whether infringement had occurred, Jacobs J was somewhat critical of the extensive references to the US decision in *Computer Associates* and warned against 'overcitation of US authority based on a statute different from ours'. The approach to be adopted was for the court to determine whether there was a sufficient degree of similarity between the two works which, coupled with evidence of access to the original work, would establish an inference of copying. The onus would then switch to the defendant to establish that the similarities were explicable by causes other than copying. Evidence that 'functional necessity' served to narrow the range of options open to the defendant would be relevant. Trivial items may well provide the most eloquent testimony. As was said in *Bilhofer v Dixon* [1990] FSR 105:

It is the resemblances in inessentials, the small, redundant, even mistaken elements of the copyright work which carry the greatest weight. This is because they are the least likely to have been the result of independent design.

7.53 In the present case, evidence was presented that the same words were misspelled in the same manner, the same headings were used in the two programs and both shared the same bit of code which served no useful purpose for the functioning of the program. Beyond this, there were considerable similarities at the level of the code itself. In respect of one element of the programs it was held that:

> . . . there are 22 identical variables, 8 identical labels, 1 identical remark, 31 identical code lines and one identical redundant variable. This to my mind plainly indicates copying and enough in itself to constitute a significant part.

The court recognised in *Ibcos* that copyright protection must extend beyond the literal aspects of the program code to aspects of 'program structure' and 'design features'. In the case of the former element, it was held that copyright subsisted in the compilation of individual programs which made up the ADS system. Although some differences existed between ADS and Unicorn, it was held that the defendant had taken 'as his starting point the ADS set and that set remains substantially in Unicorn'. Although the two programs had a different visual appearance and it was recognised that 'Unicorn is undoubtedly to the user a much friendlier program than ADS was at the time', the defendant, it was held had taken 'shortcuts by starting with ADS and making considerable additions and modifications'.

7.54 The cases of *Richardson* and *Ibcos* remain the only occasions on which the UK courts have considered the extent of copyright protection in software at any level of detail. It is to be noted that, in both cases, the copyright owner established a case of infringement although the victory in *Richardson* was limited. Where individuals are employed as software programmers as was the case in *Richardson* and *Ibcos*, it may be extremely difficult to distinguish between their own expertise and the proprietary information belonging to the employer. Most programmers when faced with a particular task will not attempt to create new code. Rather they will seek to reuse existing modules. These may be taken either from their own portfolio of work and experience or from reference manuals. Too extensive an application of intellectual property rights may inhibit significantly the future career prospects of employees.

The trouble with spreadsheets

7.55 Cases such as *Richardson* raise a number of important issues but once determinations have been made concerning the facts at issue, the application of copyright law is less problematic. More difficult conceptual issues arise in respect of the second category of action and here discussion might most usefully focus on the US litigation centring on the market leading computer spreadsheet, Lotus 1-2-3.

7.56 Although Lotus could not be classed as inventors of the spreadsheet, their product was the first to attain significant commercial success. Inevitably, competitors sought to enter the market. Whilst there was never any suggestion that there had been direct copying of any code developed by Lotus, at least two competing products produced by Paperback and Borland displayed strong similarities with the appearance and manner of functioning of the Lotus package. Lotus brought separate actions against these two companies. The cases were brought, however, in the same US court and were heard by the same judge, Judge Keeton.

7.57 The case against Paperback was the most straightforward. Although it contained a number of additional features, the Paperback product was effectively a clone of the Lotus original. The justification put forward for this situation was Paperback's belief that customers used to the Lotus interface would be reluctant to switch to a competing product if this meant having to learn new commands and methods of operation.

7.58 Borland's activities were rather more complex. It had developed an original spreadsheet package which contained few similarities with the Lotus version. Acting, however, on the same concerns as expressed by Paperback, they provided users with a function allowing them to emulate the Lotus interface. The intention was that, whilst users might originally make use of this function, especially when working on spreadsheets originally created using 1-2-3, eventually the (allegedly) superior features of 1-2-3 would encourage them to migrate to the new package.

7.59 Judge Keeton found decisively against both Paperback and Borland. His judgment can be seen as establishing the high-water mark of copyright protection of software. Copyright protection extended, he held, to all aspects of a program and its manner of functioning. It was doubted whether the assertion that market forces would compel a program to imitate a competitor but even if this were the case:

one object of copyright law is to protect expression in order to encourage innovation. It follows, then, that the more innovative the expression of an idea is, the more important is copyright protection for that expression. By arguing that 1-2-3 was so innovative that it occupied the field and set a de facto industry standard, and that, therefore, defendants were free to copy plaintiff's expression, defendants have flipped copyright on its head. Copyright protection would be perverse if it only protected mundane increments while leaving unprotected as part of the public domain those advancements that are more strikingly innovative.

7.60   The action involving Paperback stopped at this stage. Borland, however, pursued an appeal. This was successful before the Court of Appeals. By this time another US Court of Appeals had delivered its decision in the case of *Computer Associates v Altai,* discussed above. The Lotus court was not uncritical of the *abstraction-filtration-comparison* approach which, it argued, was at least impliedly based on the premise that some elements of copyrightable expression existed. This test, it was suggested, was appropriate where non-literal copying was involved but could be 'misleading' in a case such as Lotus where the fact that literal elements in the form of menu structures had been copied was not at issue. What had to be decided was whether what had been copied was protected by copyright. The majority of the court held that the Lotus menu structure was not protected. In reaching this conclusion, they applied a prohibition in the US copyright law against protecting a 'method of operation'. The Lotus menu, it was held, did not merely describe the manner in which the program functioned but provided the 'means by which users control and operate Lotus 1-2-3'. As such, Borland was free to copy the Lotus menu structure. An analogy was drawn with the control buttons on a video recorder. No one, it was suggested, could copyright the 'play', 'record' or other functions inscribed on the relevant buttons. Menu commands in a computer program performed the same function.

7.61   The judgment continued to make a number of criticisms concerning the relevance of copyright as the major vehicle for protecting rights in software. Applying copyright law to computer programs, it was stated, 'is like assembling a jigsaw puzzle whose pieces do not quite fit'. A computer program –

is a means for causing something to happen; it has a mechanical utility, an instrumental role, in accomplishing the world's work. Granting protection, in other words, can have some of the consequences of patent protection in limiting other people's ability to perform a task in the most efficient manner. Utility does not bar copyright (dictionaries may be copyrighted), but it alters the calculus.

Whilst it was acknowledged that the use of Lotus's work by others might deprive Lotus of 'a portion of its reward', it was pointed out that 'the provision of reward is one concern of copyright law, but it is not the only one'. Specific reference was made to the investment of users in acquiring expertise in the operation of a program and to the need to ensure that they did not remain 'captives of Lotus'.

7.62 A final appeal was brought by Lotus against this judgment and the case was heard by the US Supreme Court. Hopes that a definitive ruling would be obtained were dashed when it was discovered that the relative of one of the nine Supreme Court Justices owned shares in IBM (which by this time had taken over Lotus). He therefore disqualified himself from participating in the court's deliberations. Perhaps inevitably, the remaining eight justices became deadlocked, four supporting the Lotus appeal and four favouring Borland's arguments. As a result, no opinion was issued by the court.

Software copyright after *Lotus*

7.63 No case similar to *Lotus v Borland* 73 3d 355 (1995) has been brought before a UK court. As suggested above, significant differences exist between UK and US copyright laws and care should be taken not to rely to heavily on the judgment. In particular, the US is much more willing to deny protection to elements of a work than is the case under the UK system. The inconclusive ending to the litigation might have raised expectations that many further copyright disputes would be brought. In fact this has proved not to be the case. A variety of reasons might be advanced for this state of affairs. In large measure, the emergence of Windows as a standard operating system has served to impose a measure of uniformity on software developers. It is clearly in the interests of operating system producers such as Microsoft to encourage as many hardware and software producers as possible to build their own operations around the particular operating system. Rather than relying on copyright to prevent third party use of programs, this involves placing the information necessary to interact with an operating system into the public domain.

7.64 The issue of compatibility also arises between competing applications developers. In the early days of word processing software, the capabilities of the programs were limited. Most data was represented in accordance with the American Standard Convention for Information Interchange (ASCII) and as such it would be relatively easy for a document produced by one package to be opened by another. Further, it was comparatively rare for documents to be exchanged in electronic format. With more sophisticated packages and the massive increase in the electronic dissemination of information, it becomes necessary in their mutual interests for producers to exchange the data necessary to allow documents to be transported between different applications. To an extent, co-operation has replaced litigation.

Chapter 8

Patents and software

Development of the patent system

8.0 The world's first patent is reported as having been issued in Florence to Philippo Brunaleschi, the architect responsible for the design of Florence Cathedral. The claim was that he had thought of a better method for transporting goods on the River Arno (which runs through Florence). His problem was one which continues to face inventors to this day. In most cases, once an invention is put into the public domain it can readily be copied. A new product might be reverse engineered by competitors to discover its manner of construction. It is trite knowledge that it is easier to emulate than to innovate. The only other option would be to keep the idea secret. In some cases this is not incompatible with exploitation of the invention. The formula for Coca Cola is, for example, maintained under conditions of extreme secrecy. The drink is, of course, publicly available and any chemist could analyse the contents to find the ingredients used. As any cook will be aware, having a list of ingredients is only a small step in the task of cooking a meal. The manner and order in which the ingredients are combined, coupled with cooking techniques, will determine the success or failure of the culinary endeavour.

8.1 The solution arrived at in the Brunaleschi case bears many of the hallmarks of the modern system. Brunaleschi undertook to divulge details of his new system to the Florentine authorities. In return he would be granted a monopoly in respect of the exploitation of the invention within Florence for a number of years. After this, any other person would be free to exploit the invention or, preferably, to introduce further improvements to the technology.

8.2 Initial developments in the UK – or more specifically England – proceeded along different grounds. The word 'patent' is an abbreviation of the term 'letters patent' – literally 'open letter'. In the early Middle Ages, each town would have its guilds of craftsmen who would guard jealously access to the various trades. Only a member of the appropriate guild could, for example, act as a butcher or carpenter. One of the major weaknesses of such an approach was that the guilds stifled innovation. Recognising that the country was lagging behind its continental rivals in terms of technology, the practice began whereby the Sovereign would encourage foreigners to come to England bringing with them their advanced technical skills. To overcome the objections – which might extend to physical violence – of the craft guilds, letters patent would be issued. Signed with the royal seal, these would command any citizen to refrain from interfering with the bearer in the exercise of the technical skills referred to in the letter. The first recorded English patent of this kind was issued to a Flemish glazier who came to the country to install stained glass windows in Eton College. Unlike Brunaleschi's patent (and unfortunately history does not record whether his new form of transportation proved of any value), the technology covered by the patent was new to the country rather than new in itself.

8.3 In spite of moves towards the goal of rewarding inventors and making new technologies available to the public, the English patent system fell into considerable disrepute. Although some patents were granted in respect of what might be regarded as inventions; the first recorded patent of this kind being awarded to an Italian émigré, Annoni, who developed a novel system of fortification, used to safeguard the town of Berwick against the Scots invaders, the system was all too often used to boost the royal revenues by conferring for a fee a monopoly in respect of basic commodities. A prime example was the grant of a patent in respect of playing cards. The role of the patent system played a significant part in the ongoing struggles between the monarchy and Parliament. In 1687, the last Stuart king was forced into exile and Mary and William of Orange were invited to take the throne. In the effort to establish its own supremacy and to guard against the possibility of future abuses, the Statute of Monopolies was enacted by Parliament. This rendered illegal all monopolies except those:

> . . . for the term of 14 years or under . . . (for) the sole working or making of any manner of new manufactures (by) the true and first inventor.

8.4 Although the royal prerogative in respect of the grant of patents was significantly reduced, until the Patents Act 1949 patents were granted in the name of the Sovereign. The Statute of Monopolies did, however, serve to put the operation of the patent system on to a more structured basis with its day to day operation removed from the Crown and placed into the hands of a specialised organisation. Today, applications for patent protection in the UK must be submitted to the Patent Office, which is headed by the Comptroller of Patents and is located in Newport, Wales

The patent system today

8.5 Until recent times, patent systems tended to be found only in the developed world. Here, although an international agreement, the Patent Cooperation Treaty provides for a degree of harmonisation between national patent offices, there is no equivalent to the Berne Copyright Convention providing worldwide protection for inventions. A UK patent will be valid within the UK but of no effect in Japan or the US. A person wishing to secure widespread patent protection for an invention will have to undergo the time-consuming and expensive process of seeking to obtain a patent from each country where protection is desired.

8.6 A greater degree of harmonisation has occurred within Europe, where the 1973 Munich Convention on the European Patent System provided for the establishment of the European Patent Office and the award of a European Patent. This latter title, however, is something of a misnomer. An applicant is required to specify those countries in which it is intended that the patent will apply and, assuming the application is successful, the end product will be the award of a basket of national patents. Effectively, the role of the convention and the European Patent Office is to centralise the process for the award of national patents, with the costs to applicants rising in line with the number of countries in which protection is sought. As the European Commission has commented, one consequence of this process has been that 'the additional costs of protection for each designated country are prompting businesses to be selective in their choice of countries, with effects that run counter to the aims of the single market'.

8.7 Although the European Patent Convention is sometimes linked with the European Community, the two organisations are distinct. In the 1970s it was the intention of the then Community member states that the Munich Convention should be followed shortly by the establishment of a Community Patent and the Community Patent Convention (the Luxembourg Convention) was signed in 1975. This sought to establish a unitary patent system operating throughout the Community. The system would, however, be administered through the European Patent Office. In spite of the conclusion in 1989 of a further agreement (the Luxembourg Agreement), the convention has never entered into force, having been ratified by only seven of the current member states (Denmark, France, Germany, Greece, Luxembourg, the Netherlands and the UK). Recently, however, as will be discussed at the end of this chapter, the European Commission has sought to become more involved in the field and has produced proposals seeking both to resurrect the concept of the Community patent and to make patents more widely available to software related inventions.

8.8 The British law relating to patents is to be found today in the Patents Act 1977. This statute was introduced in part to update domestic law but principally to enable the UK to ratify the European Patent Convention. As will be discussed below, decisions made within the European Patent Office have proved extremely influential in the domestic system with decisions of the European Patent Office authorities being cited extensively in UK cases. In a leading UK case, the view was expressed strongly that:

> It would be absurd if, on the issue of patentability, a patent application should suffer a different fate according to whether it was made in the United Kingdom under the Act or was made in Munich for a European Parliament (United Kingdom) under the Convention.

8.9 The recently adopted Trade Related Aspects of Intellectual Property Rights (TRIPS) protocol to the General Agreement on Tariffs and Trade (GATT) seems likely to lead to an expansion in the application of the patent system. The protocol requires signatories to make patents –

> available for any inventions, whether products or processes, in all fields of technology, provided that they are new, involve an inventive step and are capable of industrial application . . . patents shall be available and patent rights enjoyable without discrimination as to the place of invention, the field of technology and whether products are imported or locally produced.

This provision was included at the behest of the developed world and was prompted by concern that companies were suffering losses through audio, software and video piracy in developing countries with little legal recourse because concepts of intellectual property law were not recognised by national laws. Effectively TRIPS requires these states to introduce intellectual property statutes as the price for benefiting from the free trade provisions of the GATT. The topic is assuming special significance in the field of biotechnology, where patented products may be based upon ingredients discovered in plants growing in a developing country.

Criteria for the award of a patent

8.10 The basic function of the patent system is to protect inventions. The Patents Act defines the word by reference both to qualities which any application must demonstrate and, more controversially in the present context, to elements which will exclude an application from protection. In terms of the first category, it is required that an application should demonstrate:

- novelty;

- inventiveness; and

- capacity for industrial application.

In negative terms, it is provided that an application will not be considered patentable in so far as it relates to a:

- discovery;

- scientific theory;

- mathematical method;

- scheme or method for performing a mental act;

- method for doing business;

- program for a computer.

The appearance of the phrase 'program for a computer' in this list might appear to render consideration of the patent system otiose in the context of the present work. As will be discussed, however, things are not as they might appear and the patent system plays a significant and, indeed, expanding role in the field of software.

8.11 Once granted, a patent will be valid for a period of four years. It may subsequently be extended on an annual basis up to a maximum of 20 years. Fees are payable for each renewal, the amount increasing with time. Statistics suggest that the average life-span of a patent is around eight years. After this time, further developments in technology may have rendered the subject matter of the patent obsolete or, as in the majority of cases, it will have been discovered that the invention has little or no commercial value.

The patent process

8.12 Unlike the copyright system, where protection is conferred from the moment a work is recorded in some form, the act of making an invention will confer no rights upon an inventor. The onus is totally upon the inventor, or anyone acting on their behalf, to make the initial application for a patent and to pursue this through all the stages of the patent procedure.

8.13 Applications are to be made to the Patent Office using the appropriate form and tendering payment of the required fee. The application will formally lay claim to a patent and is required to give details of the invention in question. At the stage of submission, it is not required that all of the detail which will subsequently form the basis of the application should be included; notification of an intention to claim a patent coupled with a description of the alleged invention will suffice. The date upon which an application for patent protection is received will be significant, in that it sets a priority date giving the inventor precedence over any similar applications which may be submitted at a later date. Although a limited submission may accompany the initial application, in order for the patent processes to continue, all of the requirements specified in the legislation must continue. This requires that the application include a specification consisting of a description of the invention together with one or more claims regarding the extent of the protection sought (an abstract, normally within 150 words, must also be submitted summarising the specification).

8.14 The specification is a key feature of the patent application. The requirement relating to description has been interpreted as requiring that the product or process should be described in such a manner as to permit the product to be made or the process operated by the average workman reasonably skilled in the area in question. To this extent the description can be regarded as a list of instructions. Merely describing the invention will not suffice for the grant of a patent. Beyond the issue of the legal requirement, simply to specify the manner in which a product is made or a process operated would leave the door open for competitors to make such modifications as are necessary to acquire the benefit of the invention without making a straight copy of the equipment. In a leading textbook on the subject it is stated that: 'for production in quantity, most larger concerns seem to prefer in any case to redesign any new product or tool to fit in with the established practice of their works.'

8.15 The description of an invention serves to indicate what may be regarded as the inventor's opinion regarding the optimum embodiment of its principles. Beyond this, claims for protection will be made regarding the functioning of the product or process – effectively what the invention does. The drafting of these claims and their relationship to the specification is one of the most critical aspects of the patent process. Often, 'headline' reports concerning a software patent refer to the specification which may describe some established form of technology such as hypertext linking. The assertion is that the applicant is seeking, or may have obtained, a patent for hypertext. When the heat and dust dies down and the patent claims are examined, it becomes clear that what is involved is a small refinement of the process. Only that minor feature will be protected by the patent.

8.16 The dilemma for an applicant may be that, if the claims are drawn too narrowly, the patent may well be awarded but prove to be worthless as competitors evade its scope. If, on the other hand, the claims are drawn too widely, the application may be rejected in the Patent Office on the ground that the claims are not sufficiently supported by the specification or that the alleged invention is not truly novel or inventive. Even in the event that the patent is granted, its validity may subsequently be challenged on this basis in the course of any legal proceedings brought by third parties, a fate which, it is suggested, may befall a number of controversial software patents issued in the US.

Examination of the application

8.17 Once an application has been received within the Patent Office it will be held there with no further action being taken until the applicant requests that a preliminary examination be made. Such request must be made within 18 months from the date when the application was filed. Applications will be subject to two forms of examination – preliminary and substantive.

8.18 The first purpose of the preliminary examination is to ensure that the application complies with all the formal requirements of the legislation (principally that the application contains an abstract, specification and claims). If this is the case the examiner will turn to consider the merits of the application. At the stage of the preliminary examination, the examiner's main task is to identify those documents and sources of information which it is considered are likely to prove of assistance in the event that a decision subsequently has to be made concerning the novelty and inventiveness of the invention. Having identified relevant documents, the examiner is instructed to scrutinise the documents to such extent as is considered will serve a purpose in determining the application. The results of the preliminary investigation are reported to the applicant.

8.19 The report subsequent to the preliminary examination will be non-judgmental. It may indicate grounds for objecting to or refusing the grant of a patent. In such circumstances, it may become clear to an applicant that the chances of the application being granted are minimal and the decision taken not to pursue the matter any further. In this respect the applicant has the option either to give notice of their wish to withdraw the application or simply to fail to apply for the process to move on to the next stage. The disadvantage of the latter course of action is that, unless notice of withdrawal is given, details of a patent application will be published 'as soon as possible' after the expiry of 18 months from the date of application. Such publication may adversely affect the prospects of any modified application which the inventor might wish to make in substitution for one which he has allowed to lapse and might also make potentially valuable information available to competitors.

8.20 In the event that the inventor wishes the patent processes to continue, a request must be made for a substantive examination. The request must be made within six months from the date of publication. It is at this stage that the examiner will make a full study whether the claimed invention is novel, involves an inventive step, is capable of industrial application and does not fall within one of the prohibited categories. The examiner will make a report to the Comptroller of Patents. In the event that this report makes objection to aspects of the application, the applicant must be afforded the opportunity to make observations or to amend the application so as to take account of the examiner's objections. In the event that the applicant fails adequately so to do, the Comptroller may refuse the application. If a patent is awarded, the Comptroller is required to cause a notice to this effect to be published in the Official Journal (Patents).

Substantive requirements

Criteria for patentability

8.21 Having considered procedural aspects of the system, attention must now be paid to more substantive issues. Patents may be awarded for inventions with the statute identifying elements which must be present in any application together with a list of items, often referred to as 'prohibited subject matter' which are excluded from patentability. At the positive level, an invention must be:

• novel;

• involve an inventive step; and

• be capable of industrial exploitation.

Novelty

8.22 Novelty is considered in purely objective terms. The question posed is whether the technology at issue is new. In order to answer this, the Patent Office employs a considerable number of scientists and engineers in the capacity of patent examiners. An examiner will take an application and consider it in the context of the state of scientific knowledge in the particular field. Any information which is in the public domain anywhere in the world is relevant to this determination. One leading UK case (*Quantel v Spaceward* [1990] RPC 83) was concerned with a patent which had been awarded in respect of a system for developing on-screen graphics. In part the system provides an example of the pace of technical development. The case was brought in 1990. The product in question could be bought at a cost of around £100,000 and its use was restricted to the likes of television companies. The features found in the system are today typically included in the software packages included in the purchase price of a basic PC. In terms of the novelty of the system at the time the patent was issued, it was argued by a party opposing (unsuccessfully) the grant of the patent that its techniques had been described – the technical term used is 'anticipated' – in a Master's dissertation produced by a student at the University of Southern California, a copy of which could be consulted in the university library. Clearly, it would be impossible to expect a patent examiner based in Wales to have either knowledge of or access to all information held anywhere in the world. In terms of the patent application, the prime source of reference will be the catalogues of previously issued patents together with a basic literature search.

8.23 Whilst the search techniques described above are well suited to mature forms of technology, the task of an examiner faced with an application relating to a fast developing field such as information technology is a daunting one. This has led to vociferous complaints, especially in the US, that patents have been awarded in respect of computing applications that were well known, albeit ill-documented, within the software community. This argument is not without merit but, as the UK case described above indicates, the award of a patent is not in itself conclusive. Any party can at any time challenge its validity by bringing forward evidence indicating that the invention was not truly novel. It may also be noted that it was only with the enactment of the Patents Act 1949 that the notion that applications should be examined within the Patent Office was accepted. Until that date, an application would be received, published and, in the absence of third party objections, awarded without further formalities.

8.24 One pitfall which has trapped many an unwary inventor is that any significant disclosure of the features of an invention prior to the submission of an application for a patent will lead to rejection of the application. Even though the publication of information may have come from the inventor, the mere fact that the details are in the public domain will be fatal to the application.

Inventive step

8.25 The distinction between the requirements that an application be novel and that it involve an inventive step is not clear cut. The Patents Act 1977 states that an invention –

> shall be taken to involve an inventive step if it is not obvious to a person skilled in the art, having regard to any matter which forms part of the state of the art.

The requirement that an invention demonstrate an inventive step imposes a qualitative hurdle for applicants. Henry Ford is often quoted for his comment that customers could have their cars in any colour, 'so long as it is black'. If we imagine that a competitor produced the first car with white paintwork, it might be possible to argue that the vehicle was novel but the development could not have been regarded as inventive.

8.26 An example of a situation where the requirement of an inventive step was not satisfied, and of the relationship with the requirement of novelty, can be seen in the case of *Genentech Inc's Patent* [1989] RPC 147. A research programme conducted by Genentech resulted in the identification and mapping of elements of DNA (the basic building block of life). The research furthered the knowledge of this basic structure and could be used as the basis for further research. he research furthered the knowledge of this basic structure and could be used as the basis for further work. One output was the development of a new drug which was designed to be used to diminish the dangers of blood clots (ironically some years after the conclusion of the patent litigation, clinical trials suggested that the new and expensive drug was no more effective than aspirin). Genentech sought unsuccessfully to patent the results of its efforts, the Court of Appeal holding that the work did not involve an inventive step. Genentech's activities were analogised with athletes running a race:

> ... they won the race. The goal was known and others were trying to reach it. Genentech got there first.

Whilst the achievement of a goal (equivalent, perhaps, to setting a new world record in a sporting event) would constitute evidence of novelty, if the target was widely known the winning of the race might say no more than that the winner was richer or more determined or luckier than others working in the same area. To this extent, therefore, the expenditure of time and effort in making a breakthrough will not, of itself, be conclusive evidence of the existence of an inventive step.

8.27 Conceptually, this approach is not without merits. If one hundred people are engaged in searching for a needle in a haystack, it is difficult to argue that the finder displayed any degree of inventiveness (unless in determining a more efficient way to search haystacks). The achievement of the goal of running a mile in less than three minutes might not be inventive but would certainly be meritorious and deserving of recognition. The problem will be encountered in a number of areas and the traditional precepts of intellectual property may not fit well with developments in information technology, yet the effect of denying access to intellectual property rights is to deny any form of legal recognition and protection for the work in question.

8.28 Also at issue in the *Genentech* litigation was the identification of the notional persons 'skilled in the art' – ie those persons to whom the making of the steps leading to the claimed invention would have been 'obvious'. It was recognised that in respect of advanced areas of technology the collected knowledge of a team of researchers might be the relevant factor, rather than the knowledge possessed by any particular individual.

Capable of industrial application

8.29 The final requirement which must be satisfied in order for a patent application to proceed is that the invention should be capable of industrial application. This reflects the goal of the patent system to reward useful technical advances. Patents may be awarded either in respect of a product or a process. Virtually any product will be capable of being sold or otherwise disposed of and, in this respect, will satisfy the applicability test. With a process, slightly different considerations will apply. If the end result of the application of the process will be a product, it is likely that the process will be considered capable of industrial application.

Inventions excluded from patent protection

8.30 In addition to demonstrating that it satisfies the criteria described above, the UK Act and the European Patent Convention specify a list of what is referred to as prohibited subject matter. It is provided that a patent will not be awarded for:

   a discovery, scientific theory or mathematical method;
   a literary, dramatic, musical or artistic work or any other aesthetic creation whatsoever;
   a scheme, rule or method for performing a mental act, playing a game or doing business, or a program for a computer; or
   the presentation of information.

8.31 It is arguable that these listings serve no useful purpose. Previous UK patent statutes – and current US patent law – appear to operate by simply identifying the positive attributes that must be present in an application. The notion of a 'discovery' would include, for example, the discovery of a previously unknown mineral. As this is something which exists in nature, it is clear that the requirement of an 'inventive step' cannot be satisfied. Scientific theories such as the famous theory of relativity are the intangible product of the application of the human brain. Although in the event that the theory should be applied – for example to develop a time machine – the latter could qualify for a patent; the raw theory is not capable of industrial application.

8.32 The inclusion of a prohibition against the award of a patent for a program for a computer might give rise to the query why patents have any relevance in the software field. The answer, perhaps, lends support to the argument that the list of prohibited subject matter is a cause of confusion rather than enlightenment. Having listed the various categories, the Act and convention go on to state that the prohibition extends only to the extent that the application related to the 'thing as such'. This qualification is crucial. Many pharmaceutical products begin life as a discovery – for example that a particular combination of ingredients relieves pain. Once the discovery is made, its practical application may be relatively simple and obvious. None the less, pharmaceutical patents are issued in considerable numbers and, historically, have been amongst the most valuable awards. The reason for this is that, whilst it is often possible for a competitor to design around an engineering patent, a well formulated pharmaceutical patent will lay claim to what is referred to as the 'family' of compounds which may produce the desired effect.

8.33 These issues will be considered in more detail below, but it is important to note at this stage that the fact that an invention makes use of (or even depends on) a computer program will not constitute a bar to patentability. In the UK, approximately 100 patent applications are published each year. In proceedings before the European Patent

Office, this figure rises to 100 per month. The report of the Parliamentary Office of Science and Technology on 'Patents, Research and Technology' indicates that 'in the last 10 years the EPO has granted around 10,000 patents for software related inventions, and has refused only 100 applications'. Even more substantial figures are quoted for the number of patents awarded in the US although, in part because the existence of the statutory prohibitions requires that software related inventions be catalogued by reference to their field of application rather than the software component, makes any calculation a somewhat subjective assessment. There is no doubt, however, that patents have a significant role to play in the field of information technology.

Software patents in the courts

8.34 The first UK cases involving the eligibility of software-related inventions for patent protection arose under the Patents Act 1949. Given the date of its passage, it is not surprising that this statute contains no mention of computer programs. In 1967 a committee, the Banks Committee, was established with the remit:

> To examine and report with recommendations upon the British patent system and patent law, in the light of the increasing need for international collaboration in patent matters, and, in particular, of the United Kingdom Government's intention to ratify the recent Council of Europe Convention on patent laws.

8.35 A chapter of the final report was devoted to an examination of the position of computer programs. This concluded that that the situation was characterised by considerable uncertainty but indicated that the majority of the evidence submitted to the committee was hostile to the notion that programs should qualify for patent protection. This view was shared by the committee, which put forward reasons of both principle and utility for denying protection. In terms of principle it was argued that no significant distinction existed between programs and methods of mathematical calculation which had always been excluded from protection. Practical difficulties were also identified, the committee commenting:

> ... were programs to be patentable, very real and substantial difficulties would be experienced by the Patent Office in searching applications for program patents even were the search material available in suitably classified form. The issues of novelty and obviousness would be so difficult of determination that patents of doubtful validity would be likely to issue.

8.36 In the event, the committee recommended that:

> A computer program, that is: a set of instructions for controlling the sequence of operations of a data processing system, in whatever form the invention is presented e.g. a method of programming computers, a computer when programmed in a certain way and where the novelty or alleged novelty lies only in the program, should not be patentable.

8.37 It was recognised, however, that a distinction should be drawn between applications for programs per se and for inventions which involve the use of a program. A new form of machine, for example, should not be denied protection simply because aspects of its functioning were controlled by computer. Although such a distinction may totally be supported, it will be seen that, once again, the seeds of doubt as to the application of patent protection have been planted.

8.38 The eligibility of software related inventions for protection under the 1977 Act was first raised in the case of *Merrill Lynch's Application* [1989] RPC 561. At issue in this case was a data processing system for making a trading market in securities and for executing orders for securities transactions. The patent application claimed:

> This invention relates to business systems and, more specifically, to an improved data processing based system for implementing an automated trading market for one or more securities. The system retrieves and stores the best current bid and asked prices; qualifies customers buy/sell orders for execution; executes the orders; and reports the trade particulars to customers and to national stock price reporting systems. The system apparatus also determines and monitors stock inventory and profit for the market maker.

8.39 The system can be seen as an early version of the automatic buying and selling of stocks and shares. All of the computer equipment used was standard, with the novelty residing only in the software components. The patent application was rejected on the basis that the subject matter of the alleged invention fell within the prohibition of the Patents Act 1977. The principal patent examiner held that the effect of this section, with its prohibition against the patenting of computer programs, was such that it would also prevent the award of a patent in the situation where the program was incorporated in some other object but where the novelty and inventive step resided in the elements of the program rather than in any of the other attributes of the subject matter. This reasoning, which was upheld in the High Court, was challenged before the Court of Appeal. The critical issue concerned the interpretation of the concluding passage of s 1(2), stating that the prohibitions against patentability extended only 'to the extent that a patent or application for a patent relates to that thing as such'. It was the applicant's contention that the claim related to apparatus operating in accordance with the requirements of the program.

8.40 Subsequent to the High Court decision in *Merrill Lynch* [1989] RPC 561, the Court of Appeal handed down its judgment in the case of *Genentech Inc's Patent* [1989] RPC 147. Although the subject matter of this case concerned developments in genetics and the effect of the statutory prohibition against the grant of a patent for a discovery, the principles discussed are highly relevant to software related inventions. The court pointed out that many developments in the pharmaceutical field followed from a discovery that a particular compound produced specific effects. Such developments had always been considered eligible for protection even though the practical application of the discovery, ie a new drug, might have been obvious once the discovery was made. Any other result, it was suggested –

> would have a very drastic effect on the patenting of new drugs and medicinal or microbiological processes.

Adopting the reasoning applied in *Genentech* the Court of Appeal held in the *Merrill Lynch* that an invention could be patentable where the novel or inventive elements lay in a computer program.

8.41 Although the application in *Merrill Lynch* survived challenge on the ground that it related to a computer program as such, the Court of Appeal held that it was barred from patentability on another ground. Attention, it was held had to be paid to the nature of the resulting application. In the present case, the result:

> . . . whatever the technical advance may be, is simply the production of a trading system. it is a data processing system for doing a specific business, that is to say making a trading market in securities. the end result, therefore, is simply 'a method . . . of doing business', and is excluded by section 1(2)(c) . . . A data processing system operating to produce a novel technical result would normally be patentable. But it cannot, it seems to me, be patentable if the result itself is a prohibited item under section 1(2). In the present case it is such a prohibited item.

Although the result of *Merrill Lynch* was to deny the grant of a patent for the particular application, the interpretation adopted by the Court of Appeal would appear to open the doors of the patent system to many forms of computer program subject always to the requirements that any claims must be couched in terms relating to the program's application.

8.42 In terms of the nature of the application, the landmark case has been the decision of the European Patent Office in the case of *Vicom Systems Inc's Application* [1987] EPOR 74. The application here related to digital image processing. The invention at issue, it was claimed, facilitated the processing of data at increased speed and produced images of greater quality than that which could be attained using traditional methods. In the application for the grant of a patent, the steps by which this result was achieved were expressed mathematically in the form of an algorithm. The application was rejected by the European Patent Office on the basis that the claims referred to a mathematical method and, as such, were excluded from patentability.

8.43 Appealing against this refusal, the applicants claimed that:

> A novel technical feature clearly exists in not only the hardware, but also in the method recited in the claims presented by this appeal. The invention, furthermore confers a technical benefit namely a substantial increase in processing speed compared with the prior art.

This contention was accepted by the Board of Appeal. The Board accepted that any processing operation which was to be carried out on an electronic signal could be expressed in terms of a mathematical formula. When the formula existed in isolation, there could be no question of it being granted a patent. Where the formula was applied, however, different considerations arose. It was stated that:

> ... if a mathematical method is used in a technical process, that process is carried out on a physical entity (which may be a material object but equally an image stored as an electronic signal) by some technical means implementing the method and provides as its end result a certain change in that entity. The technical means might include a computer comprising suitable hardware or an appropriately programmed general purpose computer.
>
> The Board, therefore, is of the opinion that even if the idea underlying an invention may be considered to lie in a mathematical method a claim directed to a technical process in which the method is used does not seek protection for the mathematical method as such.

8.44 The references in this judgment to terms such as 'technical process' and 'technical benefit' echo provisions in guidelines issued by the European Patent Office in 1985. Intended to advise patent examiners faced with software related inventions these stated that:

> A computer program claimed by itself or as a record on a carrier is unpatentable irrespective of its content. The situation is not normally changed when the computer program is loaded into a known computer.

Moving on from this, however, it was recognised that inventions in which a computer program constitutes an essential element may qualify for patent protection subject to the application of the convention's general rules. As is the case under the UK legislation, the fact that the novelty of the invention lies in the computer program will not bar a claim so long as the end result makes a 'technical contribution to the known art'. The guidelines continue:

> If, however, the subject matter as claimed makes a technical contribution to the known art, patentability should not be denied merely on the ground that a computer program is involved in its implementation. This means, for example, that program controlled machines and program controlled manufacturing and control processes should normally be regarded as a patentable subject matter. It follows also that, where the claimed subject matter is concerned only with the program controlled internal working of a known computer, the subject matter could be patentable if it produced a technical effect.

8.45 The new approach, it was stated, aimed to produce a workable system from the standpoint of the European Patent office (particularly in relation to the search and examination requirements), whilst 'responding to the reasonable desires of industry for a somewhat more liberal line than that adopted in the past'.

8.46 Although the intention to focus on what an invention does rather than the manner in which it does it is clear, the quest to identify a technical contribution has not proved an easy one. The issue is relatively straightforward when the product or process at issue produces some external effect, for example, a new X-ray system where computer programs permit the dose of radiation to be calculated and directed more precisely than has been possible in the past. Decisions become more complicated where the working is internal. Consideration of a number of decisions of the European Patent Office might serve to illustrate the point.

8.47 Case T–52/85 [1989] EPOR involved an application by IBM who sought to patent a system for automatically generating a list of expressions semantically related to an input linguistic expression together with a method for displaying such a list, ie a form of thesaurus. The actions of the computer in this case were considered to operate in the field of linguistics rather than to produce a technical contribution to the known art. The computer's functions were all conventional described as consisting of:

> storing data; comparing input data with an index for finding an address location; storing the address; accessing it with a memory; decoding the

addressed data; utilising the decoded data as an address for accessing another memory; displaying the addressed data.

8.48 Beyond the technicalities of its performance, all that the computer did was to compare data in the form of a word, with other data already programmed into a segment of its memory and displaying the results of any matches. To this extent, its operations were comparable with a person 'searching' their memory for an alternative form of expression. The Board of Appeal concluded:

> It remains, of course, true that internally a computer functions technically and this applies also to its display device. However, the effect of this function, namely the resulting information about the existence of semantically related expressions, is a purely linguistic, that is, non-technical result. The appellant agrees that the claimed system can be implemented by pure software and this implementation is the only one described and preferred. No new reconfigured hardware has been shown to be used in this case. As said before, the two memories can be different sections of a single (conventional) memory. In the opinion of the Board, this new reconfiguration by software is not a technical contribution here.

8.49 In a further case, T–6/83 [1990] EPOR 91 the application involved the interconnection of a series of computers in such a manner as to facilitate communications between programs and data held in the various computers. Obviously, the basis for the claimed invention lay in the computer programs which controlled these operations. The problem which the invention sought to resolve, it was held, was essentially a technical one, involving the transmission, reception, processing and output of data. As such the application was not patentable.

8.50 The contrary conclusion was reached in a further case, T–22/85 [1990] EPOR 98. This claim referred to a system for automatically abstracting and storing a document. Such a function was a conventional attribute of computers – although the new program might perform the task more efficiently than had previously been the case and advance was solely in the area of programming – and, as such, was excluded from patentability.

8.51 In another case involving an application by IBM, T–115/85 [1990] EPOR 107 an application was accepted which referred to a method for causing a computer automatically to display one of a number of pre-determined messages relating to the machine's status. The view was taken that:

> giving visual indications automatically about conditions prevailing in the apparatus or system is basically a technical problem.

The application proposes a solution to a specific problem of this kind, namely providing a visual indication about events occurring in the input/ output device of a text processor. The solution includes the use of a computer program and certain tables stored in a memory to build up the phrases to be displayed.

8.52 The distinction between this successful application and the unsuccessful claim in case T–52/85 [1989] EPOR 454 appears slight. The Board of Appeal was of the view that the present application was more than a computer program, but it is not clear why a development which automatically displays information regarding a computer system's state of health should be so regarded whilst a development which automatically displays the synonyms of a word inputted by a user should be rejected.

8.53 The most recent UK authority is the case of *Fujitsu's Application*, decided in 1997 [1996] RPC 511. The *Fujitsu* case illustrates well what is becoming a feature of our information society. Computers and computer programs are being used in situations and for activities which were previously the province of humans. The machine may well substitute in whole or in part for human thought. In this situation, it is very possible that the end product of the process might be classed as a scheme or method for performing a mental act and any claim for patentability rejected on this basis.

8.54 The technology at issue in *Fujitsu* will be familiar to anyone with a recollection of chemistry lessons at school and the use of three-dimensional lattices to depict molecular structures. Fujitsu's invention sought to bring this concept into the age of virtual reality, allowing chemists to depict and manipulate crystal structures on a computer screen. The effect would be to allow the analysis of the properties of new compounds without the need to create these in the real world. The novelty in the claimed invention lay only in the relevant computer programs.

8.55 The patent application was rejected in the Patent Office on the basis that it related to a program for a computer as well as to a method for performing a mental act – that of visualising molecular structure. An appeal was taken to the High Court where counsel for the Comptroller of Patents recognised that there had been 'difficulty in applying these statutory exclusions'. '[S]trict application of the guidance laid down in the authorities' it was suggested, 'leads to the exclusion from patentability of a considerable number of inventions which do in reality appear to provide a substantial contribution to the sum of technical knowledge.' The hope was expressed that the decision of the court would provide 'guidance' in determining 'the scope and application of the exclusions'.

8.56 It is unclear whether this hope has been realised. The Patent Office rejection of the application was upheld on both grounds. In respect of the computer program point it was held that:

> In VICOM, the technical contribution was provided by the generation of the enhanced display. In the present case, the combined structure is the result of the directions given by the operator and use of the program. The computer is conventional as is the display unit. The displays of crystal structures are provided by the operator. The operator then provides the appropriate way of superposition and the program does the rest. the resulting display is the combined structure shown pictorially in a form that would in the past have been produced as a model. The only advance is the computer program which enables the combined structure to be portrayed quicker.

8.57 The application fared no better in respect of the objection on the ground that it related to a scheme or method for performing a mental act. Here it was held that:

> In VICOM, the Board explained that a mathematical method could be distinguished from a patentable process based on it in that the former involved an abstract concept in which numbers were worked on to produce new numbers whereas in a patentable process a physical entity was worked on and a new physical entity was produced. Very similar concepts apply to the distinction between methods for performing mental acts and processes methods or apparatus based upon such acts. Excluded mental acts must include those mental activities which involve a significant level of abstraction and intellectual generality. Rules as to the planting of potatoes in which the operator is instructed to measure and evaluate matters such as the type of soil, location, weather and availability of irrigation is a method for performing a mental act. Directions to plant one seed potato every metre is not. It is a precise process.
>
> In this case, Fujitsu's application leaves it to the operator to select what data to work on, how to work on it, how to assess the results and which, if any, results to use. The process is abstract and the result of use of it is undefined. What is produced is not an inevitable result of taking a number of defined steps but is determined by the personal skill and assessment of the operator. As such it consists in substance of a scheme or method for performing a mental act and is unpatentable

8.58 Although adopting the same criteria as the European Patent Office, it has been suggested that the decision in *Fujitsu* adopts a more restrictive view of the scope of patentability. In some respects, the result seems somewhat paradoxical. A computer controlled potato planting machine which plants a potato every metre might be patentable. Were the identical machine to have more sophisticated software allowing account to be taken of factors such as soil conditions, weather and the presence of other crops, no patent could be awarded even though this second machine might appear more technologically advanced and deserving of protection.

Towards a more liberal approach?

8.59 During the 1990s considerable discussion took place concerning the proper role of the patent system in respect of software related inventions. In the United Kingdom, a symposium organised by the Patent Office in 1994 considered the question whether the prohibition in s 1(2) of the Patents Act 1977 against the award of patents for 'a program for a computer' should be repealed. A large majority of those attending expressed support for this approach with the argument extending also to the other forms of prohibited subject matter such as mathematical methods and schemes for performing a mental act. Reliance upon the general criteria that an invention should be novel, non-obvious and capable of industrial application, it was suggested, would be sufficient to maintain the integrity of the patent system whilst rendering it suitable for modern, information based, products.

8.60 In 1997 the European Commission published a Green Paper on Patents. In part this was concerned with efforts to re-launch the concept of a Community patent. Significant attention was also given to the role of software. Whilst restating the current prohibition against the patentability of software as such, the Green Paper indicated that:

> Faced with the increasing importance of software, the European Patent Office and the national Patent Offices of some Member States have in recent years granted thousands of patents protecting logical models composed of basic ideas and principles that constitute 'technical solutions to technical problems'. These patents were not granted for the software *per se* but in respect of software-related inventions consisting of hardware and software.
>
> The Commission note that the TRIPS agreement provides that patents should be available for 'any inventions , whether products or processes, in all fields of technology' (Art 27). This formulation does not exclude software and some commentators have argued that the present approach of the European Patent Convention contravenes the TRIPS agreement. The current US patents law makes no specific mention of computer programs and practice in the courts and Patent Office has indicated an increasing willingness to award patents for software-related inventions in situations where the role of the hardware component was extremely peripheral to the technology at issue. Japan has also adopted a favourable attitude towards the patentability of software related inventions with draft Guidelines indicating that patents should be awarded to inventions which involve a high degree of 'technological creativeness using the laws of nature.

8.61 In an increasingly global economy, one major concern was that investment and employment in the software sector might flow to those countries which offered strong intellectual property rights. In a follow-up paper published in 1999, the Commission noted that:

> In the United States, following developments at the end of the 80s, it became possible to lodge claims covering a program as such ('program product claim'). This change had a very positive impact on the development of the software industry; thus, Microsoft now holds about 400 American patents for software programs, and about 12 000 patent applications covering software are filed annually (or 6% of total applications, compared with less than 2% in Europe). In Japan, about 20 000 patent applications covering computer programs are filed each year, and the guidelines adopted in 1997 by the Japanese Patent Office follow the more liberal practice in force in the United States.

It was accordingly indicated that the Commission would bring forward a directive providing for the patentability of computer programs so long as the basic requirements of novelty, inventiveness and industrial application are satisfied.

8.62 More recent developments within the European Patent Office might have the effect of making the Commission's proposals redundant. Two decisions of the European Patent Office Board of Appeal involving applications submitted by IBM appear to indicate a more liberal interpretation of the European Patent Convention provisions.

8.63 The reasoning in the two cases was identical. Case T0935/97 concerned an application with a claim including reference to a computer program stored on a computer readable storage medium. This, it was held by the examiners, amounted to no more than a claim for a program stored on a disk, something which had always been regarded as unpatentable. The Board of Appeal disagreed.

8.64 In reaching its decision, the Board of Appeal took considerable notice of the provisions of the TRIPS agreement and the practice of the US and Japanese Patent Offices. Although it was recognised that none of these was binding on the EPO it was considered that:

> These developments represent a useful indication of modern trends. In the Board's opinion, they may contribute to the further highly desirable (world-wide) harmonisation of patent law.

8.65 After analysing a range of previous EPO authorities, dating back to the venerable *VICOM* decision, the Board of Appeal stated its view as to the proper approach to software-related applications:

A computer program claimed by itself is not excluded from patentability if the program, when running on a computer or loaded into a computer, brings about or is capable of bringing about, a technical effect which goes beyond the 'normal' physical interactions between the program (software) and the computer (hardware) on which it is run.

...

Furthermore, the Board is of the opinion that with regard to the exclusions under Article 52(2) and (3) EPC, it does no matter whether a computer program is claimed by itself , or as a record on a carrier.

It should be noted that the requirement that a program produces a technical effect remains but the decision may serve to reduce some of the word games which have been associated with the attempt to secure patent protection for a software-related invention. The floodgates have been well and truly opened.

Where next for patents?

8.66 It was suggested at the beginning of this chapter that the patent system was based largely on the notion of national patents. This is likely to remain the case and even the proposed Community patent would exist alongside, rather than replace, national patents. The increasingly global nature of commerce and industry is serving to bring about an increasing degree of harmonisation and, as shown in the discussion above of the most recent European Patent Office case law, the TRIPS agreement is providing a legal basis for harmonising initiatives. The trend throughout the world is clearly to accept that software should be brought within the ambit of the patent system. In some senses there is almost an element of competition between states as to who can provide the strongest protection. As was said in the US case of *Lotus v Paperback*:

> It is no accident that the world's strongest software industry is found in the United States, rather than in some other jurisdiction which provides weaker protection for computer programs.

8.67 As can be seen from the account of the origins of the UK patent system, monopolies can be used to stifle competition. The justification for the patent system rests on a finely drawn balance. As has been said:

> The basic theory of the patent system is simple and reasonable. It is desirable in the public interest that industrial techniques should be improved. In order to encourage improvement, and to encourage the disclosure of improvements in preference to their use in secret, any person devising an improvement in a manufactured article, or in machinery or methods for making it, may upon disclosure of the improvement at the Patent Office

demand to be given a monopoly in the use for a period of years. After that period it passes into the public domain; and the temporary monopoly is not objectionable, for if it had not been for the inventor who devised and disclosed the improvement nobody would have been able to use it at that or any other time, since nobody would have known about it. Furthermore, the giving of the monopoly encourages the putting into practice of the invention, for the only way the inventor can make a profit from it (or even recover the fees for his patent) is by putting it into practice; either by using it himself, and deriving an advantage over his competitors from its use, or by allowing others to use it in return for royalties.

8.68 Perhaps surprisingly, almost no empirical evidence exists whether the patent system is effective in either economic terms or in ensuring that information regarding technical innovations enters into the public domain. Whilst people may legitimately argue that the patent system is ill founded and therefore that all patents are wrong, there is little justification for arguing that the world's largest industry should be excluded from the most important and relevant form of intellectual property law. What the debate concerning the patentability of software should now focus on is ensuring that patent offices have the resources and expertise to apply effectively the criteria of novelty, inventiveness and industrial application which are at the core of the patent system. Poorly drafted and inadequately examined patents will serve no one's interests.

Chapter 9

Rights in databases

Introduction

9.0 From 1 January 1998, a new form of intellectual property right has been established in UK law. Implementing the provisions of the European Directive of 11 March 1996 on the legal protection of databases, the Copyright and Rights in Databases Regulations 1997 may reduce the level of copyright protection available to database owners, substituting this with a new, sui generis, right effective against the extraction and/or re-utilisation of a substantial part of the database contents.

9.1 During the late 1980s, the proportion of the gross domestic product of countries such as the US and the UK relating to the manufacturing sector dropped below 50% for the first time since the early stages of the industrial revolution. The services sector is now responsible for most of our national income. Software (and electronic information services) make up a significant and growing element of the sector. In its Green Paper, *Copyright and Related Rights in the Information Society*, the European Commission indicate that 'activities covered by copyright and related rights account for an estimated 3–5% of Community gross domestic product'. The European information services market itself has been valued at almost 2.2 billion ECU (approximately £1.5bn) per annum. Databases constitute a significant segment of the information technology economy. In 1992 European on-line services generated revenues of $3.24bn. This figure excluded earnings of US-based services such as Lexis/Nexis, which are offered within Europe. Worldwide, the legal profession has been estimated as generating some 7% of total on-line revenues.

The nature of the beast

9.2 A dictionary definition refers to the term 'database' as consisting of:

a large body of information stored in a computer, which can process it and from which particular pieces of information can be retrieved when required.

9.3 The initial draft of the European Union's Database Directive adopted a similar approach, limiting its application to:

> a collection of work or materials arranged, stored and accessed by electronic means, and the electronic materials necessary for the operation of the data base such as its thesaurus, index or system for obtaining and presenting information.

9.4 Although there might be pragmatic reasons for limiting the scope of legislation, there is no reason in principle why more traditional forms of data storage, such as a card index file, should not also be classed as a database. In the final version of the Directive, and in the Copyright and Rights in Databases Regulations 1997, which implement the provisions of the directive for the UK, a broader definition applies referring to:

> a collection of independent works, data or other materials which:
> (a)   are arranged in a systematic or methodical way, and
> (b)   are individually accessible by electronic or other means.

Examples of databases

9.5 Starting with non-automated systems, a telephone directory could be classed as a database. Here data in the form of names, addresses and telephone numbers are arranged in alphabetical order and may be retrieved by users through opening the directory at the appropriate page. Card index systems, such as those which used to occupy significant areas of floor space within libraries also function in a similar manner. On the basis of the definition cited above, one might even class the library itself as a database. With the dawning of the digital revolution and the ability to record and store any form of information in electronic format, the range and commercial value of databases has increased dramatically. Introducing the proposed regulations in Parliament, the Minister of State said that:

> The database sector is a major United Kingdom industry. Estimates of the size of the UK database market range up to £10 billion but even that may be an underestimate. It is growing at more than 11% a year. About 350 firms are believed to be active in the sector, 30 of which are large suppliers and the rest small and medium-sized enterprises. UK suppliers have a share of the wider European Union market which has been put at more than 50%.

9.6 Many electronic databases are accessible on an on-line basis. Most lawyers will, for example, be familiar with the Lexis database.

Located in Dayton, Ohio, this represents the world's largest collection of case law and statutory material. The parallel Nexis service provides access to electronic copies of the contents of a vast range of newspapers and journals. Also on the market are a wide range of CDs. Such capacity devices typically have a storage capacity of around 650 MB of data. A 500-page book would occupy somewhere in the region of 2.5MB. A single CD could, therefore, contain the text of some 300 volumes, although the figure would drop if pictures and illustrations were to be embedded in the text.

Databases and new technology

9.7 Traditionally, one of the basic requirements for a functional database has been that its contents are stored in accordance with a predetermined structure. A similar requirement applies to many automated databases where data is stored in predetermined fields. With developments in retrieval software and what are referred to as relational databases, it is less and less necessary for information to be stored in accordance with a predetermined structure. In general, the tendency is to allow users maximum flexibility in using a database rather than requiring searches to be formulated in accordance with predetermined structures. Once again, the telephone directory may provide an apposite example. With a paper directory, a user can search effectively only by means of the structure devised by the publisher – effectively, in alphabetical order by reference to subscribers' surnames. CD directories typically allow searches by reference to any item of data – or to a combination of items. Reverse searching is a popular feature which allows names to be identified from telephone numbers or a listing produced of all subscribers resident in a particular street.

9.8 Where a database comprises an amalgam of data and retrieval software it will be necessary for the software to compile indexes of words used in the data, such indexes being used in subsequent acts of retrieval. Such a system is likely to come within the definition. More problematic issues will arise where the retrieval software is separate from the data being searched. The WWW, for example, consists of tens of millions of individual items of data controlled by millions of users. It is difficult to think of a less structured network than the WWW, yet search engines such as Alta Vista provide increasingly sophisticated searching facilities. Whilst it must be likely that many items on the WWW will qualify for copyright protection in their own right, others may not, for example law reports or copies of statutes from countries which regard such materials as being in the public domain. It may be that the list of materials identified by a search engine as meeting the user's request will itself constitute a database. In this instance there might be a further issue, discussed below: who is to be considered the owner of any resulting database right?

Legal protection of databases before the directive and regulations

9.9 The preamble to the directive asserts that 'databases are at present not sufficiently protected in all Member States by existing legislation'. This may certainly have been the case in some other member states, notably Germany, which have required strict qualitative criteria for the award of copyright but is less applicable in a UK context. The basis for the legal protection of databases lies in the copyright system. As we have seen, s 3 of the 1988 Act defines a literary work as including 'a table or compilation'. Although there is little precedent on the point, there seems little doubt that a database would fall within the latter category. For this reason, therefore, it is necessary in this chapter to consider first the protection afforded to databases under traditional provisions of UK copyright law before turning to examine the new and additional rights conferred under the directive.

9.10 Copyright in respect of the contents of a database may arise in two ways. First, the individual pieces of work located therein may qualify for copyright protection in their own right. An example might be a database consisting of a collection of poems. Each poem, it may be assumed, will be protected by copyright. Additionally, the database may qualify for protection in its own right – a matter which may acquire particular importance if portions of the subject material are not so protected, for example because the author has been dead for more than 70 years or because the factual nature of the data excludes copyright protection. The names of individual companies, for example, will be unlikely to be protected by copyright but a compilation such as the FTSE 100 will enjoy protection as a compilation.

9.11 Discounting the issue whether the contents of a database might qualify for protection in their own right, the issue arises whether the degree of effort which accompanies the compilation of a database is sufficient to qualify for such a grant. Traditionally, a major element of the task facing the compiler of a database has been to determine the order in which the material is to appear and subsequently giving effect to this concept. Using modern technology, text can be scanned and converted into digital format. Whereas traditional compilations such as directories will need to be carefully structured to make it easy for users to find particular items of information, the utilisation of appropriate software will mean that the entire contents of a database may be scanned with reference to a particular word or phrase. In such a case, there is less need for the database compiler to expend effort in arranging the layout of the database.

9.12 It is also one of the features of many computerised services that they seek to take advantage of the processing and storage capabilities of computers in order to present a comprehensive collection of materials. The goal of a legal database such as Lexis is to provide a transcript of every High Court decision delivered in the English courts. Similarly, the website of the Scottish Courts Administration provides the text of every High Court and Court of Session judgment. This is to be contrasted with the more traditional law reports, which contain only a comparatively small number of decisions and where some skill and labour will be expended by the publishers to determine which cases are of sufficient importance to warrant a place in a particular volume.

The 'sweat of the brow' doctrine

9.13 In the event that a database seeks to provide a comprehensive coverage of its chosen subject area, it may be difficult to evidence any originality in the selection process. It is here that a significant divergence exists between the UK approach and that adopted in almost every other copyright system. As has been stated, the UK system imposes minimal qualitative requirements relating to originality. In the case of a compilation, the traditional justification for extending protection has been the effort that has gone into selecting the works to be incorporated therein; what has been referred to in the US as the 'sweat of the brow' doctrine. This approach is well illustrated in the case *of Waterlow Publishers v Rose* [1995] FSR 207. The plaintiff, under contract to the Law Society, had published listings, arranged geographically, of English solicitors and barristers in a publication, the *Solicitors' Diary and Directory*. A listing of all solicitors was supplied to the plaintiff by the Law Society and this was used to send out forms seeking further information about areas of specific expertise.

9.14 Prior to 1984, a company owned by the defendant had been contracted to print copies of the directory. Following a take-over of the plaintiff, this work was transferred to another firm. The defendant thereupon determined to publish a similar work, the *Lawyers' Diary* which would compete with the plaintiff's publication. The defendant's manner of work was to commence with the *Solicitors' Diary*, which constituted the only comprehensive public listing of the names and addresses of solicitors. A copy of the entry in the *Solicitors' Diary* would be sent out to the individuals concerned and they would be asked to reply, either confirming the accuracy of the information or making any changes that were felt desirable. The plaintiff alleged that this method of work meant that the resultant publication infringed their copyright.

9.15 In deciding the case, the court had to consider first the question whether copyright subsisted in the compilation of names, addresses and other information published in the *Solicitors' Diary* and, second, whether the defendant's conduct constituted infringement. Although it was recognised that the nature of compilations was such that it might be difficult to identify a single person as author, the fact that the plaintiff was identified as publisher established a presumption that copyright was owned by it. Regarding the issue of infringement, the Court of Appeal held that:

> Mr Rose argued that he only used the existing directory to get in touch with the solicitors and that his work was then based upon the forms returned to him . . . There were something like 50,000 forms and the names and addresses to which they were sent were all obtained from the Solicitors' Diary 1984 . . . In my judgement that goes beyond lawful use of an existing publication and amounted to an infringement of the plaintiff's copyright.

9.16 The effect of this and of similar decisions is that extensive copyright protection is afforded to databases compiled in the UK. A similar approach had been followed in the United States until the landmark Supreme Court case of *Feist Publications Inc v Rural Telephone Service Co Inc* 499 US 330 (1991) signalled a significant change of direction.

9.17 The case concerned the extent of copyright protection in a telephone directory. The respondent, Rural, was a telephone service provider which was required under the terms of its operating licence to publish a directory of its subscribers. A substantial number of service providers operate in the United States each publishing directories covering a small geographical area. The appellant, Feist, was a publishing company which specialised in publishing directories which covered a wider geographical area than that of typical small-scale provider such as Rural. Feist entered into negotiations seeking licences to publish from 11 different telephone utilities. Only Rural refused permission.

9.18 Despite Rural's refusal, Feist went ahead with the publication, extracting the necessary information from Rural's directory. Although it added some items of information and attempted to verify other items independently, 1,309 entries in the Feist directory were identical to their Rural counterparts. More damningly, four of these were fictitious entries inserted by Rural in order to provide a means of detecting unauthorised copying.

9.19 Rural's action alleging copyright infringement succeeded before the lower courts. The Supreme Court took a different view. Infringement, it was held, could occur only when what was copied was protected under the copyright regime. Although the level of originality required as the basis for protection was low, there was 'a narrow category of works in which the creative spark is utterly lacking or so trivial as to be virtually non-existent'. Rural's telephone directory, it was held, fell into this category. Its selection of listing 'could not be more obvious'. Rural, it was held, 'expended sufficient effort to make the . . . directory useful, but insufficient creativity to make it original'.

9.20 The decision in *Feist* has produced considerable comment within the US. Certain aspects of the court's reasoning are potentially significant for the UK system. In particular, the court explicitly rejected the notion that the expenditure of effort, the 'sweat of the brow', could suffice for the grant of copyright. Even so, the court makes it clear that only a modicum of creativity is required. Although copyright does not subsist in an alphabetical listing of subscribers, subsequent cases have held that 'yellow pages'-type listings where subscribers are grouped according to the nature of their business or profession will attract protection.

9.21 A further illustration of the new US approach can be found in the case of *ProCD v Zeidenberg* (1996) 86 F 3d 1447. As was stated in the case report:

> Plaintiff spent millions of dollars creating a comprehensive, national directory of residential and business listings. Plaintiff compiled over 95,000,000 residential and commercial listings from approximately 3,000 publicly available telephone books. The listings include full names, street addresses, telephone numbers, zip codes and industry or 'SIC' codes where appropriate. Plaintiff sells these listings on CD-ROM discs under the trademark 'Select Phone TM,' as well as under other trade names and trademarks.

The plaintiff's pricing strategy was to sell copies of the CD at a low price for consumer use but levy higher rates for those seeking to make commercial use of the product. The defendant purchased a copy of the consumer CD which retailed for less than $100. Using its own retrieval software it placed a copy of the plaintiff's listings on an Internet site from where it allowed users to extract up to 1,000 listings free of charge. More extensive access, typically for commercial purposes, could be obtained at a cost less than that charged by the plaintiff. The site was soon attracting up to 20,000 visitors a day and, fearing significant adverse effects on sales of its CD, the plaintiff sought an injunction preventing its continued operation. Although at first instance the injunction was refused, the Court of Appeals eventually found in favour of the plaintiff on the ground that the defendant was bound by the terms of a licence accompanying the CD which prohibited its use for commercial purposes, it was common ground that no copyright subsisted in the data itself.

9.22 As indicated in *ProCD*, one of the consequences of the *Feist* decision has been the emergence of a new market in the US for CD- and Internet-based compilations of telephone directories. Selling for a few dollars, these will contain hundreds of millions of names and numbers, often providing additional facilities, such as a reverse search option allowing a person's address to be identified from a telephone number. In the UK, British Telecom has continued to assert copyright in telephone directories and has threatened copyright actions against parties planning to introduce competing products. This situation has now changed, not through the operation of copyright law, but as a result of the actions of the Director General of Telecommunications, who inserted a clause in British Telecom's licence requiring it to make directory information available to third parties.

9.23 A major goal of the directive is to eliminate obstacles to the creation of a single market by harmonising the level of protection afforded to databases. Although not explicitly stated in the preamble, there was undoubtedly the feeling that the UK's 50% share of the EU database market was due in part to the fact that strong legal protection provided an incentive for database producers to locate their businesses in the UK. An alternative explanation might refer to the advantages of working in the English language and the larger market available to such databases.

The new regime

9.24 The directive's provisions can be grouped into three categories: first, it makes provision regarding the application of copyright to the contents of databases; second, it provides for the extent of and exceptions to such copyrights; finally, a new sui generis right is established to benefit some databases which are excluded from the copyright regime.

Copyright and databases

9.25 Article 1 of the directive provides that:

> databases which, by reason of the selection or arrangement of their contents, constitute the author's own intellectual creation shall be protected as such by copyright.

The key phrase in this provision refers to work being 'the author's own intellectual creation'. This term is not defined further. In the implementing UK regulations, it is provided that:

> For the purposes of this Part, a literary work consisting of a database is original if, and only if, by reason of the selection or arrangements of the contents of the database the database constitutes the author's own intellectual creation.

9.26 The formula that work will be protected when it is the authors 'own intellectual creation' is also used in the software protection directive, which provides that computer programs are to be protected as literary works. When the directive was implemented into UK law, this phrase was not included. Introducing the regulations in Parliament, however, the Minister of State commented that:

> Some people felt that no amendment of the (1988 Act) was needed to introduce the test and that the current test for the originality of literary works was enough.
> The Government do not share that view. The Directive is clear. It requires copyright protection for databases 'which by reason of selection or arrangement of their contents, constitute the author's own intellectual creations.

This is intended to exclude so-called sweat of the brow databases – that is, ones that involve time, money or effort but no intellectual creation, such as the white pages telephone directory.

9.27 Assuming this view is correct, it gives rise to the suggestion that the UK has failed adequately to implement the software protection directive. If the view is incorrect, the effect of the regulations has been to introduce unnecessary complexity into copyright law. Prior to implementation of the directive, s 3 of the 1988 Act provided that the term 'literary work' was to encompass:

> any work, other than a dramatic or musical work, which is written, spoken or sung, and accordingly includes:
> (a) a table or compilation,
> (b) a computer program,
> (c) preparatory design material for a computer program.

9.28 This is now amended to read:

any work, other than a dramatic or musical work, which is written, spoken or sung, and accordingly includes
(a)   a table or compilation other than a database,
(b)   a computer program,
(c)   preparatory design material for a computer program, and
(d)   a database.

For the purposes of this Part, a literary work consisting of a database is original if, and only if, by reason of the selection or arrangements of the contents of the database the database constitutes the author's own intellectual creation.

9.29 Given that databases were hitherto regarded as a form of compilation, this approach might not be considered entirely satisfactory and it may be unclear where the division between the two categories lies. The preamble to the directive recites that:

as a rule, the compilation of several recordings of musical performances on a CD does not come within the scope of this Directive, both because as a compilation, it does not meet the requirements for copyright protection and because it does not represent a substantial enough investment to be eligible under the sui generis right.

9.30 Under previous UK law, there is little doubt that such a work would benefit from protection as a compilation. The question which will be discussed below is whether implementation of the directive will alter this situation.

Licensing and Databases

9.31 In previous versions of the directive, provision was made for database owners to be required to grant licences to users in certain circumstances:

If the works or materials contained in a database which is made publicly available cannot be independently created, collected or obtained from any other source, the right to extract and re-utilize, in whole or substantial part, works or materials from that database for commercial purposes shall be licensed on fair and non-discriminatory terms.

It was also provided that licenses should require to be issued:

if the database is made publicly available by a public body which is either established to assemble or disclose information pursuant to legislation or is under a general duty to do so.

9.32 At least in respect of the first category, compulsory licences would only be available in very limited circumstances. It might be commented in particular that in most cases where only one party could obtain data, this might fall into the category of confidential information or be regarded as a trade secret and would certainly not be made available to the public. In the event, the proposal was dropped following objections from the Parliament, although it is provided that the issue is to be kept under review by the Commission, which is to report to the Council and Parliament within the first three years of the directive's operation, indicating whether the operation of the new regime –

> has led to abuse of a dominant position or other interference with free competition which would justify appropriate measures being taken including the establishment of non-voluntary licensing arrangements.

9.33 Extensive provisions are made in the 1988 Act for the handling of licensing agreements between copyright owners and those wishing to make use of their materials. The Copyright Tribunal is established to determine disputes as to the nature and extent of such schemes. The regulations extend the scope of the statutory provisions and of the tribunal's jurisdiction to matters relating to database licences.

Other copyright changes

9.34 A number of other changes are made to the provisions of the 1988 Act. In order to implement the provisions of the software protection directive amendments were made by the Copyright (Computer Programs) Regulations 1992, which had the effect of allowing the lawful user of a program to perform acts which might otherwise be restricted by copyright. In particular, this would sanction such copying of the program as was necessary for its use. Similar considerations will apply with electronic databases (whether on-line or held on disk) and the regulations add equivalent authorising provisions to the 1988 Act. Any attempt contractually to restrict or exclude the operation of these rights is declared void.

The new database right

9.35 Implementation of the directive is likely to have the effect of removing the protection of copyright from certain databases. Balancing this, a new database right is created which will arise when:

> there has been a substantial investment in obtaining, verifying or presenting the contents of the database.

The maker of the database will be the first owner of the database right except in the case where the work is created by an employee in which event the employer will own the right.

9.36 It is not clear how much investment will be required to justify application of the adjective 'substantial'. The directive's assertion that a musical compilation will not require substantial investment has been cited above. Dependent upon the popularity of the music involved, it may be, however, that a high price will require to be paid to obtain the necessary copyright licences.

9.37 The database right is not presently found in any international agreements, although WIPO has proposed a draft Treaty which would establish such a right. Pending the adoption of this instrument, which has been the subject of considerably hostility from certain quarters in the US, where it is seen as marking a retreat from the principles of free access to data enshrined in the *Feist* decision, protection is limited to individuals or undertakings who are nationals of or incorporated in a state within the European Economic Area. Assuming that the effect of the changes to the 1988 Act discussed above do have the effect of taking databases outwith the scope of copyright protection, the effect will be to reduce the level of protection afforded to databases owned by non-EEA nationals or undertakings without conferring the compensatory benefit of the new database right. To this extent, non-EEA database owners may be significant losers under the new regime. This may cause difficulties where databases are maintained on the WWW. Implementation of the directive in the UK might have the effect of removing some such databases from the copyright regime but, where the database is controlled by a non-EEA national, the compensatory database right will not be available. The effect of the new regime will therefore be to reduce the level of protection afforded within the UK to, for example, US-based database providers.

9.38 It is immaterial for the existence of this right, which is stated to be a 'property right', whether the database or its contents are protected by the law of copyright. The right will be infringed by a person who:

> without the consent of the owner . . . extracts or re-utilises all or a substantial part of the contents of the database.

This may take the form either of a single act or a succession of smaller extractions. Where conduct by a lawful user would not infringe the database right, it is provided that any term or condition which seeks to restrict this will be null and void. The traditional copyright exemption permitting such use as comes under the heading of fair dealing is restated in modified form for the new right. This provides that:

Database right in a database which has been made available to the public in any manner is not infringed by fair dealing with a substantial part of the database for the purposes of illustration for teaching or research, other than teaching or research for a commercial purpose, provided that the source is indicated.

9.39 Infringement of the database right will expose the perpetrator to actions for damages, injunctions or accounting of profits as specified in s 96 of the 1988 Act. Significantly, however, although the directive confers considerable discretion on member states as to the nature of the rights and remedies adopted in respect of the new right, the 1988 Act's provisions relating to criminal penalties do not extend to infringements of the database. Also unavailable are the rights of seizure of infringing copies and the right to demand delivery up. It may be that such rights are of limited relevance to on-line databases but, as has been discussed, the right extends to a wide range of electronic and manual products.

Duration of the right

9.40 The right will come into existence when a database is made available to the public and will subsist for a period of 15 years. It is provided, however, that:

Any substantial change to the contents of a database, including a substantial change resulting from the accumulation of successive additions, deletions or alterations, which would result in the database being considered to be a substantial new investment shall qualify the database resulting from that investment for its own term of protection.

9.41 The application of this provision should be non-problematic where databases (perhaps a telephone directory) are issued on an annual basis. Its application to on-line databases may be more contentious and the provision cited above was amended from earlier proposals to try to cover the situation where a database was subject to continual minor amendment. The example might be taken of an on-line database of law reports such as Lexis. In most areas cases are stored for the last 50 years. If reports are added on a daily basis, each day will see a database which is very slightly different from the earlier one. On a rough and ready calculation, the change from one day to another will be in the region of 0.0001% of the total database. This can surely not be considered substantial. As additions accumulate and are accompanied, perhaps, by changes to the structure of the database itself, it must be likely that the criteria will be satisfied before the expiry of the 15-year period. Assuming continuing development of the database it will obtain perpetual protection.

9.42 In practice it must be likely that the issue whether the contents of a database remain protected by the database right will be significant only when legal proceedings are brought alleging infringement. A database might, for example, be made available to the public in the year 2000 and subjected to continual minor amendments. In 2020 the database owner might institute proceedings against a third party alleging breach of the database right. In this event, evidence could be submitted to the court of the state of the database in 2000 compared with its 2015 incarnation. In the event this indicated substantial additional investment, the court would have to conclude that a new period of protection began in 2015 and that infringement had occurred.

Implementation of the new right

9.43 The database right came into existence on 1 January 1998. Any databases being made available to the public after this date will come under its ambit. In respect of existing databases, any database completed on or after 1 January 1983 will obtain a full term of protection, ie will be regarded as a new database for the purpose of protection. A further transitional provision will benefit databases created on or before 27 March 1996 (the date of the directive's publication in the Official Journal). Any copyright interests in such databases will continue for the full period of life plus 70 years.

Conclusion

9.44 Many aspects of the new regime remain unclear, in particular what impact the new definition of originality will have in the UK. Since the US Supreme Court moved away from the 'sweat of the brow' doctrine in its decision in *Feist*, the UK (and to an extent Commonwealth jurisdictions) have been isolated in terms of the extent of copyright protection. It is difficult to consider a telephone directory as a literary work and the terms of the database right which refer to concepts of extraction and re-utilisation are perhaps more relevant to functional works. Whilst UK-based database producers may see a reduction in the availability of copyright protection, this may be compensated by the fact that works which would previously have been unprotected in other European states will now be protected under the database right. The duration of protection will be less than copyright's life plus 70 years but should be quite adequate for most functional works. The time is fast approaching, however, when a more fundamental examination of the precepts of copyright law will be required in order to develop principles and practices that will be appropriate for our emerging information societies.

Chapter 10

Liability for defective software

Introduction

10.0 As the preceding discussions have indicated, computers are used increasingly in situations where any malfunction may result in financial or physical loss, damage or injury. The terms 'mission' and 'safety critical' are often used. In such circumstances, a lawyer's fancy lightly turns to thoughts of liability. As discussed in Chapter 1, two main forms of liability can be identified. The law of contract serves to confer rights and impose duties upon contracting parties. In the software context, contracts are likely to exist between software developers and their clients and between software suppliers and their customers. Whilst the nature and extent of rights and obligations may be determined in large part by the expressed wishes of the parties, these may be constrained by the provisions of statutes such as the Sale of Goods Act and the Unfair Contract Terms Acts.

10.1 In the situation where no contract exists, attention must turn to non-contractual remedies. Until recently, the basis of these has rested in the law of tort. The prerequisite for a successful action in tort is evidence of negligence on the part of the defender (absent exceptional circumstances where strict liability has attached to this party's actions). The passage of the Consumer Protection Act 1987 has radically transformed the non-contractual position. Based on the provisions of an EC Directive, this serves to impose a strict liability regime upon the producer of a product for certain categories of loss resulting from the presence of a defect within the product.

10.2 Prior to considering these issues, it is helpful to give brief consideration to the nature of computer software and to the differences which exist between software and the tangible products with which society and the law are more familiar. The first difference of substance may be identified at the level of testing. With a product such as a motor car, it is at least theoretically possible to examine every component so as to provide definitive information about its properties. Often, however, testing entails destruction of the item involved and even where this is not the case, it will seldom be commercially feasible to test every specimen of the product. In production, it is possible that some components will be of inferior quality to those tested. A further point is that many, probably most, instances of defects occur as a result of errors at the production stage. Only a portion of products will possess any particular defect and these may not be the ones which are selected for inspection. The conclusion from this analysis is that it is possible to test one item exhaustively but that the results have limited applicability regarding other items of the same type.

10.3   The situation is radically different where software is concerned. It is impossible to test even the simplest program in an exhaustive fashion. This is because of the myriad possibilities for interaction (whether desired or not) between the various elements of the program. In the world of popular science much publicity has been given in recent years to what is known as chaos theory. This suggests that every event influences every other event; that the beating of a butterfly's wings has an impact upon the development of a hurricane. On such an analysis, totally accurate weather forecasting will never be practicable because of the impossibility of taking account of all the variables affecting the climate. The theory's hypothesis is reality in a software context. Although software can and should be tested, it has to be accepted that every piece of software will contain errors which may not materialise until a particular and perhaps unrepeatable set of circumstances occurs. Especially where software is used in safety-critical functions, it is sometimes advocated that where an error is discovered it is preferable to devise procedures to prevent the circumstances recurring than to attempt to modify the software. The argument is that any change to the software may have unanticipated consequences resulting in another error manifesting itself at some time in the future. The cause of a massive failure which paralysed sections of the US telecommunications system in 1991 was ultimately traced to changes which had been made in the call routing-software. The software contained several million lines of code. Three apparently insignificant lines were changed and chaos ensued. By way of contrast, the operators of London's Docklands Light Railway, whose trains are driven under computer control, took the decision that they would not make any changes to the software after it had passed its acceptance tests. The result was that for several years trains stopped on an open stretch of line, paused for a few seconds and then continued with their journey. It had been intended to build a station at the site. After the software was accepted the plans were abandoned but the trains remained ignorant of this fact.

10.4   The plus side of software testing and production is, that although the testing has limitations, the nature of the copying is such as to give a very high degree of assurance that every copy which is made will be identical. Production defects are virtually unknown so that test results will be valid for every copy of the software.

Contractual liability

10.5   The doctrine of freedom of contract is one of the cornerstones of this branch of the law. Parties should be able to determine the terms under which they wish to do business with the task of the law and the courts being to give effect to their agreement. As will be discussed, however, contracts may not make specific provision for certain eventualities and the court's task of interpreting the agreement may be no simple matter. Very many contracts are entered into in an extremely informal manner. To give an example, a customer might enter a computer shop, select a copy of a computer program from a display, tender payment at a cash desk and leave with the software. Barring a possible exchange of pleasantries with the checkout assistant, no words will have been exchanged regarding the purchase. If the software fails to live up to the customer's expectations, the question will arise what forms of legal guarantees might be applicable? Even where contracts are entered into in a more formal manner, important issues relating to the transaction may be omitted. As will be discussed below, the contract is often unclear concerning what will be delivered, when, and to what level of quality and performance

10.6   As indicated in Chapter 1, one of the first tasks of a court will be to determine what terms might be implied into a contract. To date three cases concerning issues of contractual liability for software have reached the Court of Appeal and discussion of these will serve to illustrate the legal situations involved.

Terminate in haste – repent at leisure

10.7   The first case to be considered is that of *Saphena v Allied Collection Agencies* [1995] FSR 616 a case dating back to 1998. The appellant, Saphena Computing, was a small firm specialising in the supply of third-party hardware and software either produced or customised by themselves. The respondent was engaged in the business of debt collection. Under an initial contract between the parties, it was agreed that Saphena would supply a quantity of software. The software was ordered in January 1985 and installed between February and April. Despite initial teething problems it was functioning satisfactorily by May 1985. In August 1985 a second contract was made for the supply of further software. It was intended that this would upgrade the defendant's system. Upon installation of the system, a degree of modification was required caused by difficulties in attaining compatibility with the existing system and through changes in the defendant's requirements.

10.8 Although attempts were made to remedy the problems, it was common ground between the parties that the system was not operating in a satisfactory manner by February 1986. On 11 February a telephone conversation took place between representatives of the parties. In the course of this it was agreed that the relationship should be terminated. Unfortunately, untangling the legal consequences was to prove no simple matter, and when the dispute went to trial proceedings before the High Court lasted for 17 days.

10.9 Subsequent to the conversation, another programmer was contracted to work on the system. In the course of this work, the source code of the programs produced by the plaintiff was copied. Responding to this action, the plaintiff instituted proceedings alleging breach of copyright in their programs. It was further claimed that the defendant had acted wrongfully in terminating the contract and that the plaintiffs were entitled to the price of the goods or services supplied under the contract. This latter contention was challenged by the defendant, who counterclaimed for damages, alleging that the software supplied was not to be considered fit for its purpose. The plaintiff succeeding in all significant aspects of its claim; the defendant appealed to the Court of Appeal, which unanimously affirmed the findings of the lower court. In particular, it was held there was an implied term as to the fitness for the purpose for which the software was required. It had to be reasonably fit for such purposes as had been notified to the suppliers before the orders were placed or were notified subsequently and accepted by the supplier. These obligations had not fulfilled by the supplier at 11 February, when the relationship was terminated. Although the software was usable at this stage, it was not entirely fit for the defendant's purposes. There remained faults which required correction. However, the defendant was not entitled, at that stage, to terminate the agreement on this basis. Software, it was held by Staughton LJ –

> is not a commodity which is delivered once, only once, and once and for all, but one which will necessarily be accompanied by a degree of testing and modification.

10.10 Thus, it would not be a breach of contract to deliver software in the first instance with a defect in it. In this respect, software must be distinguished from other products, in that the concept of delivery is a much more fluid one. In part, this is due to the necessary interaction between supplier and customer. Just as no software developer can reasonably expect a buyer to tell him what is required without a process of feedback and reassessment, so no buyer should expect a supplier to get his programs right first time.

The eradication of defects may be a lengthy and laborious process. In the absence of specific provisions relating to acceptance tests and procedures it is debatable as to how long the buyer must allow this process to continue. Certainly, the message from *Saphena* would indicate that the buyer must exercise caution and restraint before seeking to terminate a contractual relationship. In this instance the effect of termination was that:

> the defendant thereby agreed to accept the software in the condition in which it then was and, by agreement, put it out of the plaintiff's power to render the software fit for its purpose. The original agreements were thereby varied by deleting the fitness term.

10.11 In the event, the plaintiff was held entitled to payment of a reasonable sum in respect of their work on the software and were freed from the requirement to conduct any further work on the system. The defendant's counterclaim for damages in respect of losses caused by the alleged unfitness of the software was dismissed.

Computers are not always the solution

10.12 A broadly similar situation arose in the later case of *Salvage Association v CAP Financial Services Ltd* [1995] FSR 654. The parties initially contracted in March 1987 for the defendants to develop a specification for the computerisation of the plaintiffs' accounting system. This work was carried out and the specifications delivered by July 1987. These were accepted by the plaintiffs, with the defendant being asked to commence work on its implementation in July 1987, although a formal contract to this effect was not concluded until July 1988. The work was scheduled to be completed in a number of stages, with the system coming on-line to replace the existing accounting system in May 1988. Owing to a number of factors outside the control of the defendants, including the availability of suitable telecommunications links, it was recognised that the introduction would be delayed, although significantly the judge held that 'time for completion of the project was of the essence'.

10.13 Apart from external factors, work on the project progressed slowly. With hindsight it became apparent that the original specification was seriously flawed and, despite extensive efforts by the defendant, the system proved incapable of meeting the agreed performance standards. The case report catalogues a lengthy list of problems and unsuccessful rescue attempts. A number of scheduled completion dates came and went, causing increasing problems for the plaintiffs, who had based much of their future business strategy upon the implementation of the new system. In May 1989 the defendants proposed a new programme of 're-analysis, redesign and recoding' with a completion date of 31 December 1989.

10.14 The new programme soon fell behind schedule, due to staff departures and illnesses. The plaintiffs engaged independent consultants to report on the project. This cast serious doubt on the ability of the defendants to meet the new completion data. Following a series of meetings between the parties, the plaintiffs gave notice terminating the contract in July 1989. Legal proceedings resulted with the trial taking no less than 72 days.

10.15 Much of the dispute in the case was concerned with the validity of the limitation clauses contained in the defendants' standard terms and conditions which were incorporated into the agreement between the parties. These purported to limit the extent of their liability to a maximum of £25,000. The plaintiffs alleged that their losses resulting from the defendants' breach of contract amounted to some £800,000. The limitation clause was held to be invalid as failing to satisfy the requirement of the Unfair Contract Terms Act 1977 that such clauses be fair and reasonable. In respect of the system itself, it was unequivocally held that it was not functional, that the plaintiff were entitled to have lost confidence in the ability of the defendant to produce a working system within any reasonable time scale, and that they were entitled to terminate the contract on account of the defendants' failures.

Problems with the community charge

10.16 The community charge, more commonly known as the poll tax, proved one of the less popular forms of taxation in recent British history. In fiscal terms, the tax is no longer operative, but it has made a significant contribution to the law. The case *of St Albans District Council v ICL* [1996] 4 All ER 481 was concerned with the acceptability of hardware software supplied by the defendant to the plaintiff for the purpose of administering the operation of the tax. The case is undoubtedly the most significant precedent in the field of information technology law and deserves detailed consideration.

10.17 The key (and controversial) element of the poll tax was that, subject to a very limited number of exceptions, all those aged 18 or above living in a local government district were required to pay a single sum by way of poll tax. No account was taken of a taxpayer's income, so that a person earning £100,000 per annum would pay the same as a person earning £10,000. In administrative terms, this approach simplified the task of the local authorities. Effectively, all that was required was to calculate the income required and the number of persons liable to pay the tax and divide the one by the other.

10.18 If ever a task could be seen as made for the computer, this was surely it, and without exception local authorities invested heavily in IT systems to administer the tax. Many of the authorities, St Albans included, entered into contracts with the computer supplier ICL, who promoted an IT system referred to as 'The ICL Solution'. At the time the contract was signed, the elements of the system required to cope with the specific demands of the community charge had not been completed or tested. This fact was promoted as a positive benefit to the authority. The developers would use a 70-strong development team to produce the necessary software and, by entering into the contract, the council would be able 'to input into the development process in order to be sure that this product meets your specific requirements'.

10.19 The contract, valued at some £1.3m, was concluded subject to ICL's standard terms and conditions, which excluded all liability for consequential loss and limited liability for other losses to a maximum of £100,000. The system was delivered to the council timeously but, as envisaged in the contract, the software required was to be delivered and installed in stages as various elements were completed and in line with legislative requirements relating to the introduction of the new tax. Initial elements were to be completed in Autumn 1988, with the full system being operable by February 1990.

10.20 One of the first tasks which had to be conducted by local authorities was to calculate the numbers of persons in their area liable to pay the tax. Many local authorities were politically opposed to the new system, and in order to prevent them delaying its introduction, the legislation provided a rigid timetable for the various actions required, with penalties being imposed upon recalcitrant authorities. St Albans Council was therefore faced with the requirement to complete their count by a certain date. Once the figure had been calculated, the legislation provided that it could not be altered.

10.21 The calculation was carried out using the ICL system in early December 1989 and a figure of 97,384.7 was produced. Unfortunately, the version of the software used had a bug and for some unknown reason a new release which would have cured the problem was not installed on the council's computers prior to the calculation. The correct figure, it was subsequently discovered, was almost 3,000 lower at 94,418.7. The financial effects were significant. The council were effectively caught in a double-edged trap. Their income was reduced because the 3,000 phantom taxpayers would clearly not produce any income. To compound matters, part of the community charge income was destined to be transferred to the larger Hertfordshire County Council and this figure was also calculated on the basis that St Albans' taxpaying population was greater than it actually was. When the accounts were finally completed, it was calculated that the loss to St Albans was over £1.3m. Legal proceedings were brought against ICL seeking recovery of this sum.

10.22 Three key issues were raised before the courts. First, were the defendants in breach of their contractual obligation? Second, were their exclusion and limitation clauses effective and, finally, were they responsible for all of the losses identified by the plaintiff? The High Court found in favour of the plaintiff on all counts and an appeal was made to the Court of Appeal

10.23 Although the defendants did not dispute the fact that the software involved in the calculation had been defective, they argued that their obligation was merely to supply a system which would be fully operative at the end of February 1990. Until then, as was recognised in the contract, the system would be in the course of development. Save where it could be shown that the supplier had acted negligently, it was argued, 'the plaintiffs had impliedly agreed to accept the software supplied, bugs and all'. This contention was rejected by the court, which held that:

> Parties who respectively agree to supply and acquire a system recognising that it is still in the course of development cannot be taken, merely by virtue of that recognition, to intend that the supplier shall be at liberty to supply software which cannot perform the function expected of it at the stage of development at which it is supplied.

10.24 In terms of deciding the particular case, the court could have terminated this section of the judgment with the finding that the defendants were in breach of an express contractual obligation to supply a system fit for the purpose of calculating the number of prospective taxpayers. This, indeed, has been the approach adopted in most software-related disputes, with judges declining to express a view on the status of software as a product or service on the ground that they were required only to interpret the provisions of a specific contract. The Court of Appeal was braver – or more foolhardy. In his judgment, Sir Iain Glidewell considered the question 'is software goods?' The Sale of Goods Act 1979 adopts a definition of goods as 'all personal chattels (property)'. On this basis, there is no doubt that a computer disc or tape would be regarded as goods. Equally, it is clear that a program per se, cannot be classed as goods. He continued:

> If a disc carrying the program is transferred, by way of sale or hire, and the program is in some way defective, so that it will not instruct or enable the computer to achieve the intended purpose, is this a defect in the disc? Put more precisely, would the seller or hirer of the disc be in breach of the terms of quality or fitness implied by s 14 of the Sale of Goods Act.

10.25 There was, he recognised, no English or indeed any common law precedent on this point. An analogy was drawn, however, with another form of informational product:

> Suppose I buy an instruction manual on the maintenance and repair of a particular make of car. The instructions are wrong in an important respect. Anybody who follows them is likely to cause serious damage to the engine of his car. In my view the instructions are an integral part of the manual. The manual including the instructions, whether in a book or a video cassette, would in my opinion be 'goods' within the meaning of the Sale of Goods Act and the defective instructions would result in breach of the implied terms.
>
> If this is correct, I can see no logical reason why it should not also be correct in relation to a computer disc onto which a program designed and intended to instruct or enable a computer to achieve particular functions has been encoded. If the disc is sold or hired by the compute manufacturer, but the program is defective, in my opinion there would prima facie be a breach of the terms as to quality and fitness for purpose implied by the Sale of Goods Act.

10.26 In an increasing number of situations, software may be downloaded over the Internet so that no disk or tangible object is transferred to the acquirer. In the present case, for example, the practice for installing software was that an ICL engineer would visit, load the software from disk and retain the disk. In such cases, there could be no transfer of goods. In such situations, it was indicated, in determining the extent of the parties' obligations:

> The answer must be sought in the common law. The terms implied by the Sale of Goods Act . . . were originally evolved by the Courts of Common Law and have since by analogy been implied by the courts into other types of contract . . . In the absence of any express term as to quality

or fitness for purpose, or of any term to the contrary, such a contract is subject to an implied term that the program will be reasonably fit for, ie reasonably capable of achieving the intended purpose.

10.27 The effect of this dicta would be to impose a high degree of liability upon software producers and suppliers. Faced with such extensive liability, the attractions for suppliers of exclusion or limitation clauses are readily apparent. Here, again, the court's findings offer scant consolation. In the UK, exclusion and limitation clauses are either prohibited or subjected to the application of a test of reasonableness in all cases involving consumers. For non-consumer contracts, exclusion clauses will be upheld except where the contract is classed as a standard form contract. In the St Albans' case, the council published a call for tenders, negotiated – albeit fairly incompetently – with a number of potential suppliers, engaged in further negotiations with ICL and concluded a contract one clause of which stated that it was subject to ICL's standard terms and conditions. This contract was held to be a standard form contract and, upholding the findings of the trial judge, the Court of Appeal held that it did not satisfy the statutory criterion of reasonableness. In part, the basis for this finding was the belief that:

> On whom is it better that a loss of this size should fall, a local authority or an international computer company. The latter is well able to insure (and in this case was insured) and pass on the premium cost to the customers. If the loss is to fall the other way it will ultimately be borne by the local population either by increased taxation or reduced services. I do not think it unreasonable that he who stands to make the profit (ICL) should carry the risk.

10.28 Although it is possible to conceive of contractual tactics through which producers might make exclusion or limitation clauses less vulnerable to attack by the courts, the case does show that the concept of a standard form contract will be defined expansively and that the courts will not hesitate to interfere in contractual relationships even when the customer is a large organisation.

10.29 English law's doctrine of judicial precedence provides that only those elements of a decision which are necessary to the result are binding in future cases. In the particular case, ICL were found to have accepted express contractual obligations to provide a computer system which would maintain a reliable database of the names of those liable to pay the community charge. Express terms will, subject to the operation of the unfair contract terms legislation, override any implied terms. The passages in Sir Iain Glidewell's judgment in which he indicates that contracts for the sale of software will be regulated by the terms of the Sale of Goods Act with its implied terms of merchantable (since 1994 replaced by the term 'satisfactory') quality and fitness for purpose were not essential to the judgment and will not be binding in future cases. The same will apply to his other suggestion that even where – perhaps because software is downloaded from a server rather than being supplied on a disk or tape – the law relating to sale or supply of goods cannot apply, equivalent terms relating to quality will be implied on a common law basis.

10.30 Assuming that Sir Iain Glidewell's views are followed in subsequent cases, it remains uncertain how qualitative requirements will apply in an informational context. The requirements that goods should be of satisfactory quality and fit for the purpose for which they are supplied do not require perfection. The analogy drawn with a motor instruction book may be appropriate. In the circumstances described, where following the instructions will result in serious damage, there could be little argument that the book is not fit for its purpose. The decision becomes much closer if the complaint is that the book describes an inefficient method for performing work. Another problematic case might be where an instruction is so obviously wrong that no reasonable person would follow it. Equivalents in a software context might be inefficient methods of saving word processed documents or defects which require a user to 'work around' them. Assuming Sir Iain Glidewell's dicta is followed, we can say that software must be of satisfactory quality and fit for the purpose for which it is supplied. Further cases will be required before we can attempt a plausible answer to the questions what these qualitative requirements mean in a software context.

Non-contractual liability

10.31 In an increasing number of cases software is being used in situations where failure may result in some form of personal injury or damage to physical property. In one case reported in the computer press, a factory worker was killed when he strayed into an area where a robot was operating and was pinned between the robot and a steel pole. The cause of the accident was that the robot had been programmed to complete its work without stopping. Notices had been displayed warning employees against entering the robot's area of operation but the question might arise, not least under the requirements of the health and safety at work legislation, whether this was sufficient to ensure a safe system of work.

10.32 In other situations, computer programs may perform similar functions in a more opaque fashion. An example might be where computers control the flight of an aeroplane. At a more down-to-earth level, many motor cars rely upon computers to control the operation of items such as anti-lock braking systems. In both examples, the potentially fatal consequences of a failure on the part of the computer system are all too obvious. In one recent air crash, it has been speculated that a dispute between the human and the automatic pilots may have been responsible for the accident and it is a frequent complaint that those responsible for designing (specifying) computer systems take inadequate account of human frailties and our propensity to push the wrong button or stray from normal procedures.

10.33 In a number of the scenarios described above there may well be contractual relationships which may found an action on the grounds described in the previous sections. In the absence of any contract, for example a pedestrian being injured following the failure of a car's braking system, attention will need to be paid to the liabilities arising on a non-contractual basis. Initially, consideration will be given to the product liability regime established under the Consumer Protection Act 1987. This will be followed by consideration of the liabilities arising under the general law of tort.

Product liability

10.34 Since the enactment of the Consumer Protection Act the producer of a defective product has been held strictly liable for any personal injury resulting from its operation. Liability is also imposed in respect of any damage to private (non-commercial) property. As discussed above, there is uncertainty whether a computer program might be regarded as a product for the purposes of either the Consumer Protection Act or the Sale of Goods Act. This is a matter of little significance in the situation where the program controls directly the operation of a physical object which in turn causes death or personal injury. What is of more significance is the determination when the product is to be considered defective and, given that liability under the Consumer Protection Act is strict rather than absolute, whether any defences might be available.

10.35 Under the terms of the Consumer Protection Act, a product is to be considered defective when it fails to provide the level of safety that 'persons generally are entitled to expect'. In most cases this must mean that a party will not come to any harm as a result of coming into contact with the product. Account must be taken of the manner in which the product is used. If a user cuts a finger whilst wielding a knife, it would generally be recognised that the fault lay with the user rather than the product. In similar fashion, although air passengers might reasonably expect that they will be carried safely to their destination, the producer of an aeroplane would not be held responsible for an accident caused by pilot error.

10.36 In real life it may seldom be the case that a single factor is responsible for an accident. The Consumer Protection Act is concerned only with the liability which may be incurred by the producer (or in some cases the supplier or importer of a product). In many instances, other forms of liability may also arise. In the example of the robot, it is likely that the worker would have been in a contractual relationship with the factory owner who might be liable for breach of the statutory duty to provide a safe system of work. In the aeroplane example, passengers would have had a contract of carriage (itself subject to the terms of international conventions) with the airline involved.

10.37 It is also the case that risks may be inherent to an activity. The Act provides that a product is not to be considered defective solely because 'the safety of a product which is supplied after that time is greater than the safety of the product in question'. The example might be put forward of two cars travelling side by side along a road, each travelling at 80 kph. Without warning, a hole appears in the road 30 metres ahead. Seconds later, one car has stopped short of the obstacle whilst the other has disappeared into the bowels of the earth. Discounting factors such as driver reaction, this might appear indicative that the second car is defective. Further investigations reveal that the first car was produced in 1994 and the second in 1954. If it is further discovered that the average stopping distance for a 1954-built car travelling at 80 kph was 35 metres, the conclusion may have to be revised. Products have to be assessed against their contemporaries rather than their successors, although a distinction must be drawn between the situation described above, where a certain level of performance represents the state of the art, and that where a failure might be in accordance with expectations. The concept of perfection is seldom a realistic goal and it may be anticipated, for example, that an aeroplane engine will fail once in 10,000 hours of flight. It might be further calculated that the risks of both engines failing on a twin-engined plane would be once for every 100 million hours of flight. In the event such a dual failure occurred and injury resulted, it would be no defence for the producer to establish that the failure rate was in line with the calculations and that the state of the technical art did not permit them to build a more robust product.

10.38 As computer applications become more sophisticated, the risk analysis referred to above may become a matter of increasing complexity. It has been suggested that the technology is such that robot surgeons could perform operations to narrower tolerances than any human could attain. This is perceived as having particular advantages in surgery for the removal of brain tumours. By being able to cut more precisely, a robot could remove a greater proportion of the tumour, thereby improving the patient's prognosis. Any operation can go wrong. In the event that a surgical procedure goes wrong, a patient seeking compensation has presently to establish negligence on the part of the surgeon. If the surgeon is a robot, it may be that the provisions of the Consumer Protection Act will impose strict liability. The robot will thus be judged more harshly than the human. Other ethical and legal considerations aside, such a possibility may well deter hospital authorities from utilising the new technology. It may be that the law and lawyers are better equipped to assess the nebulous nature of human conduct than the statistical precision which characterises computer applications.

The development risks defence and computer software

10.39 One of the most controversial aspects of the Consumer Protection Act concerns the provision of a development risks defence. In part the controversy arises from a difference in terminology between the European Directive and the implementing UK legislation. The former provides the producer with a defence where it is established that:

> . . . the state of scientific and technical knowledge at the time when he put the product into circulation was not such as to enable the existence of the defect to be established. (art 7(e))

10.40 The Consumer Protection Act provides that the defence is to apply where a producer is able to establish that:

> . . . the state of scientific and technical knowledge at the relevant time was not such that a producer of products of the same description as the product in question might have been expected to discover the defect if it had existed in his products while they were under his control . . . (s 4(1)(e))

Use of the phrase 'might have been expected' appears to render the UK provision more favourable to a producer than the original version. The European Commission at one stage threatened proceedings against the UK government, alleging that the change in terminology constituted a failure fully to implement the provisions of the directive. To date, no action has ensued.

10.41 The question how far the defence (in whatever version) may be relevant in a software context has been the subject of extensive debate. Given the recognition that the state of scientific and technical knowledge does not permit the exhaustive testing of software, some commentators have argued that the defence will be of considerable utility. The contrary view is that a distinction exists between risks whose occurrence was not foreseeable and defects whose existence was undiscoverable. The case of *Smedleys v Breed* [1974] AC 839 provides a helpful illustration of this rather opaque distinction. The appellants had been convicted of an offence under the terms of the Food and Drugs Act 1955. Section 2(1) of that Act prohibited the selling of food which was not of the nature, substance or quality demanded by the purchaser. At issue in the case was a can of peas which contained an unadvertised extra ingredient in the form of a caterpillar (deceased). Liability under the Act was strict but the appellants argued before the House of Lords that they were entitled to the benefit of a statutory defence applying where it could be demonstrated that the presence of the extraneous object 'was an unavoidable consequence of the process of collection or preparation' (s 3(3)).

10.42 In the year in question, 1971, the appellants had produced some 3,500,000 cans of peas and received only four complaints involving the presence of foreign bodies. Extensive checks involving both mechanical devices and human inspection were conducted by them but, presumably owing to a momentary lapse of attention by one of their checkers, the caterpillar escaped discovery. Statistically, the appellants' performance was impressive, with a complaint rate of little more than one in a million cans. It was accepted that nothing more could feasibly be done to improve the control system.

10.43 However, as was stated by Lord Hailsham:

> What has to be shown in order to constitute a defence under section 3(3) of the Act is not that *some* failures are unavoidable and that, owing to the excellence of the system, statistically the failures have been few. This is a matter for mitigation. What has to be shown under section 3(3) is that 'the presence of that matter' (ie, the particular piece of extraneous matter) in the particular parcel of food the subject of the charge was 'the unavoidable consequence of the process.' As I ventured to point out in the argument, over a long enough run any sort of process, however excellent, will statistically result in some failures, human or otherwise, and these are statistically predictable in the light of experience. But that will not necessarily be a defence under section 3(3).

10.44 In the case of software it is the vast number of possible interactions which defeats any attempt at exhaustive testing, rather than the intrinsic difficulty of the task of identifying a particular defect. A further argument may also be advanced against the application of the development risks defence. To an extent greater than with any other product, software is a creation of the human mind. Any defects are introduced by its creator(s). It would appear contrary to the aims of the legislation to allow a party to be allowed both to create a defect and subsequently claim that this was unforeseeable.

Liability in tort

10.45 There will be many situations when the Consumer Protection Act will be of little relevance. It may be that the damage caused falls outside the somewhat narrow boundaries established by the statute. It may also be that the damage resulted from the act or omission of someone other than a producer. The following section will consider the rights and remedies which may exist when parties are in a contractual relationship. Initially, however, consideration will be given to the application of principles of non-contractual liability.

10.46 In order to establish liability under the law of tort/delict, a pursuer is generally required to establish that the defender was negligent. The basis for this may lie either in an act or an omission. Two candidates may be identified for the role of defender. First, consideration will be given to the liability of a producer or supplier of software and, second, to the liability of a party using (or failing to use) software in the course of their work.

A reasonable software producer?

10.47 The concept of the 'reasonable man' is one of the most famous creations of the common law. A defender will be liable if he or she failed to display the level of skill and care reasonably to be expected of them. The value of the concept lies in part in its flexibility. Effectively, individuals will be judged by the standards of their peers. Such an approach can be of maximum effectiveness in the case of an established profession or activity. In the present context, the question 'what would a reasonable software producer (or supplier) do?' has to be prefaced by that of 'who is a software producer?' Although a number of professional bodies, such as the British Computer Society, operate in the area, these lack the status of the regulatory bodies associated with the older professions, such as law, accountancy and medicine.

Liability for use or non-use of software

10.48 A common issue in debate on the use of and failures in safety-critical software systems is the alleged over-dependence of human operators on the computer elements. An example recently cited concerned an experiment conducted on subjects who, without their knowledge, were given specially programmed calculators, then told to compute a few simple sums. The results indicated that most people trusted the machine even when a simple mental calculation would have given a different and correct answer. The experiment raises interesting questions concerning the possibility of such attitudes prevailing even in the highest levels of science. Is it wise to allow computer modelling to replace human observation? Of course, it is widely accepted that the use of new technology is essential if scientific advances are to be made. It has been said that the development of the Space Shuttle would not have been possible without Computer Aided Engineering. Bearing this in mind, what standards are to be expected of those who design or engineer systems which may be safety critical and how does the law apportion liability?

10.49 Of course, a decision to adopt an innovative technique, as yet not extensively used, in itself will rarely be classed as negligence, but special care must be given to its application. If the innovative technique fails, and it is established that no reasonable member of that profession would have employed such a method, then the use of such a technique may be judged to be negligent.

10.50 Although the use of new technology always carries a certain degree of risk, it may well be that, overall, the level of risk is reduced. The system may be safer, although not totally risk free, if designed by new technology and by the application of new methods. Bearing this in mind, might it ever be considered negligent *not* to use a computer-based technology? A number of earlier cases concerned with the shipping industry and its relationship with new technology provide useful parallels with the use of computers and computer-simulated models.

10.51 In the case of *TJ Hooper* 60 F 2d 737 (1932) two barges were lost at sea, partly because their tugs had not been equipped with working radio receivers. If radios had been installed, it would have been possible to listen to weather forecasts, thus enabling them to seek shelter from the storm. At that time the installation of radios on tugs was not common practice. In spite of this, the owners were held to be negligent on the basis that 'A whole calling may have unduly lagged in the adoption of new and available services'.

10.52 However, in the case of *United States Fire Insurance Co v United States* coastguards who failed to identify the location of a hazard to navigation were held not to be negligent, even though it was agreed that an available computerised method was superior in its accuracy to the manual technique actually used by the coastguards. At an earlier stage, a court had found the coastguard to be negligent by not marking the position of the wreckage correctly, but the Appeal Court held that the coastguard was not under an absolute duty to mark wreckage, but only to exercise due care in searching for it. The point was made that:

> . . . the district court must consider what actually transpired, not simply against what would have transpired [had the marker been in the correct location] but rather against what probably would have occurred had the Coast Guard exercised due care.

10.53 The fact that the desired result (in light of hindsight) did not occur does not imply that reasonable skill and care was not used, nor is it sufficient merely to establish that a new method which could have been adopted is superior to the old method. It must be established that, in the circumstances, the risk was identifiable, that the failure to adopt the new method or the new technology was in itself a breach of a duty of care, and that in the absence of such a breach, the loss or injury would not have occurred.

10.54 The likelihood of establishing negligence may depend on the extent to which the use of the new technology would have minimised the risk of loss or injury. Would use of the new technology have been very likely to have prevented such an error, or would it merely have reduced the risk but not eliminated it? Of course, such questions can only be resolved after the event on the basis of available expert evidence.

10.55 However, it should be said that manufacturer and designers must endeavour to keep themselves informed of new technical developments, as it is possible that a failure to adopt a new method could be considered negligent if an injury or loss occurred which would have been very unlikely to have occurred had the new technology been employed. Judging by *TJ Hooper* 60 F 2d 737 (1932) this may apply even if the use of such technology is not yet standard practice. Failure to respond to an identifiable risk may well be considered to be negligent.

Conclusions – and a brief Y2K legal post mortem

10.56 During the months leading up to the millennium, it was virtually impossible to open a newspaper or watch or listen to a news programme without finding mention of the disruption anticipated to accompany the date change on New Year's Eve. Estimates of the cost of the so-called Millennium Bug were high. In terms of prevention, the British Bankers Association estimated that UK banks spent some £1bn checking and repairing systems. British Telecom budgeted for expenditure of £300m. Worldwide, costs are estimated at some £400bn. Even more speculative were the costs in the event the problem is not eradicated. One estimate suggested that the effect of the bug would cause 8% of Western European companies to fail. The prospect of global recession was frequently raised in reports. In addition to financial cost, the widespread use of software in safety-critical applications conjured up the spectre of hospital patients dying because of failures of medical devices, trains, planes and automobiles crashing, massive power cuts, shortage of food and drink due to failures in retailers' distribution systems. Altogether, a recipe for a less than 'Happy New Year'.

10.57 Accompanying the publicity concerning the consequences of software's inability to cope with the change in date was considerable discussion regarding potential legal consequences. There seems little doubt that software (or software-controlled products) which ceased working on the fateful evening could not be considered of satisfactory quality or fit for its purpose. A problem may arise with the statutory periods of limitation which require that actions alleging breach of contract must be brought within six years of the date when the factual situation constituting the breach occurred. It is immaterial that the defect did not materialise until a later date. On this basis, the breach of contract would have occurred when the software was supplied. No action would therefore lie in respect of any software supplied before 1994.

10.58 In the event, it does not appear that the predicted consequences of the bug have materialised. There may remain legal issues. As indicated above, vast sums of money have been expended, especially in the UK and US in checking software to ensure conformity. Other countries, it is reported, have spent much less and suffered no more disruption. Could companies and other software users seek reimbursement of costs incurred? To a small degree, the answer may be positive. If checking indicated specific defects which were repaired, it would be reasonable to claim in respect of these on the basis that software with a latent defect is not of satisfactory quality. It would appear, however, that only a tiny porting of the expenditure incurred could have been attributed to actual defects. Most checking discovered no faults. An alternative line of legal argument might suggest that software companies and consultants were negligent in advising users to incur the expenses they did in preparing for the millennium. Given, at least at the time, that the preponderance of opinion seemed to suggest that a significant problem existed, it would be difficult to sustain the argument that no reasonable software company would have recommended the degree of expenditure.

10.59 If software suppliers and developers might escape lightly from the millennium issue, the last decade has seen an increasing acceptance by the courts that software is to be regarded as a product and subject to the stringent requirements of the Sale of Goods Act that it be of satisfactory quality and fit for its purpose. There has also been increasing judicial willingness to intervene in the contractual relationship to control the enforceability of exclusion clauses. Whilst this may be seen as bad news for the software industry, it also reflects the increasing economic and practical importance of software. It has been estimated that the value of the microprocessors installed in a modern car exceeds that of the metal used in the vehicle's construction. There can be little justification for imposing a lower requirement as to quality on silicon than on metal.

Chapter 11

Defamation

Introduction

11.0 The notion of freedom of expression is widely recognised as a fundamental human right, the European Convention on Human Rights providing for example, that:

> 1. Everyone has the right to freedom of expression. This right shall include freedom to hold opinions and to receive and impart information and ideas without interference by public authority and regardless of frontiers.

11.1 As with other rights, however, the right cannot be absolute. The convention goes on to provide that:

> 2. The exercise of these freedoms, since it carries with it duties and responsibilities, may be subject to such formalities, conditions, restrictions or penalties as are prescribed by law and are necessary in a democratic society, in the interests of national security, territorial integrity or public safety, for the prevention of disorder or crime, for the protection of health or morals, for the protection of the reputation or rights of others, for preventing the disclosure of information received in confidence, or for maintaining the authority and impartiality of the judiciary.

11.2 Prohibitions against the publication of pornographic or obscene materials constitute an example of a case where restrictions and penalties might be justified on the ground of the protection of morals. The law relating to defamation constitutes a further example relating to the 'protection of the rights or reputations of others'. As with national rules relating to obscenity, considerable variations exist between states. In the US, for example, comments made concerning public figures will attract liability only if it can be shown that they were motivated by malice. This is a very difficult hurdle for any litigant to overcome. Although UK law recognises that certain forms of communication should benefit from a similar form of protection, as a general rule no distinction is drawn between public figures and

212

private individuals. A consequence is that statements which might be made with impunity in the US could attract legal sanctions if published in the UK. Differences exist also between the UK and many continental legal systems. In the UK, defamation is almost entirely a matter for the civil courts, whereas in countries such as Germany it is primarily a criminal matter. Again, countries such as France offer protection under the law of privacy in the event information about an individual's private life is brought into the public domain.

11.3 National variations in the treatment of published comments has created problems over the years. A recent example concerns the decision of the US publishers of a biography of the Royal Family not to permit the book to be sold within the UK. The decision was based on fear that certain comments in the book might expose them to liability for defamation. The efforts to restrict publication even extended to on-line bookshops such as Amazon.com refusing to supply the book to UK addresses.

The nature of defamation

11.4 The term 'defamation' tends to be used as a generic descriptor for actions in which it is alleged that the making of untrue and unwarranted comments about an individual have tended to lower that person's standing in the eyes of right thinking members of society. The question what sorts of comments would produce this effect is not easy to answer and will vary with changing social attitudes. Until the start of the Second World War, it was not considered defamatory to accuse someone of being anti-semetic. The term 'computer hacker' was originally used to describe someone who was particularly skilled in operating computers and finding solutions to problems. In this context, the phrase could not be considered defamatory. Today, of course, the generally accepted meaning has changed and the accusation that someone is a computer hacker might have legal consequences.

11.5 In English law a distinction exists between libel and slander. The law of libel applies to comments which are recorded in some permanent form – in print or on tape – whilst slander is reserved for comments which are more transient in nature. In general, the law of libel operates on a stricter basis than that of slander, based in part on the assessment that statements which are recorded are likely to be more damaging to the subject than those which are not. Developments in recording and broadcasting technology have served to blur both the distinction between libel and slander and the rationale for distinct treatment. A statement on a live television broadcast might be heard by tens of millions of viewers and be far more damaging to the reputation of the subject than would be the case with a letter published in a local newspaper.

11.6   In the case of broadcasting, the Defamation Act 1952 provided that the law of libel was to apply in respect of any statements made. In the case of e-mail and the contents of the Internet and WWW, it seems beyond question that there is a sufficient degree of recording to ensure that the law of libel will apply. Some doubt, perhaps, remains concerning the status of services such as chat rooms, where the atmosphere at least is closer to a conversational forum and where no permanent record is maintained. In cases of slander a defence is available, commonly referred to as 'vulgar abuse'. The essence of the defence is that words, albeit defamatory in content, were neither intended as such nor would be so regarded by anyone listening to the exchange. Such a defence might seem appropriate in relation to many postings to Internet newsgroups, where the concept of the 'flame war' is well established. Anyone perusing computer newsgroups will be aware that forthright expression is often the order of the day and that 'flame wars', in which discussion is reduced to a level of personal abuse, are not uncommon. One newsgroup, alt.flame, even specialises on this topic. Although the existence of a culture encouraging robust and blunt debate cannot affect the determination whether a message is defamatory, there may be an element of consent on the part of those participating in such *fora*. With newsgroups, although there would seem no doubt that postings are written and the range of dissemination is comparable (perhaps even wider) than that associated with the written word, the attitudes and practices coupled with the speed of communication are perhaps more akin to the spoken word.

Who can be defamed?

11.7   Given the basis of the action for defamation, it is apparent that it is effectively an individual action. A company may, however, bring an action for defamation if it can be shown that comments are likely to have the effect of damaging its trading reputation. A recent example of such an action can be seen in the case of *McDonald's Corp v Steel* [1995] 3 All ER 615, in which the hamburger giant brought libel proceedings against two individuals who had made accusations concerning McDonald's trading practices. Other forms of organisation such as clubs, local authorities and trade unions cannot bring actions for defamation. An assertion, for example, that a particular golf club was 'a haven for cheats and liars' will not give rise to liability. This is, however, subject to the important qualification that an individual member of the club could sue successfully if it could be shown that any reasonable person to whom the comments might be communicated would associate them with that person. This might be the case if a particular member had been the subject of publicity concerning allegations of cheating.

Communication

11.8 In order to be actionable, it is necessary that a statement be communicated to at least one person other than the subject. The range of dissemination need not be wide. A letter or e-mail to a third party will suffice, as would posting a comment on a public noticeboard. Indeed, in terms of impact on an individual, a letter to an employer making false and defamatory comments might have far more serious consequences than a communication accessible to a wider audience.

11.9 The Internet provides a superbly effective communications medium. E-mail permits cheap and swift communications of messages between individuals, whilst newsgroups allow anyone to express views on almost any topic under the sun and the WWW permits individuals to establish themselves as electronic publishers. Given the volume and variety of traffic carried by the Internet, it would be a source of considerable surprise were its contents to be free of defamatory comments. The essence of defamation is that a statement is published which is both inaccurate and likely to have the effect of lowering the standing of its subject in the eyes of right thinking members of society.

Who is liable for defamatory comments?

Liability of the poster

11.10 There is no doubt that a person making a defamatory comment will incur liability. It has, for example, been reported that a student has been warned by the office of a government minister that postings to a politics newsgroup were considered to be defamatory, although no legal proceedings followed. In addition to cases concerning the liability of service operators, which will be discussed below, in the US a journalist has been reportedly faced a legal bill in excess of $25,000 after settling a libel suit resulting from a posting which he made on the Internet.

11.11 Although it may be stated that the poster of a defamatory message runs the risk of legal action, the task of identifying the party responsible may not be an easy one. Even if a message appears to originate from a particular individual, it may be necessary to establish that it is genuine. In the US case of *Stratton Oakmont v Prodigy* (1995) 195 NY Misc LEXIS 229 discussed below, a message appeared to have been sent from a particular user's account. The user, however, denied that the message had been sent by him or from his equipment. In the particular case, the issue was not of great significance, as the action proceeded against the service provider who, it appears, had always been the major target of the litigation. In other cases, it may be necessary for a plaintiff to establish that a message was sent by the party whose identifiers appear. It appears that it is possible for a user's identity to be impersonated. Instances have been reported of forged e-mail messages purporting to have originated from the White House. Another technical facility which may complicate any legal proceedings is the use of anonymous remailing services. These services, which may be based anywhere in the world, accept messages from users, strip out the details of the original poster and forward them to the addressee with no indication of the identity of the original poster. Such a technique makes it impossible to identify the author without the co-operation of the operator of the remailing service. Such co-operation may not readily be forthcoming and considerable controversy has surrounded attempts by the Church of Scientology to discover the identity of a user who posted documents relating to the organisation, allegedly in breach of copyright. On this occasion, the remailing service involved was based in Finland.

11.12 In the example given above of a private person making comments in a letter (or e-mail) to a third party, that will be the extent of liability. In other situations, however, other parties may contribute to the dissemination of the comment or may incur liability for the actions of the individual's concerned. A typical example of the latter situations might see an employer being held vicariously liable for comments made by employees in the course of their employment. In other cases, the third party might provide facilities for the distribution of the comment. Examples here might include a newspaper publishing a letter to the editor or a publisher a book with defamatory sections. The chain of liability may stretch even further to encompass a bookshop or newsagent stocking the contested publication. One of the major attractions for a plaintiff in bringing proceedings against a publisher or broadcaster rather than the individual responsible for a comment is the likelihood that the organisation will be more likely to have the resources to satisfy an award for damages than a possibly impoverished individual.

Employer's liability

11.13 As more and more companies make use of e-mail as a method of communication between staff, so there will be increasing exposure to action on the basis of vicarious liability in respect of the use or misuse made of the communications network. In 1997 the Norwich Union insurance company reached a settlement in a libel action brought by a health insurance company, Western Provident Association. Under the terms of the agreement, Norwich Union agreed to pay £450,000 in damages and costs in respect of libellous messages concerning the association's financial stability which had been contained in e-mail messages exchanged between members of Norwich Union's staff.

11.14 The fact that a settlement was reached prior to trial means that the case is of no value as a legal precedent. The lesson for those engaging in e-mail discussions is obvious: that although communications may be approached as a form of conversation, everything is recorded almost without limit of time and can be retrieved at a later date. A similar example of this phenomenon can be seen in the discovery of internal Microsoft e-mails during the legal investigations into their commercial practices. One significant factor limiting the extent of liability for defamatory communications made by employees may be that the vicarious liability applies only in respect of acts committed in the course of employment. In the Norwich Union case, the communications were clearly work-related but it is unlikely that an employer would be held liable in the event, for example, that employees used e-mail facilities to exchange defamatory comments on subjects unconnected with work. To minimise the risks of liability, it would be advisable for employers to indicate clearly in contracts of employment or staff handbooks what uses may or may not be made of electronic communications.

11.15 Faced with concern at their potential liabilities for misuse of electronic communications, it is commonplace for employers to monitor use of the facilities. In the US a number of actions have been reported of corporations being sued 'for millions of dollars' by employees alleging that fellow workers have been engaging in some form of electronic harassment involving the posting of abusive or offensive messages. It has been suggested that:

> Lawyers are bracing themselves for a wave of litigation as people catch on to the fact that they can redress grievances – and possibly become very rich – by producing e-mail evidence of prejudice based on gender, sexual preference, race, nationality or age. Proving cases that depend on spoken jests and casual remarks has always presented its difficulties in court. The beauty of e-mail is that all plaintiffs have to do is retrieve it from their

company's computer systems and then print it out. Plenty of material is certain to be available in a country where 80 per cent of organisation use e-mail, and where it is expected that by the year 2000 more than one billion messages will be sent a week.

11.16 Faced with such exposure, employers may well be tempted to use packages to monitor e-mail communications within the workplace. One such package, it is reported:

> . . . may be programmed to suit the offensiveness threshold of each particular firm. Thus it might be that a message between two secretaries that contained the words 'sex' or 'black' – or something profane – would immediately appear on their boss's computer screen for inspection.

11.17 Under present UK law it would appear that use of such a system would not be unlawful. Although the provisions of the Interception of Communications Act 1985 will govern the interception of e-mail messages passing through a public telecommunications network, this statute does not apply to private networks. In the case of *Halford v UK* (1997) 24 EHRR 523, however, the European Court of Human Rights held that the convention's requirements relating to protection of privacy had been breached where telephone calls made from work premises by a senior police officer had been 'bugged' on the authority of her Chief Constable. Argument on behalf of the UK to the effect that the telephones in question belonged to the employer, in this case the government, did not sway the court. It would appear that any monitoring of e-mail might be challenged on this basis, although it is not clear whether the giving of notice to employees that phone calls or e-mail messages might be monitored would remove their 'reasonable expectation' of privacy in their communications.

Liability of service providers

11.18 With the exception of the issue whether a defence should be available for those who post defamatory messages in the heat of a flame war, there can be little dispute that the author of such a posting should face the legal consequences. More controversial is the question how far the operators of an on-line service should incur liabilities akin to those of traditional publishers in respect of messages appearing on their systems. Two decisions from the US have received widespread publicity, *Cubby v CompuServe* 776 F Supp 135 (1991) and *Stratton Oakmont v Prodigy* (1995) 195 NY Misc LEXIS 229.

11.19 In the first case, the service provider was sued in respect of an item appearing in its appropriately named forum 'Rumorville USA'.

Rumorville was originally published in printed format by a third party and provided on CompuServe by another party, CCI, which had contracted to 'manage, review, edit, delete and otherwise control the contents' of this and other forums 'in accordance with editorial and technical standards and conventions of style as established by CompuServe'. Rumorville was loaded directly onto CompuServe, whose operators had no opportunity to review its contents. The plaintiffs, who intended to establish a service which would compete with Rumorville, alleged that statements regarding its business and activities appearing on Rumorville were defamatory.

11.20 Proceedings were initiated on a variety of grounds and against a variety of defendants. CompuServe sought summary judgment on all the claims brought against it claiming that it acted as a distributor rather than as a publisher of the statements. In the absence of evidence that CompuServe knew of the statements there was, it was argued, no basis in law for the action. This argument was accepted in the District Court with Judge Leisure holding that the constitutional guarantee of freedom of speech had long dictated that distributors should not, in the absence of actual knowledge, be held liable for the contents of materials supplied by them. Technology, it was stated:

> . . . is rapidly transforming the information industry. A computerized database is the functional equivalent of a more traditional news vendor, and the inconsistent application of a lower standard of liability to an electronic news distributor such as CompuServe than that which is applied to a public library, book store or newsstand would impose an undue burden on the free flow of information.

11.21 Thoughts that the decision in *Cubby v CompuServe* would confer immunity on the operators of on-line services in the event contents supplied by third parties may have to be revised following the decision of the Supreme Court of New York in *Stratton Oakmont v Prodigy Services Co*. The defendant, Prodigy, operates one of the world's largest commercial on-line information services. Amongst its features was a discussion forum or bulletin board, 'Money Talk', where subscribers could post and read comments on financial topics. Certain statements appearing in the forum, it was alleged, were defamatory both of the plaintiff company and its president.

11.22 Prodigy began operations in 1990. At that time, its service was promoted as a 'family oriented computer network'. Unlike many of its competitors, it exercised editorial control over messages posted on its bulletin boards. The court was referred to a newspaper article written by Prodigy's Director of Market Programs and Communications, in which it was stated that the company:

. . . make no apology for pursuing a value system that reflects the culture of the millions of American families we aspire to serve. Certainly, no responsible newspaper does less when it chooses the type of advertising it publishes, the letters it prints, the degree of nudity and unsupported gossip its editors tolerate.

11.23 Prodigy's attempt to exercise control over the contents of postings operated at a number of levels. Guidelines were issued to users indicating that notes which were insulting or which 'harass other members or are deemed to be in bad taste or grossly repugnant to community standards or are deemed harmful to maintaining a harmonious on-line community, will be removed'. All messages submitted to bulletin boards were screened by a software program which removed automatically language regarded as offensive. The operation of this program was not entirely unproblematic. Deletion of the word 'bitch' caused some difficulty and annoyance to those seeking to post messages to a forum devoted to those with an interest in dogs.

11.24 Additionally, Prodigy entered into contracts with individuals who acted as 'board leaders'. The board leaders were not employees of Prodigy, but were engaged to promote on-line discussion (there was a contractual obligation to post a minimum of 120 messages a month to the relevant board) and to enforce Prodigy's guidelines. Board leaders were provided with a tool referred to as an 'emergency delete function' to allow the removal of messages considered unsuitable.

11.25 The various levels of intervention operated by Prodigy, it was argued by the plaintiff, meant that it should be regarded as publisher rather than as mere distributor of the information contained in its system. Although Prodigy claimed that the increase in traffic volume on its system (some 60,000 messages a day were posted on its various bulletin boards at the time in question) had forced it to modify its intention to monitor the contents of bulletin boards, this contention was accepted by the court. The decision in *Cubby v CompuServe* was approved but distinguished on two factual grounds. First, Prodigy held itself out to the public and its members as controlling the content of its computer bulletin boards. Second, Prodigy implemented this control.

11.26 Prodigy had made a conscious choice to gain the benefits of editorial control. It is one of the major complaints of users of on-line services – especially Internet newsgroups – that the ratio of 'signal to noise' is frequently low. Especially when a user is incurring charges for time spent on-line, the attraction of a filter system is apparent. Having claimed to provide facilities for monitoring its contents, Prodigy was obliged to accept the legal consequences of any failure so to do.

11.27 Although it may be argued that Prodigy had brought misfortune upon itself, the decision can be criticised on a number of grounds. The use of automatic filters to delete obscene or offensive terms would seem to have little connection with the excision of defamatory material. The defamatory comments in the present case made reference to 'major criminal fraud' and 'soon to be proven criminal'. None of these words could be considered objectionable per se. Even the accusation that the plaintiffs were a 'cult of brokers who either lie for a living or get fired' does not contain a single word which could be considered obscene. The role of the board leaders may be considered more pivotal. Even here, it may be that the analogy with the editorial role found in newspapers and other forms of publication is somewhat stretched. In particular, few newspapers or magazines rely on contributions from their readers to such an extent as a bulletin board service. Whilst it might be reasonable to expect board leaders to identify and remove offensive items (and it may be that at least some of the comments at issue in this case should have been viewed in that light), it would appear excessive to require them also to be familiar with all the nuances of the law of defamation. This point may also be made in relation to-so called 'moderated newsgroups' appearing on the Internet. Although the moderator's function is to determine what postings will be accepted for publication, the goal in many instances is primarily to prevent messages unrelated to the newsgroup's topic from swamping the system rather than to identify defamatory messages. In any event, it would appear that the *Prodigy* decision is founded in a particular set of facts which wise service operators will ensure are not repeated. Judge Ain stated specifically that:

> Let it be clear that this Court is in full agreement with Cubby . . . Computer bulletin boards should generally be regarded in the same context as bookstores, libraries and network affiliates . . . It is Prodigy's own policies, technology and staffing decisions which have altered the scenario and mandated the finding that it is a publisher.

11.28 Most matters concerned with the *Prodigy* decision appear to be shrouded in a measure of confusion. It was never established how the offending message came to appear on the system or who was responsible for it. Again, it was unclear whether Prodigy had ever eschewed the monitoring policy described above. Although some commentators have seen the decision as posing a threat to the Internet's culture of free speech, it should be recognised that on-line services such as CompuServe and Prodigy have a user base greater than that of many newspapers or even television or radio stations. The consequences of a defamatory statement may be profound, even more so when the editorial input claimed for the service may add an air of authority to statements, and it may be considered unreasonable that a commercial organisation which seeks to profit from the provision of on-line services should be able to abdicate responsibility for a failure to conform to its self-defined standards.

UK authority

11.29 The first UK case to reach the stage of High Court proceedings is that of *Godfrey v Demon*. Although settled prior to trial, preliminary hearings have raised a number of interesting and potentially significant issues concerned with the extent of an Internet service provider's liability for defamatory postings carried on its services.

11.30 The plaintiff, Laurence Godfrey, is a UK-based lecturer in computer science, mathematics and physics. He appears to be a keen poster to Usenet, with reference being made in the court proceedings to a posting record of more than 3,000 messages. A number of Godfrey's postings, it was suggested by the defendant, were intended to provoke a violent response from other posters:

> The words complained of were posted to a newsgroup. Newsgroup users have come to abide by an informal code of conduct known as 'netiquette', which is intended to introduce an element of restraint and moderation with regard to the content of postings. Those who persist in breaching netiquette are almost invariably exposed to irate (and sometimes offensive or aggressive) postings from aggrieved users: this practice is known as 'flaming'. As a regular newsgroup user, it is to be inferred that the Plaintiff would at all material times have known of the foregoing facts and matters.

11.31 Rather than perpetuating a flame war, Mr Godfrey had, on at least seven occasions, instituted proceedings against both posters and ISPs, alleging that comments defamed him. The defence alleged that:

> . . . the Plaintiff has cynically pursued the tactic of posting deliberately provocative, offensive, obnoxious and frequently puerile comments about other countries, their citizens and cultures; and has done so with a view to provoking others to trade insults which he can then claim are defamatory and seek to use as the basis for bringing vexatious libel actions against them and against access or service providers such as the Defendant.

11.32 The conduct at issue in the *Demon* case was slightly different. A message purporting to come from Godfrey had appeared in the newsgroup 'soc.cuture.thai'. The message was a forgery and in its tone and content was described by the judge as being 'squalid, obscene and defamatory of the plaintiff'. The basis for the defamation would lie in the argument that the plaintiff's standing in the eyes of right-thinking members of society would be damaged if it was thought that he held the views attributed to him in the e-mail. The defendant, Demon is a well-known ISP. Messages in 'soc.culture.thai' could be accessed by its subscribers, the postings being held on Demon's servers for around 14 days.

11.33 The posting at issue, which originated in the US, appeared in the newsgroup on 13 January 1997. On 17 January, Godfrey faxed the defendant's managing director with the demand that the posting be removed from Demon's servers. It was accepted by both sides that this could have been done. Although Demon acknowledged that the fax had been received, it appeared that it never reached its managing director's desk and the message remained on its site until routinely deleted after a fortnight. The plaintiff subsequently brought proceedings seeking damages in respect of the damage to his reputation caused by the defendant's actions. The defendant denied liability on two grounds. First, it was argued, its conduct was covered by a defence established under the Defamation Act 1996. Second, it was denied that there had been any publication of the comment by it.

The Defamation Act 1996

11.34 The Defamation Act was enacted in 1996 in an attempt to update the law relating to defamation. It followed a study conducted by the Law Commission which recommended the introduction of a new defence of 'innocent dissemination'. In terms of the statutory defence, s 1 of the Act provides a defence often referred to as 'innocent dissemination'. This provides that:

　　(1) In defamation proceedings a person has a defence if he shows that—

　　(a)　he was not the author, editor or publisher of the statement complained of,
　　(b)　he took reasonable care in relation to its publication, and
　　(c)　he did not know, and had no reason to believe, that what he did caused or contributed to the publication of a defamatory statement.

11.35 The section goes on to provide that, for the purposes of s 1, a person will not be classed as an author, editor or publisher if the involvement with the work is 'only' in specified capacities. Included in this list is that the party acted:

(2) (c) in processing, making copies of, distributing or selling any electronic medium in or on which the statement is recorded, or in operating or providing any equipment, system or service by means of which the statement is retrieved, copied, distributed or made available in electronic form.

(e) as the operator or provider of access to a communications system by means of which the statement is transmitted or made available, by a person over whom he had no effective control.

11.36 It was held by the court that Demon fell within the scope of this latter definition. The onus of proof under s 1 lies with the defendant, and it was held that the requirements of s 1 were cumulative rather than alternative. The provisions of para (a) having been satisfied, attention required to be given to paras (b) and (c), quoted above. In respect of these, the Act provided further that: 'in determining whether a person took reasonable care or had had reason to believe that his actions would cause or contribute to the publication of a defamatory statement, account should be taken of:

(a) the nature of his responsibility for the contents of the statement or the decision to publish it;
(b) the nature and circumstances of its publication; and
(c) the previous conduct or character of the author, editor or publisher.

11.37 Given the circumstances of the case, it is perhaps not surprising that the court held that the defence could not be sustained. The defamation action related only to the period after 17 January when the plaintiff's fax arrived and, as the defendant had taken no action to examine the matter, it was not in a position to demonstrate that reasonable care had been taken.

11.38 The more interesting and controversial question might relate to what could have been expected of the defendants if their administrative procedures had been more effective. It is clear from the calendar of events described above that the case concerned a period of around ten days. There would have been limited opportunity for the defendant to undertake in-depth enquiries. As noted above, the offending message entered the Internet via a US-based ISP. Without the active co-operation of this party, there may well have been little that the defendant could do to verify the true identity of the sender. Even with co-operation, with the proliferation of ISPs offering free access to the Internet with a minimum of registration procedures, which could themselves be falsified with minimal effort, it would appear that an ISP in receipt of a complaint regarding a posting would have little choice other than between doing nothing and removing the posting from its servers. The first action obviously carries the risk of an action for defamation, but the automatic removal of messages upon receipt of a complaint is something which carries its own problems and dangers.

Publication

11.39 The defence of innocent dissemination was introduced in the 1996 Act in the attempt to update the law to take account of changes in technology. In a consultation document issued prior to the introduction of the Defamation Bill, it was stated that:

> The new defence to replace and modernise innocent dissemination takes account of the rapid advances which have been made in the technology of communications. Most recently the extraordinary expansion of computer network systems has focused attention on the possibility of defamatory material appearing or being available at an almost infinite number of widely dispersed outlets. We invite comments as to whether it would be considered helpful if there were legislation to clarify any doubts as to when and where publication has taken place.

11.40 It was recognised, however, that the defence was a first attempt to deal with the problem and might require to be amended in the light of experience. The definition of 'publisher' discussed above in the context of the innocent dissemination defence applies only to that defence. The question when and by whom a statement is published requires also to be considered in relation to the general law of defamation. Reference was made to a number of authorities, the most relevant being the case of *Byrne v Deane* [1937] 1 KB 818, where the directors of a golf club were held liable as publishers in respect of a defamatory message placed by a third party on a notice board in the club. Here the court held that:

> It is said that as a general proposition where the act of the person alleged to have published a libel has not been any positive act, but has merely been the refraining from doing some act, he cannot be guilty of publication. I am quite unable to accept any such general proposition. It may very well be that in some circumstances a person, by refraining from removing or obliterating the defamatory matter, is not committing any publication at all. In other circumstances he may be doing so. The test it appears to me is this: having regard to all the facts of the case is the proper inference that by not removing the defamatory matter the defendant really made himself responsible for its continued presence in the place where it had been put?

In the present case the conclusion was reached that:

> In my judgment the Defendants, whenever they transmit and whenever there is transmitted from the storage of their news server a defamatory posting, publish that posting to any subscriber to their ISP who accesses the newsgroup containing that posting. Thus everytime one of the Defendants' customers accesses 'soc culture.thai' and sees that posting defamatory of the Plaintiff there is a publication to that customer.
>
> I do not accept [the] argument that the Defendants were merely owners of an electronic device through which postings were transmitted. The Defendants chose to store 'soc.culture.thai' postings within their computer. Such postings could be accessed on that newsgroup. The Defendants could obliterate and indeed did so about a fortnight after receipt.

11.41 It has subsequently been reported that a second defamation action has been brought by the same plaintiff against Demon, on this occasion complaining of posting by a person who it is alleged 'was a repeat offender, well known to Demon because of previous complaints from other users'. Although the full details of the complaint have not been published, this adds another element to the problem faced by ISPs. If the claim were to be successful, it would almost be a requirement that an ISP should maintain a 'black-list' of persons whose postings had given rise to complaints in the past.

Offer of amends

11.42 If it may be that little can be done to prevent defamatory messages appearing on an on-line service, the Defamation Act seeks to enhance the possibility that a defendant may make an 'offer of amends' in response to an allegation of defamation. This will constitute a damage-limitation measure rather than any form of defence and involves the making of an offer to publish a suitable correction of the offending statement and apology to the party offended, coupled with an attempt to inform persons who have received copies of the statement of its allegedly defamatory nature and an offer of compensation. If the party defamed does not accept the offer, or contests the amount of compensation offered, this may be determined by the court. In assessing the amount of compensation, account is to be taken of the effectiveness of the notice of correction and apology.

The future of defamation in cyberspace

11.43 The High Court decision in *Godfrey v Demon* undoubtedly imposes a high degree of liability on Internet service providers. The liability is considerably higher than that imposed in the US. Some measure of relief may come through proposals contained in the draft European Directive on Electronic Commerce. Article 12 of that measure provides that:

> 1. Where an Information Society service is provided that consists of the transmission in a communication network of information provided by the recipient of the service, or the provision of access to a communication network, Member States shall provide in their legislation that the provider of such a service shall not be liable, otherwise than under a prohibitory injunction, for the information transmitted, on condition that the provider:
> (a) does not initiate the transmission;
> (b) does not select the receiver of the transmission; and
> (c) does not select or modify the information contained in the transmission.

> 2. The acts of transmission and of provision of access referred to in paragraph 1 include the automatic, intermediate and transient storage of the information transmitted in so far as this takes place for the sole purpose of carrying out the transmission in the communication network, and provided that the information is not stored for any period longer than is reasonably necessary for the transmission.

11.44 Article 15 provides further that:

> Member States shall not impose a general obligation on providers, when providing the services covered by Articles 12 to 14, to monitor the information which they transmit or store, nor a general obligation actively to seek facts or circumstances indicating illegal activity.

> 2. Paragraph 1 shall not affect any targeted, temporary surveillance activities required by national judicial authorities in accordance with national legislation to safeguard national security, defence, public security and for the prevention, investigation, detection and prosecution of criminal offences.

11.45 This provision relates more directly to the situation where material such as child pornography is stored or accessed by customers of an Internet service srovider. In general, whilst providers will not be entitled to turn a blind eye to activities being conducted over their facilities, they will not be under any obligation actively to monitor and control these.

Defamation in cyberspace

11.46 Finally, reference should be made to the jurisdictional issues involved. As has been stated previously, the operations of the Internet pay little regard to national boundaries. A comment may be posted by a user in any country and read in every other country where the Internet operates. In an Australian defamation action, *Rindos v*

Hardwick (31 March 1994, unreported) a posting by to a mailing list by a US-based academic was defamatory of an Australian-based colleague and resulted in the Australian courts awarding damages of $40,000.

11.47 The English law of defamation is generally regarded as being considerably stricter than that applying in most other jurisdictions. Assuming the necessary connection with the jurisdiction can be established by a plaintiff, the general rule applied by the courts to jurisdictional issues was described by Lord Goff in the case of *Spiliada Maritime Corpn v Consulex Ltd* [1987] AC 460 in the following terms:

> The basic principle is that a stay will only be granted on the ground of forum non conveniens where the court is satisfied that there is some other available forum, having competent jurisdiction, which is the appropriate forum for the trial of the action, ie in which the case may be tried more suitably for the interests of all the parties and the ends of justice.

11.48 Although there will often be considerable practical difficulties in pursuing and enforcing an action against a foreign-based party, the suggestion has been made by one lawyer that:

> Plaintiffs will be able to choose countries with repressive libel laws, like Britain. Anyone with an international reputation will sue here, because, relatively speaking, it's like falling off a log.

11.49 As with so many aspects of the topic, we are once again brought to the realisation that national boundaries may be of little effect in the era of the global information infrastructure. As always, however, there may be a significant gap between an individual considering himself or herself to be the victim of defamation finding a plaintiff-friendly jurisdiction and securing enforcement of any award made in other jurisdictions. US courts have in the past refused to enforce an award of damages made against a US citizen by an English court in respect of a defamatory comment on the ground that the liability for defamation is unduly extensive.

Chapter 12

The commercialisation of cyberspace

Introduction

12.0 Until 1991 the Internet remained the exclusive province of the academic/military/governmental sectors. The prime justification for this approach was that the infrastructure used for data transmission was funded by the public sector. Aspects of the technology have been used in the private sector for a number of years. The computerised legal information retrieval service, Lexis, for example, began operations in 1973. Services such as CompuServe and America Online also began operations in the 1980s, using proprietary communications software and operating over the normal telephone network. Effectively, this would mean that a CompuServe member could send e-mail to another member but not to a subscriber to another service.

12.1 In 1991 the decision was taken in the US to allow commercial users to access the Internet. Almost without exception, organisations such as CompuServe and America Online have migrated to the Internet through the adoption of the TCP/IP standards and have been joined by many thousands of other organisations offering individual subscribers the possibility of Internet access. At the time of writing there are around 150 Internet service providers operating in the UK. The range of services provided by these organisations varies significantly. Some provide significant value-added services. These might include technical help desks and access to proprietary information services as well as access to the Internet. Users pay fees generally based upon the level of usage. More recently, a number of operators have come into the market offering a service which is effectively limited to Internet access. These services are offered on a free basis except for the telephone charges incurred by the user whilst on-line. A number of Internet service providers are now offering free connections (by means of an 0800 number) to the Internet at evenings and weekends. At present it is estimated that around 18% of local telephone calls are made for the purpose of establishing connection with the Internet, a figure which is likely to rise significantly. It is perhaps not surprising that domestic Internet usage is considerably higher in the US, where local telephone calls are generally free of charge.

Why is the internet valuable for commercial users?

12.2 Today, the .com domain which web hosts sites of commercial relevance is the largest single Internet domain, with some 12 million hosts. 84% of sites registered in 1998 were in the .com domain. In the UK domain, however, the academic domain .ac.uk remains the largest sector with slightly over 700,000 hosts, as opposed to 585,000 in .co.uk.

12.3 A number of elements can be identified which make the Internet valuable for the commercial sector. As many users of e-mail will be aware, the Internet provides marketeers with a cheap promotional device, albeit referred to under the derogatory epithet of 'spamming'. Also from the marketing perspective, the owner of a web site can, through the judicious use of 'cookies', obtain a considerable amount of information about those visiting the site. More directly, of course, the Internet can be used for the conclusion of contracts for the sale and supply of goods and services.

12.4 One of the most notable aspects of electronic commerce has been the facility it offers for relatively small and newly established companies to establish what is effectively a global presence. An excellent example is the electronic bookshop Amazon.com. Located in Seattle (chosen because this city is home to some of the biggest US book wholesalers), Amazon originally consisted of little more than a computer and small warehouse. It can compete, however, with more traditional booksellers around the globe and in November 1999 'Fortune' Magazine reported that it had a market value five times greater than the largest real life bookshop chain, Barnes and Noble – which has responded to Amazon by instituting its own Internet bookstore. Amazon have in turn, greatly expanded the range of goods and services on offer, either by providing these in its own right or through a link to a third party provider. Its aim reportedly, is to become a 'one-stop' service for all goods and services which a user may wish to acquire on-line.

12.5 In discussing this aspect of the Internet's role a distinction can be drawn between three forms of transaction. In the first category, as epitomised by the on-line sale of books, Internet businesses allow contracts of sale to be entered into electronically, with the goods involved being delivered using traditional mechanisms. Such transactions can be equated with existing forms of catalogue system and, save for the introduction of an international dimension, raise few novel legal issues. A second category relates to the provision of services. As with the previous situation, the contract will be concluded electronically but there will remain some element of physical performance of the contract. Perhaps the best example, being one of the major sectors of e-commerce, concerns the sale of airline tickets. Most airlines now operate a system of on-line booking of plane tickets. Such a facility can provide considerable cost benefits to the airline, which will need to employ and support fewer reservations staff and, in a number of cases, passengers are offered a discount for ordering on-line. In many cases, the next step is for the airline to post tickets to the customer, who then completes the journey in the normal manner. There is increased reliance, however, on what are referred to as electronic tickets. On receiving electronic confirmation of a successful booking, the customer will receive a booking number. No ticket will be issued and on arrival at the airport the customer need only quote the booking number in order to receive a boarding pass for the flight. Similar cost benefits to the service provider can be identified in many sectors. A recent survey by Salomon, Smith Barclay has suggested that the costs to a bank of an average transaction carried out within a branch is 67.5 pence, with telephone banking the cost is reduced to 37 pence and with Internet banking there is a further reduction to 2 pence. It is scarcely surprising that many banks are promoting the merits of this form of service.

12.6 The trend towards increasing de-materialisation of the contract performance phase reaches its ultimate in the third category of contracts. The phenomenon of digitisation is concerned with the practice where by information is recorded in digital format. Any form of information, images, sound or text, may be recorded in this way. We are all familiar with musical CDs and electronic encyclopaedias such as *Microsoft Encarta* or *Britannica Online*. The latter example may serve to illustrate one of the major economic aspects of digitisation. A full set of the *Encyclopaedia Britannica* in paper format cost £850. The CD equivalent costs £49 and elements are available free of charge over the Internet. Electronic publishing has indeed killed off the traditional publication, with *Britannica* now being available only in electronic form.

12.7 The Internet is based around the transfer of information in digital format and, as transmission speeds increase, so more and more complex and substantial forms of data may be transmitted on-line. It is commonplace for individuals or undertakings to purchase and download copies of software from a remote site (normally making payment by means of a credit card number). Subscriptions may be taken out to on-line databases. Until recently, it was not considered viable to transmit music or video programs of more than a few seconds in length over the Internet. Developments in the technology of compressing data, coupled with increased transmission capacity, are changing the situation. The MP3 system allows music to be transmitted over the Internet in real time, a prospect which is causing considerable concern to the owners of copyright in musical works. Systems of video on demand have been tested. With these customers can download a video of their choice over normal telephone lines whilst retaining the freedom to make or receive 'normal' calls at the same time.

The scale of Internet commerce

12.8 Increasingly, electronic commerce is being conducted over the Internet with WWW sites offering a range of products and services. As the range of services expands, so, it appears, does the number of estimates as to its scale. In the US, the Federal Trade Commission has estimated that sales transactions worth $3b took place over the Internet in 1995 and that sales will expand to 'tens to hundreds of billions of dollars' within the next decade. Other reports suggest that consumer sales over the Internet might reach $50b by 2002. At present, most Internet transactions are in the services sector. Travel, software and flower delivery services are amongst the major sectors. There are signs that e-commerce is expanding into other areas. It has been estimated that 15% of new car sales in the US are concluded over the Internet, a figure expected to rise to 50% by next year. Perhaps more impressively from the seller's perspective, it is further estimated that 85% of people who went through a 'full search of a car web site' purchased a vehicle within the next three months. Only 20% of customers visiting car showrooms made a purchase within the same time-scale. Similar systems also operate in the UK, with a service recently being announced which will allow customers to obtain on-line quotes in respect of personal imports of vehicles from abroad. Vauxhall have also become the first major UK car producer to offer to sell vehicles over the Internet at a discount of up to £1,300. At present only limited edition models – badged 'astra.com', 'corsa.com' and 'vectra.com' – are available and sales are channelled through the company's dealer network. The potential for expansion is obvious, as is the threat to the continued survival of intermediaries such as car dealers.

12.9 For Europe it has been estimated that commerce over the Internet was worth $349m in 1996 with this figure expected to grow to $26bn by the year 2001. The EU have estimated that global Internet commerce 'could be worth 200 billion ECU by the year 2000'. In the UK, the DTI have reported estimates that: 'some research suggests that the Internet will take 5-10% of all retail traffic by 2000.' Whilst the value of any statistics might be challenged, there seems little doubt that e-commerce will continue to grow. Although they tend to receive most of the headlines, consumer-related transactions represent only a small proportion of Internet-based transactions. Building on the foundation of a body of Electronic Data Interchange agreements, industry and commerce have adopted Internet based-communications with alacrity. In the US, business to business transactions worth an estimated $3 trillion dollars are predicted for 2003.

From EDI to electronic commerce

12.10 EDI represents one of the earliest forms of electronic commerce. Dating from the 1960s, the beginnings of EDI can be seen in airline reservation systems and debit clearing systems within the banking sector. A range of definitions have been essayed of EDI. The UNCITRAL Model Law on Electronic Commerce provides that it is to be considered:

> the electronic transfer from computer to computer of information using an agreed standard to structure the information.

12.11 It is the degree of structure which distinguishes EDI from other forms of electronic communications such as electronic mail. Usage of standard formats suitable for automated processing means that transactions can be processed automatically by the recipient's computer system without the need for any information to be rekeyed or, indeed, for there to be any degree of human intervention. A typical application might see a supermarket's computer system monitoring sales and linking with a supplier's system to place orders whenever stock levels fell below a specified figure. This initial act might well be followed by others generating invoices for goods delivered and causing payment to be made by means of an electronic fund transfer. It has been estimated that paper documentation and associated handling procedures can represent up to 10% of the total costs of goods. Costs savings on this element of up to 50% can be attained through a switch to EDI. Another producer has estimated that it costs $70 to process a paper purchase order as opposed to 93 cents when the order is submitted by EDI. In other cases, the figures might be even higher. In June 1997 the National Audit Office criticised procurement practices within the Ministry of Defence citing a case where £73.50 was spent processing an order for a padlock worth just 98 pence.

12.12 It is now estimated that some 4% of all business transactions in the UK take place via EDI. An indication of the range of users can be garnered from another statistic suggesting that some 3,500 dentists use the technology. EDI is heavily used in the banking sector, with the Clearing House Automated Payment System (CHAPS) handling some £100b-worth of transactions every day. At an international level the SWIFT network links some 1,900 banks and financial institutions around the world. In the Stock Exchange, the recently initiated CREST system uses EDI to facilitate share dealings. The insurance industry constitutes another sector which makes extensive use of EDI.

Format of EDI arrangements

12.13 For EDI to be effective, there is need for the parties to reach agreement concerning the format and structure of the system. Additionally, as will be discussed in more detail below, the substitution of electronic communications for the previous paper-based transactions poses significant legal problems. Many statutes and international conventions were devised before the computer age and utilise concepts such as 'writing' 'document' and 'signature', which do not fit easily into the computer context. The lack of computer specific coverage is compounded by a lack of case law providing guidance on the interpretation and application of legal concepts. Interchange agreements provide a means for parties to establish their own legal regime providing agreed definitions as to the constitution and implications of their commercial relationships. A further problem, which cannot be resolved by such agreements arises where legal provisions require the observance of procedures and formalities which cannot be satisfied without recourse to paper. An example might be found in requirements that contracts relating to the purchase of land must be entered into in writing and signed by the parties involved. This form of legal barrier to electronic trading will be discussed below.

12.14 The basis for many interchange agreements can be found in the Uniform Rules of Conduct for Interchange of Trade Data by Teletransmission (UNCID) rules drawn up in 1987 under the auspices of the International Chamber of Commerce. In the UK, the Legal Advisory Group of the UK EDI Association drew up the Standard Interchange Agreement (SIA), the third edition of which was published in 1993. A European Model Interchange Agreement developed under the auspices of the EU's Tedis programme had been published with a Commission Recommendation that it be used by 'economic operators and organizations'. A Model Interchange Agreement for the

Commercial Use of Electronic Data Interchange has been adopted by the United Nations Economic Commission for Europe Working Party on Facilitation of Electronic Trade Procedures.

12.15 Although the various models differ in details, there is considerable commonality concerning the area of coverage and basic provisions. In large measure this is consequential upon the adoption of the United Nations Electronic Data Interchange for Administration, Commerce and Transport standards (UN/EDIFACT) within all of the above-mentioned interchange agreements. The EDIFACT standards comprise:

> a set of standards, directories and guidelines for the electronic interchange of structured data, and in particular that related to trade in goods or services, between independent computerized information systems.

12.16 These lengthy technical documents define standard message terms and prescribe rules of syntax designed to ensure that the possibilities for misunderstanding the meaning of an EDI message are reduced and that such messages can be processed by the recipient system without need for any human involvement. EDIFACT directories provide definitions of the meanings ascribed to particular message terms. Some 200 'messages' (some of which are divided into sub-sets) have been devised relating to aspects of commercial transactions. Thus the message:

PRICAT

refers to a price catalogue whilst

RQOTE

indicates a request for a quotation.

12.17 Considering the content and format of interchange agreements, the EU model may be taken as illustrative. By art 3, the contracting parties agree that they will accept messages transmitted by EDI as valid. Further, art 4 provides that records of such communications will be, within limits set by national laws, admissible as evidence in the event of a dispute. It is also agreed that messages are to be processed by the recipient as quickly as practicable but that, save where specifically requested, acknowledgment of receipt is not required. Other provisions relate to the security and confidentiality of messages and the extent to which they are to be recorded and retained by the recipient. Because EDI messages may be acted upon without any human intervention or control, it is important also that participants should be able to rely upon the integrity of messages and the fact that they have not been altered during their passage through the telecommunications system. This requires the making of a further agreement with the provider(s) of the telecommunications network(s) used for the transmission of the messages. Particular care requires to be taken in the situation where messages may be transferred between two or more network providers. The phrase 'dump and pray' is used to refer to the undesirable situation where one provider passes a transmission onto another without there being any technical or legal safeguards to ensure the integrity of the message during the remainder of its journey.

12.18 Beyond the legal issues involved in applying concepts such as 'writing', signature', 'document' and 'original' in an electronic context, one of the major tasks facing organisations wishing to utilise EDI is the conclusion of an interchange agreement. As is stated in the commentary to the EDI Association standard agreement:

> Any method of communication requires discipline in order to be effective. The discipline is achieved by applying rules of conduct which by their use have become customary or by law have been imposed . . . EDI . . . has not yet been in existence long enough to have acquired in these ways a collection of standard rules of conduct. An interchange agreement provides them.

12.19 The values of EDI are most apparent when an ongoing relationship exists between the parties. A typical situation might be where EDI arrangements are used between a retailer and suppliers to ensure that product stocks are maintained at an optimal level. The need for messages to be structured precisely in accordance with predetermined parameters means that EDI is less relevant in the situation where single transactions are made. The range of transactions spans the whole commercial spectrum, with an increasing number of retailers and service providers offering customers the facility of placing orders using electronic communications.

12.20 Until recently, EDI agreements operated over dedicated networks using proprietary communications protocols. Effectively, only members of a network could communicate with each other. As has been stated above, the Internet is a global communications network and recent years have seen a shift to Internet-based communications. A leading example of such a system is the 'Trading Process Network' established by the industrial conglomerate General Electric. Originally designed to serve as a vehicle for communication between General Electric and its existing and potential component suppliers, the network has been opened up to provide an electronic home for other organisations wishing to conduct business on this basis. Claimed savings are impressive:

How much can a company save by using TPN? GE, which reportedly shells out $30 billion a year for procurement, offers a few clues. While nobody at GE will confirm that figure or project overall savings, Laurent P.M. Rotival, the company's manager of strategic sourcing, figures that the streamlining of indirect purchasing alone – which probably accounts for less than half of total buying – could save GE between $500 million and $700 million over the next three years.

12.21 Opening up communications beyond existing partners has been identified as a major benefit. It is reported that:

... In February the new Internet-based bidding system paid off in dramatic fashion when some machinery broke down at a [GE] Lighting factory in Cleveland. ...With no time to lose in getting repair parts, purchasing officials posted specifications and requests for quotes on their Website [TPN]. Of the seven new suppliers that responded, Lighting chose one in Hungary, where GE now makes lamps. The Hungarian supplier charged $320,000, 20% less than the next-highest bid, and delivered promptly as well.

The requisitioning process for machine parts, which formerly took more than seven days, has been reduced to two hours, reports Ronald J. Stettler, Lighting's manager of global sourcing. 'Sourcing can now simply point and click and send out a bid package to suppliers around the world,' he says. All the data are encrypted to keep them from competitors and hackers. After the bids are evaluated, orders can now go out in 24 hours instead of one or two days later, as in the past. Suppliers don't mind one bit.

12.22 A key phrase in this quote refers to the fact that data are encrypted. One of the major concerns that has deterred consumers from participating in electronic commerce has been that information transmitted over the Internet might be intercepted by computer hackers. Where the data takes the form of, for example, credit card information, the potential for loss is obvious. Reality does not necessarily accord with perception. No instances have been recorded of data being intercepted in transmission, although there are numerous instances of fraud conducted by parties involved in e-commerce. It is a very simple matter for a criminal to set up a website offering to supply goods or services at attractive prices, solicit orders with payment by credit card and make off with a rich harvest of numbers.

12.23 Faced with the fear of fraud, encryption has been seen as a major form of protection and many e-commerce sites indicate that all communications will be encrypted. Encryption will not, of course, be of any assistance in the situations described above, but there is general recognition that many electronic communications are insecure. E-mail is often analogised in security terms with a post card. Use of encryption increases security dramatically and a considerable variety of systems exist. Many of these have been the centre of considerable controversy. Whilst individuals have a legitimate expectation to privacy in their communications, the state also has legitimate interest in – and indeed obligation to ensure – law enforcement. On occasion, law enforcement agencies may wish to engage in the interception of communications in the course of investigations into actual or potential criminal conduct. Regulation of such actions has been a controversial matter.

Legal issues of electronic commerce

12.24 Distance selling, principally in the form of mail order and catalogue selling has been a feature of commercial life for many years. Given this, it is tempting to suggest that the fact that commercial transactions may now take place the medium of the Internet raises no new legal issues. To an extent this is indeed the case. A CD remains a CD, whether it is bought from an on-line or a High Street music store. The legal models regulating commerce have tended to be shaped to suit a particular set of assumptions. The bulk of trade has been concerned with goods rather than services, whilst international trade has tended to be the province of the commercial sector. Electronic commerce challenges the continued validity of some legal assumptions. Whilst this does not of itself require that legal principles be overturned, the nature and emphasis of aspects of commercial law do require to be re-oriented.

12.25 The following chapters will consider some of the key legal issues. The question when and where a contract is made is one which assumes significance when parties deal other than on a face-to-face basis. In some cases, the law has imposed requirements that contracts be concluded in a particular manner. This typically requires that contracts be concluded in writing, often with the additional obligation that the parties sign the document to evidence their wish to accept and be bound by its terms. The issue arises here whether a document existing purely in electronic form, for example an e-mail, can satisfy statutory requirements. In respect of these and other topics, a variety of legislative initiatives can be identified at international, European and UK level. The Electronic Communications Bill was introduced into Parliament in November 1999 and was scheduled to be the UK's first twenty-first century statute until emergency legislation to suspend the Northern Ireland Assembly took its place on the statute book. Within the European Union, a directive on the legal status on electronic signatures has been adopted, together with a directive on distance selling and a draft directive on electronic commerce. At a perhaps more practical level, the increasing globalisation of trade poses difficulties for the application of national taxation regimes. An increasing number of UK-based bookmakers, for example, are setting up operations in low- or no-tax jurisdictions and accepting wagers from their customers via the medium of a website. In general, it appears that the globalisation of electronic commerce has significant implications for national tax bases.

Chapter 13

Electronic contracts

Introduction

13.0 During the 1970s and 1980s a raft of national and international data protection statutes marked the first attempts to regulate aspects of computer-related conduct. The next decade saw considerable attention paid to the topic of computer crime. As we emerge into the next century much legislative focus is aimed at ensuring the development of effective regulatory regimes both for electronic commerce and for the relationships between individuals and companies and government agencies.

13.1 Given the international nature of the topic, it is not surprising that many of the activities in the field of electronic commerce have been initiated by international organisations. The United Nations Commission on International Trade Law (UNCITRAL) has adopted a model law on electronic commerce, whilst in December 1999 the OECD agreed Guidelines on Electronic Commerce. The goal of the guidelines, it was stated –

> is that consumers shopping on-line should enjoy transparent and effective protection that is not less than the level of protection that they have in other areas of commerce. Among other things, they stress the importance of transparency and information disclosure.

13.2 The model law and the guidelines have no binding force. In focusing on regulatory activity, attention must concentrate on the activities of the EU and of national legislatures. EU involvement in the field of electronic commerce can be traced primarily to a Commission Communication, 'A European Initiative in Electronic Commerce', published in April 1997. Itself building on earlier information society initiatives, this outlined a programme for regulatory action across a range of topics. In what might be considered chronological order, action was required to ensure that organisations were enabled to establish electronic businesses in any of the member states, that legal barriers to electronic trade should be removed, and that provision should be made for the manner in which contracts should be negotiated and concluded. Finally, legislation might be required in the field of electronic payments.

13.3 The mechanics of electronic commerce constitute one aspect of the regulatory task. It was also recognised that other more general principles would need to be applied in the context of commercial applications. Issues such as data protection arise whenever personal data is transmitted and received. Again, as will be discussed below, the use of cryptographic techniques as a means of security, both to preserve privacy and to enhance consumer and business confidence in the integrity of electronic communications, raises significant and controversial regulatory questions.

Formation of a contract

13.4 In order for a contract to be concluded, it is required that there should be an unconditional offer and acceptance. In many instances, of course, there may be several iterations of offer, and counter-offer before the parties reach agreement on all important matters concerned with the contract.

13.5 In the situation where a customer purchases goods in a shop there is little problem in determining the question where a contract is made. The question when the contract is concluded is a little more problematic. Where goods are displayed in retail premises, it is normally the case that the display constitutes what is referred to as an 'invitation to treat'. An offer to purchase will be made by the customer which may be accepted (or rejected) by the seller. There are sound reasons for such an approach, not least due to the possibility that goods might be out of stock or that the wrong price tag may have been placed on an item by mistake (or through the action of some third party). In practical terms it can be said that a contract will typically be concluded when the customer's offer of payment is accepted by the seller.

13.6 Subject to any other mechanism agreed between the parties, it is generally the case that acceptance becomes effective when it is communicated to the offeror. Clearly in the case of a face-to-face transaction this occurs at the point where the acceptor indicates – whether by words or actions – that the offer is acceptable. Matters become rather more complex when the parties transact at a distance. Until the end of the twentieth century, the postal system constituted the only significant communication network. A set of special rules was devised by the courts to cope with the situation where the parties concluded a contract by means of an exchange of letters. The so-called 'postal rule' provides that the contract is deemed to have been concluded at the moment the acceptance is placed into the postal system. The main rationale for such an approach is that, once the message has been posted, it moves out of the control of the sender. The effect of this is, of course, that a contract will be concluded before the offeror is aware of the fact of acceptance. It is also the case that, having been posted, an acceptance cannot be withdrawn, even though this may have been brought to the attention of the offeror prior to delivery of the acceptance.

13.7 Starting with the telegraph and moving through the telephone, telex and fax machines to electronic mail, a wide range of other communications technologies are now available. Responding to the emergence of the telex and telephone systems, the courts developed another rule of contract formation, generally referred to as the 'instantaneous communication rule'. In *Entores Ltd v Miles Far East Corp* [1995] 2 All ER 493 the question at issue was where a contract made following communications by telex should be regarded as having been concluded. The plaintiffs, who were located in London, had made an offer which had been accepted by the defendants in Amsterdam. Holding that the contract was made when the acceptance was received by the plaintiffs in London, Parker LJ held that where –

> . . . parties are in each other's presence or, though separated in space, communication between them is in effect instantaneous, there is no need for any such rule of convenience. To hold otherwise would leave no room for the operation of the general rule that notification of the acceptance must be received. An acceptor could say: 'I spoke the words of acceptance in your presence, albeit softly, and you did not hear me'; or 'I telephoned to you and accepted, and it matters not that the telephone went dead and you did not get my message' . . . So far as Telex messages are concerned, though the despatch and receipt of a message is not completely instantaneous, the parties are to all intents and purposes in each other's presence just as if they were in telephonic communication, and I can see no reason for departing from the general rule that there is no binding contract until notice of the acceptance was received by the offeror.

13.8 This view was endorsed by the House of Lords in *Brinkibon Ltd v Stahag Stahl und Stahlwarenhandel GmbH* [1982] 1 All ER 293, although it was recognised by Lord Wilberforce that the result might have to be reviewed in the event it could be established that there was:

> some error or default at the recipient's end which prevents receipt at the time contemplated and believed in by the sender . . . No universal rule can cover all such cases; they must be resolved by reference to the intentions of the parties, by sound business practice and in some cases a judgement where the risks should lie.

13.9 In the context of the present work, the key question will be whether e-mails and other forms of message transmitted over the Internet will be classed as coming under the postal rule or whether the provisions relating to instantaneous communications will apply? Although the issue of determining when an e-mail contract is concluded might appear to be in the 'number of angels on a pinhead' category, this is not always the case, especially when, as in the *Entores* and *Brinkibon* cases, transactions possess an international dimension. In such cases the questions will arise which law will govern the transaction and which courts will have jurisdiction in the event of a dispute. In the event that a contract is silent on the point, the location where a contract is concluded will be a major factor in determining the choice of law question. This issue will be considered in more detail below.

13.10 In terms of speed of transmission, e-mail might generally be equated with fax or telex transmission. In the event of problems or congestion on the networks, messages may be delayed by hours or even days and, in terms of the nature of transmission, the more accurate parallel may be with the postal system. An e-mail message will be passed on from point to point across the network with its contents being copied and forwarded a number of times before being delivered to the ultimate recipient. There is no single direct link or connection between sender and receiver.

13.11 In its proposal for a Directive on Electronic Commerce, the European Commission proposes a somewhat complex mechanism for determining the moment at which a contract is concluded. Article 11 provides that:

> Member States shall lay down in their legislation that, save where otherwise agreed by professional persons, in cases where a recipient, in accepting a service provider's offer, is required to give his consent through technological means, such as clicking on an icon, the contract is concluded when the recipient of the service has received from the service provider, electronically, an acknowledgement of receipt of the recipient's acceptance.

13.12 Such an approach would pose problems for the UK system which, as stated above, sees offers emanating from the customer rather than the supplier. There appears also to be an element of unnecessary complication by adding the requirement of acknowledgment of receipt of acceptance as a condition for the conclusion of a contract. The original proposal was even more prolonged, stating that the contract would not be concluded until acknowledgment was made of receipt of the acknowledgment! Receipt of acceptance would seem quite sufficient for this legal purpose. An alternative and perhaps preferable approach is advocated by the International Chamber of Commerce, whose Uniform Rules for Electronic Trade and Settlement propose that:

> An electronic offer and/or acceptance becomes effective when it enters the information system of the recipient in a form capable of being processed by that system.

13.13 Although intended primarily for business-to-business contracts rather than the EU's consumer contract focus, the ICC approach seems to achieve the legal requirements in a rather simpler fashion. Simplest of all, however, would be the UK approach, which would allow the seller to combine acceptance of the customer's offer with acknowledgment of the terms of the transaction.

13.14 A further obligation is proposed in the European Directive. Article 11(2) requires member states to ensure that national laws require that:

> the service provider shall make available to the recipient of the service appropriate means that are effective and accessible allowing him to identify and correct handling errors and accidental transactions before the conclusion of the contract. Contract terms and general conditions provided to the consumer must be made available in a way that allows him to store and reproduce them.

13.15 Whilst the provision is well meaning, it is difficult to identify how the result might be achieved. The provisions relating to the moment of formation of contract discussed above require that 'the service provider is obliged to immediately send the acknowledgment of receipt'. We can assume that, in most cases, this will be transmitted automatically. This affords very little time for the customer to identify and seek to correct any mistakes which have been made.

Formal requirements for contract validity

13.16 In most situations, parties are free to enter into contracts in such manner and under such terms as they may choose. Agreements may be entered into in writing, verbally, or may even be implied from the parties' actions. In these situations, the fact that a contract is entered into electronically will have no impact upon its legal validity, with any legal concerns relating to the manner in which its terms might be evidenced. In a number of situations, however, legal provisions may require that a contract is constituted in writing and that it be signed by the parties involved. In a 1990 report, the United Nations Commission on International Trade Law (UNCITRAL) identified four reasons which had, historically, prompted a requirement that contracts be concluded in writing. These were the desire to reduce disputes, to make the parties aware of the consequences of their dealings, to provide evidence upon which third parties might rely upon the agreement and to facilitate tax, accounting and regulatory purposes. Assuming that satisfactory safeguards could be built into systems for electronic contracting, there would seem no reason to doubt that these objectives could not be attained. As will be discussed, however, current legal requirements may pose insuperable barriers to electronic contracting in certain areas.

13.17 Calls for national action to remove such barriers have been a feature of much of the UN's work in the field, with calls being made to member governments to remove legal barriers to electronic commerce. Initially, the calls focused specifically on EDI, with the publication of a draft UNCITRAL 'Model Law on Legal Aspects of Electronic Data Interchange (EDI) and Related Means of Communication'. By the time the measure was adopted in June 1996, the title had been changed to the more generic 'Model Law on Electronic Commerce'.

13.18 This chapter will examine legal barriers to electronic contracting under a number of headings. First, consideration will be given to those contracts which are required to be constituted in writing. Second, consideration will be given to the notion of a signature. This will require an expedition into the world of cryptography. Finally, an examination will be made of the law relating to documentary evidence with a view to determining, in particular, whether information stored in electronic format might satisfy legal requirements for a document. Linked to this is the issue whether the making of electronic copies of paper originals will satisfy evidential requirements.

When is writing required?

13.19 In Scotland the Requirements of Writing (Scotland) Act 1995 codified the existing common law requirements and provided that writing will only be required for the validity of three categories of legal act:

- gratuitous unilateral obligations (an enforceable promise) except where these are entered into in the course of a business;

- contracts relating to dealings in land;

- the making of a will or establishment of a trust.

The rationale behind these exceptions is broadly similar to those identified in the United Nations' report cited above. Similar requirements are found in English law. Additionally, a wide range of statutory provisions make provision for information to be supplied 'in writing', eg company accounts. In a number of instances, specific statutory provision has been made for the acceptance of computer-generated information. In the taxation field, for example, electronic copies of invoices will be accepted for purposes connected with Value Added Tax. Generally, however, statutory requirements for the supply of information in writing will be subject to the terms of the Interpretation Act 1978, which defines writing as including:

> typing, printing, lithography, photography and other modes of representing or reproducing words in a visible form, and expressions referring to writing are construed accordingly.

13.20 A document which exists solely in digital form, for example an e-mail message stored on the hard disk of the recipient's computer, will not be capable of coming within this definition as the electronic impulses representing its contents are not visible.

13.21 It seems clear that the 1978 definition was introduced at a time when communications between computers was limited and, as with other statutory definitions of that era relating to concepts of recording and storage, is ill suited to the modern age. The UN Model Law introduces the concept of 'a data message' which is defined as:

> information generated, sent, received or stored by electronic, optical or similar means including, but not limited to, electronic document interchange (EDI), electronic mail, telegram, telex or telecopy.

and goes on to provide that:

> Where the law requires information to be in writing, that requirement is met by a data message if the information contained therein is accessible so as to be usable for subsequent reference.

13.22 As will be discussed below, the Electronic Communications Bill proposes a somewhat different approach to the topic, although the intention is also that requirements for writing should be satisfied by the creation of an electronic document. In the event that a contract is concerned with rights over property, for example land, which will exist indefinitely, it is clear that there will be the need for details to be retained over a long period. This is perhaps a technical rather than a legal problem. Just as paper needs to be stored under controlled conditions to prevent its decay, so computer storage devices will need to be preserved.

Requirements for signature

13.23 In addition to requiring that a contract be made in writing, it may also be a requirement that it be signed by or on behalf of a contracting party. For the vast majority of cases there is no specific legal requirement for signature and the prime purpose of the signature will be to evidence the fact that the document has originated from, or been approved by, a particular individual. In some instances, statutory provisions may require that a document be signed as a prerequisite to its validity. In particular, requirements for signature invariably accompany requirements that contracts be constituted in writing. In this section, consideration will be given, first, to the question what is a signature and, secondly, to the emerging concept of a 'digital signature'. Typically, this will involve the use of encryption techniques to provide a degree of assurance that a message was composed by a particular individual and has not subsequently been modified.

13.24 Even before the advent of the digital age, it was a relatively simple matter to forge documents, either by creating a new text by or altering an existing one. Alteration might, of course, leave physical traces. An enhanced (although obviously not total) degree of security could be obtained by requiring that the parties to a document sign their names to indicate their adoption of its terms. Extending the requirement to include a signature on every page of a document and perhaps also the involvement of witnesses adds further to the level of trust that can be placed in the accuracy of a document.

13.25 The nature of the requirement varies from situation to situation. In a number of instances it has been provided that a variety of methods of signature may be applied. Under the terms of the United Nations Convention on the Carriage of Goods by Sea it is provided that a signature may be made by 'handwriting . . . or . . . by any other mechanical or electrical means'. Comparatively few statutory definitions exist in the UK, but a substantial body of case law has sanctioned the use of mechanical aids to produce a signature. In *Goodman v Eban* [1954] 1 QB 550 the Court of Appeal held that a solicitor satisfied the requirement under the Solicitors Act 1932 that bills be signed by using a rubber stamp embossed with the name of his firm. As was stated:

> where an Act of Parliament requires that any particular document be 'signed' by a person, then, prima facie, the requirement of the Act is satisfied if the person himself places on the document an engraved representation of his signature by means of a rubber stamp . . . the essential requirement of signing is the affixing in some way, whether by writing with a pen or pencil or by otherwise impressing upon the document, one's name or 'signature' so as personally to authenticate the document.

13.26 In the case *Re a Debtor (No 2021 of 1995)* [1996] 2 All ER 345 it was held that a faxed copy of a signed proxy form complied with statutory requirements for signature:

> Once it is accepted that the close physical linkage of hand, pen and paper is not necessary for the form to be signed, it is difficult to see why some forms of non-human agency for impressing the mark on the paper should be acceptable while others are not.

It is a simple matter today for a fax to be transmitted directly from a computer without the need for a paper original. Coupled to this, a copy of a signature can be digitised, and when appended to such a transmission, will be printed out as a facsimile of the original signature on the recipient's machine. This will be the only paper-based copy of the document and signature. Such a copy, it was suggested, should be regarded as having been 'signed' by its author.

13.27 The case law indicates that the concept of a signature will be interpreted very broadly, so long as there is the attachment to paper of some physical mark which can be identified as indicating its adoption or approval. Although it would be normal for a signature to take the form of the signatory's name, a glance at many signatures will indicate that legibility is seldom a feature of these instruments and, in general, any mark will be acceptable so long as it can be evidenced that this is the signatory's normal method of endorsing documents. The letter 'X' has traditionally been used as a means for imprinting the mark of an illiterate person.

13.28 In addition to the question whether a document requires to be signed, the issue may also arise whether there is need to retain a paper copy. For many organisations, especially in the financial and insurance sectors, the requirement to maintain paper copies of documents is a significant expense. If assurance could be given that electronic copies represented an exact replica of the original document, significant cost savings could be secured. With respect to all of these issues, encryption may have a role to play. We are therefore looking for techniques which can provide assurance both as to the identity of the creator of a document and as to the fact that it has not subsequently been modified. The task is not a simple one and, prior to considering some of the legal dimensions to the problem, it will be necessary to give some consideration to the complex world of cryptography.

The nature of encryption

13.29 Techniques of encryption date back many centuries. An early user was Julius Caesar, who wrote his despatches from Gaul in what is now referred to as the Caesar code. This involves shifting letters an agreed number of spaces along the alphabet. Placing the two alphabets above each other we might have:

ABCDEFGHIJKLMNOPQRSTUVWXYZ

DEFGHIJKLMNOPQRSTUVWXYZABC

With a shift of three, for example, the letter C would become F, A become D and T, W. CAT would read FDW.

13.30 The Caesar code is an example of what is referred to as a substitution cipher. The other main form of encryption has involved a process of transposition. Effectively, this involves taking a phrase, such as –

WET DAY IN GLASGOW

omitting spaces and placing the letters into blocks of five produces:

WETDA YINGL ASGOW

The letters in each block are then shuffled in a predetermined manner. If the first letter is moved to the fourth space, second to fifth, third to first, fourth to second and fifth to third we arrive at:

TDAWE NGLYI GOWAS

13.31 Obviously, a real-life example would need to add far more in the way of complexity but, until recent times, all codes were based on substitution or transposition techniques. Throughout history there has been a constant battle between those seeking to use encryption to preserve secrecy and those wishing to break the codes.

13.32 In the pre-computer age, the battle between code makers and breakers could well have been regarded as an intellectual pursuit akin to solving a crossword puzzle. The advent of the computer served to change the situation. Much has been written concerning the British and US cryptographic operations during the Second World War. These led to the development of the world's first practical computing machines. Although limited by today's standards, the processing power of these computers transformed code breaking from what had been an intellectual pursuit into an exercise in number crunching. The analogy might be made with a combination lock on a safe and the contrast between the stereotypical image of a skilled safe breaker using a stethoscope to detect the correct combination and the random selection of numbers continued until the correct combination is achieved. Whilst the effort of trying several million possible combinations would be too great for humans, the task is comparatively simple for a computer.

13.33 In response to the vulnerability of traditional forms of encryption, modern systems place reliance upon mathematical techniques rather than alphabetical manipulation. This is rendered practicable because of the manner in which digital computers process every item of information as a combination of the characters 0 and 1. One of the first of a new generation of cryptographic techniques was implemented in the US Data Encryption Standard (DES). DES has been a source of some controversy since its inception in 1977, with allegations that its effectiveness was deliberately reduced at the behest of the US National Security Agency. The level of security is basically as great as the complexity of the encryption software. The analogy might be made with a combination lock. A lock with three dials provides some security but one with five considerably more so. The original version of DES used what is described as a 56-bit key. This has some 70 quadrillion combinations. A massive figure for human calculators but one which provides a more manageable challenge to modern computers. The selection of a 56-bit key is rumoured to have been influenced by the US National Security Agency. The agency is reported to possess the world's most powerful computers, machines capable of decoding a message encoded using a 56-bit key within a matter of hours. As computer technology develops it has become more possible for other organisations to acquire the processing power required. The Electronic Frontier Foundation, a civil liberties pressure group, claimed in 1998 to have build a 'DES cracker' for $250,000, whilst in yet another significant demonstration of the power of the Internet, it has been reported that messages have been successfully decoded using several thousand computers linked together over the Internet and operating throughout the night whilst their normal users slept.

13.34 DES and other forms of substitution and transposition codes are examples of single key or symetric encryption systems. In the same way that the same key is used to open and lock a door, a message is encoded and decoded using the same key. So long as only the sender and recipient know the key, the system is secure. Apart from the vulnerability of codes to attack by code breakers, another significant point of weakness has concerned the fact that a single key is used to encode and decode the message. If a sender wishes the recipient to be able to decipher his messages, it is necessary to deliver a copy of the key. The possibility that the key might be intercepted or misused creates another major point of vulnerability. Whilst systems such as DES might be used within closed networks of trusted parties – EDI agreements would be an obvious example – it can be of limited value in the wider world of electronic commerce. Here, just as is the case in the High Street, the intention is that customers and suppliers who have no prior knowledge of each other can conduct business. Clearly, no sensible users of encryption would send a key to a party whom they had not met previously.

13.35 A solution to this problem emerged with the development of public key or asymmetric cryptography. The concept was initially devised identified in 1976 by two mathematicians, Diffie and Hellman, and was brought to practical fruition by three further mathematicians, Rivest, Shamir and Adleman, after whom the RSA system is named. It has recently been reported that similar work had been conducted in the UK at the GCHQ, although details were withheld on grounds of national security.

13.36 The RSA system has proved controversial in a number of respects. Although the system was developed using public funds, the algorithms have been patented (the patents expire in the year 2000) and are owned by a private company which markets the software on a commercial basis. The system was first marketed in 1977 and required levels of processing power which effectively limited its use to large organisations and government departments. A modified form of public key encryption, still based on the RSA algorithms but suitable for use on personal computers, was developed by Phil Zimmerman and is generally referred to by the acronym PGP (Pretty Good Privacy). Zimmerman's original intention was reportedly to offer the system on a commercial basis. In 1991, however, he became concerned at legislative proposals being discussed in the US Congress which, if enacted, would have restricted the availability of encryption software. Zimmerman's response was to persuade a friend to place a copy of PGP on the Internet. From that date, the cryptographic genie has been well and truly out of the bottle and copies of PGP can be downloaded free of charge from a wide range of Internet sites.

13.37 For a number of years Zimmerman faced threats of patent infringement action by RSA but eventually the parties concluded a licence allowing the use of the RSA algorithms in non-commercial copies of PGP. This has been dropped. The US government also places restrictions on the strength of RSA software which may lawfully be exported from the US and threatened action against Zimmerman. Doubts were raised, however, whether causing a copy of PGP to be placed on the Internet constituted an act of exporting as defined in the relevant legislation and, given that the system could not be un-invented, the decision was taken to drop proceedings.

13.38 A user of either PGP or RSA software will generate two keys, a public and a private key. The act of generating the keys typically requires nothing more than random movements of the computer mouse. Messages can be encrypted using either key but possession of the other key will be required in order to decrypt them. Although the mathematics are beyond the comprehension of mere lawyers, the system is claimed to be significantly more secure than single key systems, although it also operates considerably more slowly.

13.39 If consideration is given to the nature of the public key system, strengths and weaknesses can be identified. The scenario might be postulated whereby A receives a message which purports to have been sent by B and encrypted using the latter's private key. Assuming A had details of the public key, the message can be decrypted and A can be certain that the message has not been tampered with following its encryption. A cannot, however, be certain that B has not let the private key fall into a third party's hands. Again, given the ease with which PGP software and e-mail accounts can be acquired or forged, if A and B have not dealt previously, A cannot be confident that B is who he or she claims to be. A final weakness may be most relevant in the commercial context. B may be a company and the key used to encrypt a message ordering 100,000 widgets from A. A will have no means of knowing that the person sending the message on A's behalf is authorised to engage in such transactions.

13.40 The same issues will apply in the event that A replies to B, encrypting the message with A's public key. Again, there can be confidence that the message has not been intercepted and amended in transit but less reliance upon the identity of the claimed sender. Indeed, given that the essence of the public key is that it is public, it might be a foolhardy person who would place too much credence on the origin of a message. From the point of view of the sender, he or she may be given details of a public key and told that it belongs to Ian Lloyd, a well-known supplier of memorabilia of Glasgow Celtic Football Club. Encouraged by the prospect of secure communications, credit card details may be transmitted with a view to acquiring a selection of materials. Unfortunately, the key may have been generated by someone assuming the identity of the supplier in order to entice gullible consumers to transmit details of their credit card numbers which will then be used for fraudulent purposes.

Trusted third parties

13.41 If the aim of encryption is to authenticate the accuracy of a transmission and to identify its sender, systems of public key cryptography score one out of two. To provide mechanisms for promoting trust in the identity and status of the parties involved, the involvement of trusted third parties (TTP), also referred to as certification agencies, has emerged. The TTP will seek evidence that the party sending a message is who he or she claims to be and will cause a certificate to that effect to be attached to a message. Even today the market is significant, with the market leader, Verisign, reporting a turnover of $30m in 1998. For the UK, banks, some solicitors and accountancy firms and even the Post Office have expressed interest in acting as TTPs.

13.42 The basic operation of TTPs is non-controversial and can be equated with traditional professions such as that of notary or even with the role of a witness to a document. TTPs will almost inevitably obtain information about their customers' keys and some offer what is referred to as a 'key recovery' service. This effectively involves them keeping secure a copy of a private key. In the event that the user forgets the key or – perhaps more likely – details are destroyed by a disaffected or departing employee, the loss can be made good.

13.43 As with many issues concerned with the Internet, initial moves in the field came from the US. Here, enormous controversy followed proposals to introduce a new system of encryption, the Escrowed Encryption Standard, more commonly referred to as the 'Clipper Chip'. The attraction of this system, which would be based on public key cryptography, would be that any form of digitised data would be encrypted in such a way as to ensure a high level of security. The less welcome aspect of the system was that its structure would enable 'keys' to be made available to government agencies, enabling messages readily to be deciphered. Concerns were expressed whether the legal controls envisaged concerning release of the keys would provide adequate safeguards. Although legislation implementing the clipper proposals did not pass through Congress, it was announced in Autumn 1996 that export controls on encryption software would be reduced in return for an industry commitment to the introduction of a key recovery system requiring that copies of all keys be held by a 'Trusted Third Party'. It would appear in this case that the prime motive was that the third party should be trusted by the government rather than by the contracting parties.

13.44 Much of the legislative debate in the late 1990s has concerned the role of TTPs and systems of key recovery and escrow. In March 1997, the Council of the OECD adopted 'Guidelines for Cryptography Policy'. In a manner similar to that adopted in the field of data protection, the guidelines identify eight principles which should inform national legislation in this field.

1.   Cryptographic methods should be trustworthy in order to generate confidence in the use of information and communications systems.
2.   Users should have a right to choose any cryptographic method, subject to applicable law.
3.   Cryptographic methods should be developed in response to the needs, demands and responsibilities of individuals, businesses and governments.
4.   Technical standards, criteria and protocols for cryptographic methods should be developed and promulgated at the national and international level.
5.   The fundamental rights of individuals to privacy, including secrecy of communications and protection of personal data, should be respected in national cryptographic policies and in the implementation and use of cryptographic methods.
6.   National cryptographic policies may allow lawful access to plain text, or cryptographic keys, of encrypted data. These policies must respect the other principles contained in the guidelines to the greatest extent possible.
7.   Whether established by contract or legislation, the liability of individuals and entities that offer cryptographic services or hold or access cryptographic keys should be clearly stated.
8.   Governments should co-operate to co-ordinate cryptographic policies. As part of this effort, governments should remove, or avoid creating in the name of cryptography policy, unjustified obstacles to trade.

13.45 A strong relationship can be identified between these principles and a number of those applying in the data protection field. Although the guidelines recognise the need for some legal controls over the use of cryptography, it is stressed throughout that these must 'respect user choice to the greatest extent'. To this extent, the guidelines are seen as moving away from the US-sponsored notion of mandatory key escrow, a move which is also followed in recent European and UK legislation and proposals.

13.46 It is not the purpose of this book to discuss in detail the political aspects of encryption policy. It is suggested, however, that both sides are failing to come to terms with the reality of modern life. Those advocating extensive powers for law enforcement agencies are in many respects looking back to a form of golden age when governments could exercise genuine control over communications. Terrestrial broadcasting was largely a state-controlled monopoly and the limits of transmitter power meant that foreign broadcasts could be received only in border regions. Postal and telecommunication services were also state controlled and international communications were conducted only on a small scale. The world has moved on and attempts to re-exert control are likely to be doomed to failure.

13.47 Those opposed to the interception of encrypted messages may suffer from a similarly dated view of the world, harking back to a golden era of individual anonymity. In many western countries this can be considered to have reached its apogee in the 1960s. The last 30 years have seen a massive increase in the amount of personal data recorded and processed. Privacy in the traditional sense has largely vanished. In part, this is as a result of public sector activity, but a large and growing threat comes from the private sector. There has never been a situation in which all communications receive immunity from interception. Whilst there is certainly need for controls to be introduced concerning interception and decryption of encoded messages, the notion that individuals should be assured of absolute privacy for their communications has never been a feature of societal life.

Encryption and electronic commerce

13.48 Moving from the politics to the practicalities of the topic, many states are introducing legislation designed to promote electronic commerce. In the UK, the Electronic Communications Bill has been introduced into Parliament and will be discussed in more detail below. Two directives are currently progressing through the European Union's legislative process. The proposal for a directive 'on certain legal aspects of electronic commerce in the internal market' is concerned primarily with tissues relating to the formation of contracts in an electronic context and questions of the liability of Internet service. Its provisions are discussed primarily in Chapter 14 but in the present context it is significant to note its provisions relating to the recognition of electronic signatures. It provides in art 9 that:

> 1. Member States shall ensure that their legislation allows contracts to be concluded electronically. Member States shall in particular ensure that the legal requirements applicable to the contractual process neither prevent the effective use of electronic contracts nor result in such contracts being deprived of legal effect and validity on account of their having been made electronically.
> 2. Member States may lay down that paragraph 1 shall not apply to the following contracts:
>
> (a) contracts requiring the involvement of a notary;
> (b) contracts which, in order to be valid, are required to be registered with a public authority;

    (c) contracts governed by family law;

    (d) contracts governed by the law of succession.

13.49 The effect of this provision would be to ensure that most forms of electronic commerce can be conducted without requiring to comply with any additional requirements relating to form. This general rule may, at the option of a member state, be subject to exceptions. The situations specified in the proposed directive relate to contracts which are regarded as being of special importance. In respect of these, national laws typically require that the terms of the contract be recorded in writing and signed by the contracting parties.

13.50 A more relevant instrument is the directive 'on a common framework for electronic signatures'. Although its provisions generally conjure up images of systems of public key encryption, the directive seeks to be technologically neutral. Its implementation would have the effect of providing for electronic equivalents to writing and signature to be accepted within the member states.

13.51 Although the directive uses the term 'electronic signature', the phrase 'digital signature' is perhaps more widely used. The International Standards Organization defines the concept of a digital signature as 'data appended to, or a cryptographic transformation of a data unit that allows a recipient of the data unit to prove the source and integrity of the data unit and protect against forgery'.

13.52 Although the purpose of a digital signature is equivalent to that of the more traditional version, the manner in which this is accomplished is somewhat different. A human signature is generally appended to a document in order to indicate that the text originates from a particular individual. With public key encryption, the text of a data message is encrypted in such a way that a recipient can be confident that it did originate from the identified sender and that it has not been subject to any modification or amendment during the course of transmission. To this extent, the entire message becomes the digital signature.

13.53 The directive identifies two forms of signature, electronic and advanced electronic signatures. These are defined:

    1. 'electronic signature' means data in electronic form which are attached to or logically associated with other electronic data and which serve as a method of authentication;

    2. 'advanced electronic signature' means an electronic signature which meets the following requirements:

    (a) it is uniquely linked to the signatory;

    (b) it is capable of identifying the signatory;

(c) it is created using means that the signatory can maintain under his sole control; and
(d) it is linked to the data to which it relates in such a manner that any subsequent change of the data is detectable;

13.54 The term 'electronic signature' is very broad. It would encompass, for example, the use of scanning equipment to create a digital image of a person's signature with this image being reproduced at the end of a word processed letter. Advanced forms of signature will require the use of some form of encryption.

13.55 An advanced electronic signature will give a considerable degree of assurance that the signature is that of a particular person. There cannot be assurance that its use has been authorised by the owner, either generally or in the context of a particular transaction. It might be, for example, that an unauthorised third party has obtained a copy of a private key. Alternatively, a company may have a private key which is used by an employee to place an order for goods but where the employee is acting in excess of his authority. To overcome these difficulties, the notion has been advanced that the use of a signature should be certified by an independent agency. The directive identifies criteria which must be met in what is called a 'qualified certificate':

(a) an indication that the certificate is issued as a qualified certificate;
(b) the identification of the certification-service provider and the State in which it is established;
(c) the name of the signatory or a pseudonym, which shall be identified as such;
(d) provision for a specific attribute of the signatory to be included if relevant, depending on the purpose for which the certificate is provided;
(e) signature-verification data which correspond to the signature-creation data under the control of the signatory;
(f) an indication of the beginning and end of the period of validity of the certificate;
(g) the identity code of the certificate;
(h) the advanced electronic signature of the certification-service-provider issuing it;
(i) limitations on the scope of use of the certificate if applicable;
(l) limits on the value of transactions for which the certificate can be used, if applicable.

13.56 What this means is that the certification service provider, whose technical and organisational competencies must match requirements laid down in Annex 2 of the directive, verifies that the advanced electronic signature has been used by the rightful owner.

13.57 As well as being intended to promote user confidence in the integrity and reliability of electronic signatures, the directive provides further that a certified advanced signature is to be accepted as equivalent to a hand written signature in respect of any legal requirements for such formality.

13.58 The directive was adopted by the Council of Ministers at the end of November 1999. Its provisions require to be implemented in the member states within a period of 18 months. For the UK, implementation is likely to take the form of the Electronic Communications Bill. This was introduced into Parliament in November 1999 as a key plank in the government's programme to make the UK the world's most e-commerce friendly country.

13.59 The Bill's subsequent progress has been rapid, with its Committee stage being completed on 16 December 1999. The speed of the parliamentary process can be contrasted with a somewhat lengthy (and contentious) preliminary stage. The genesis of the measure can be traced to a consultation paper published by the previous administration in March 1997 on the 'Licensing of Trusted Third Parties for the Provision of Encryption Services'. In April 1998 the Department of Trade and Industry published a statement on 'Secure Electronic Commerce'. This marked the first occasion when the term 'electronic commerce' was used in an official statement. It was indicated that:

> 2. The Government places considerable importance on the successful development of electronic commerce. It will, if successfully promoted, allow us to exploit fully the advantages of the information age for the benefit of the whole community.
> 3. The Government is committed to the successful development and promotion of a framework within which electronic commerce can thrive. Electronic commerce, as indicated below, is crucial to the future growth and prosperity of both the national economy and our businesses. Although the prime economic driver for electronic commerce may currently lie with business-to-business transactions, it is clear that consumers (whether ordering books or arranging pensions) will also directly benefit.

13.60 Although the statement used the term 'electronic commerce', its contents were almost exclusively concerned with security issues:

> To achieve our goals, however, electronic commerce, and the electronic networks which it relies, have to be secure and trusted. Whether it be the entrepreneur E-mailing his sales information to a potential supplier or the citizen receiving private advice from their doctor; the communications need to be secure. In a recent DTI survey 69% of UK companies cited security as a major inhibitor to purchasing across Internet.

Security can have a number of components and the statement referred approvingly to BS7799, which was referred to as the 'national standard on information security'. As well as organisational and technical measures, however, the statement focussed on encryption policy. As discussed in Chapter 3, this has been, and remains, a contentious political issue and the paper was criticised widely as appearing to promote a scheme of mandatory key escrow.

13.61 The next significant event occurred in March 1999, when a Consultation Paper, 'Building Confidence in Electronic Commerce' was published. This indicated that 'The Government is committed to introducing legislation in the current Parliamentary session'. Comments were sought within a three-week period. Although cryptography policy again featured prominently in the document, significant provisions were also introduced concerning procedural issues of electronic commerce, specifically relating to the removal of requirements that contracts be concluded in writing or be accompanied by a signature.

13.62 The Consultation Paper was the subject of critical comment by the House of Commons Select Committee on Trade and Industry. 252 comments were made by other organisations. In July 1999 a further consultation document was published, 'Promoting Electronic Commerce'. Although a draft Bill (now referred to as the Electronic Communications Bill) was appended to this paper, the commitment to introduce legislation in the 1998–99 parliamentary session was abandoned, apparently because of refusal by the opposition to allow it to be certified as non-controversial and thereby permitted to continue its progress over two sessions. Comments this time were requested to be submitted by October 1999. A further report was tabled by the Select Committee in November 1999 and the Electronic Communications Bill was introduced in the House of Commons on 18 November receiving its Second Reading on 29 November 1999.

13.63 As the legislative proposals have developed, the main changes have been in respect of the controls imposed over those operating cryptographic services. Concerns were expressed in many quarters that those using encryption would be required to lodge copies of their keys with agencies, from where they might be passed on the law enforcement or national security agencies. It would appear that this is now off the legislative agenda. In a speech delivered in September 1999, Patricia Hewitt, the newly appointed Minister for Small Firms and E-Commerce, proclaimed:

> Let me confirm that mandatory key escrow is NOT part of the bill. Many of you will have taken part in the campaign against mandatory key escrow – the previous cross-party policy to coerce people to give copies of the keys to their encrypted mail to a third party. This issue assumed such importance

that the PIU set up a special taskforce to look at it. Back in May the PIU concluded that these plans were not going to work.

Let me repeat what the Prime Minister said last week:

'No company or individual will be forced, directly or indirectly, to escrow keys.'

The Electronic Communications Bill is not about key escrow. Mandatory key escrow is off the agenda.

13.64 The draft Bill contained extensive provisions relating to the circumstances under which law enforcement agencies could seek access to keys held by persons (TTPs) providing cryptography services. These provisions have been deleted from the Bill as tabled in Parliament, although it has been indicated that measures may be included in new Interception of Communications legislation being considered by the Home Office. For the Electronic Communications Bill, clause 13, headed 'Prohibition on key escrow requirements', states that no power shall be provided to 'impose a requirement on any person to deposit a key for electronic data with another person'.

13.65 The removal of the provisions relating to interception seems to have drawn the teeth from most of the opposition to the Bill, although this may well be transferred to the new Interception of Communications Bill. The remaining provisions have been generally welcomed, with Bill Gates, the President of Microsoft, referring to it as a 'model for Europe'. This may be somewhat exaggerated as, in many respects, the legislation provides only a framework which will require to be filled in by secondary legislation.

Scope of the Electronic Communications Bill

13.66 The Bill contains three parts. Part I contains provisions relating to the use of encryption, Part II is designed to facilitate electronic commerce, whilst Part III contains miscellaneous provisions mainly concerned with a change to the telecommunications licensing regime. This topic is largely outwith the scope of the present work, with the Bill trying to resolve a procedural problem which has been identified by Oftel. All telecommunications activities require to be conducted under the terms of a licence. Licences are divided into two categories, individual and class. Many class licences may apply to hundreds or even thousands of users. If the Director General of Telecommunications proposes to amend the terms of a class licence, this will require to be notified to the Competition Commission unless all licence holders indicate agreement to the change. Experience suggests that, with large numbers of licences, obtaining a 100% response rate is virtually impossible. Some licence holders may, unknown to the Director

General, have gone out of business or may simply fail to reply to communications. It is now proposed that the requirement to obtain approval prior to making a change be replaced by a provision that change may be made without reference to the Competition Commission where no licence holder has intimate objection to the proposal.

Cryptography service providers

13.67 As discussed above, the emergence of the concept of cryptographic service providers (often referred to as Trusted Third Parties (TTPs)) has been a major feature of discussions concerning the legal status of encryption. Although the European Electronic Signatures Directive and the Electronic Communications Bill strive to be technologically neutral and make no reference to any particular forms of encryption, both refer extensively to the role of certification agencies or of cryptography service providers in enhancing user confidence by verifying the identity and status of persons using encryption technology.

13.68 Part I of the Bill relates to the provision of 'cryptographic support services'. This term is defined in clause 6 as encompassing –

> ... any service which is provided to the senders or recipients of electronic communications, or to those storing electronic data, and is designed to facilitate the use of cryptographic techniques for the purpose of –
>
> (a) securing that such communications or data can be accessed, or can be put into an intelligible form, only by certain persons; or
> (b) securing that the authenticity or integrity of such communications or data is capable of being ascertained.

The service must either be provided from premises within the UK or be provided to persons carrying on a business in the UK. A German service provider marketing services to UK-based companies would come within the second element of this definition.

13.69 Anyone is entitled to establish a cryptography support service. Equally, there is no obligation imposed on users of encryption to involve such a service in their transactions. Especially in cases where parties have a background of previous dealings or operate as part of an EDI network, such third party involvement may well be rendered otiose.

13.70 At present, no restrictions – and virtually no legislation – applies to the use of encryption or cryptography services. Maintenance of the status quo would not justify such flagship legislation. What is envisaged in P I of the Bill is the establishment of a voluntary register of accredited cryptography service providers. Whilst the decision to seek registration will be voluntary, the intention is that the existence of such a scheme will promote public confidence in what must be regarded as an embryonic profession.

13.71 The Bill provides in clauses 2 and 3 that responsibility for the establishment of such a register is to vest in the Secretary of State (or such other body to whom performance of the task may be delegated). It has been indicated, however, that the intention is that the register should be operated on a voluntary basis. Clause 15 provides that the provisions will come into force on such day as may be fixed by Order but that if no Order is made within five years from the date of Royal Assent, the Order making power will lapse.

13.72 Government speakers in the Commons indicated a strong desire that a voluntary scheme should be introduced as soon as possible. Discussions are ongoing with the Alliance for Electronic Business, which has proposed a 'non-statutory self-regulating scheme (tScheme) for Trust services'. The scope of the proposal is described as being to 'operate and enforce a voluntary approval scheme for trust services', whilst the overall objective is to provide a mechanism that will:

•   set minimum criteria for trust and confidence;

•   be responsible for:

    – the approval of electronic trust services against those criteria,

    – the monitoring of approved services;

    – provide a means of redress where services fall below those criteria; and

•   thereby promote the benefits of using an approved electronic trust service.

The scheme will encompass:

•   the Electronic Signatures Directive notion of the discretionary voluntary accreditation scheme aiming at enhanced levels of certification service provision;

•   the UK Electronic Communication Bill notion of a register of approved providers of cryptography support services; and

•   a method of approving other trust services offered by organisations in addition to those which conform to both the European Signatures Directive definition of a Certification Service Provider and the Electronic Communication Bill definition of a Cryptography Support Service Provider.

13.73 The criteria which are to be applied in determining whether an applicant should be admitted to the register also awaits elucidation. An indication of the nature of the likely requirements can be found in Annex 2 of the draft Digital Signatures Directive (with which the Bill is designed to be compatible). This refers to the need for demonstrable reliability of the systems, technologies and personnel involved in the provision of the service, the acceptance of liability for losses caused through errors in the service provision and the observance of a proper degree of confidentiality regarding details of the customer's business. Further indication regarding the criteria which might be applied can again be taken from the Alliance for Electronic Business Scheme, which states that:

> It is anticipated that the criteria will address business, management, operational and technical issues necessary for approval. Criteria will relate to both the services offered and the organisations offering them and will be based as far as possible on existing criteria in the marketplace.
>
> The actual criteria used for assessment will be a selection of elements from publicly available, and wherever possible international, technical or management standards. (eg ISO 9000, BS 7799, X.509, FIPS 140; and from other appropriate criteria published by bodies such as FSA and OFTEL).
>
> In addition to adopting previously defined standards the organisation will, when necessary, create criteria not already existing in the marketplace. It is vital to the success of (the) scheme, and its take up by providers, that it does not duplicate existing approval and regulatory structures, but builds on their foundations.
>
> The selection of criteria, termed an Approval Profile, will be unique for each different type of service. Criteria will be selected by reference to specific versions of standards, and reviewed periodically to ensure that the most relevant and appropriate criteria are applied, as the standardisation process and services develop. A list of the criteria selected, including any necessary identifying publication information (eg dates, versions, etc.) will be maintained and publicly available.

13.74 It is clear from the proposal that there will be no single scheme of certification. Given the vast range of transactions that may be carried out electronically, such an approach is necessary and desirable. It is to be expected and hoped that standards will emerge over time to give appropriate guidance to the courts and other agencies regarding what reliance might reasonably be placed upon a particular form of certificate.

Electronic signatures

13.75 The involvement of a TTP clearly gives a greater measure of assurance concerning the reliability of an encrypted message. This is recognised in the European draft Digital Signature Directive, which refers to the notion of a 'qualified certificate'. This is defined as:

> A digital attestation which links a signature verification device to a person, confirms the identity of that person and meets the requirements laid down in Annex 1. (art 2(5))

The Annex refers to the items of information which must be provided in a digital attestation.

13.76 The directive continues to provide that a qualified certificate, which is issued by a certification service provider, may receive an enhanced legal status. Article 5 of the draft directive provides that signatures based on such a certificate are to be recognised as satisfying legal requirements for hand written signatures and are to be admissible as evidence in the same way as their hand written equivalents.

13.77 Once again, the Bill provides few detailed provisions regarding the implementation of the provisions. Clause 7 provides that:

> In any legal proceeding –
> (a) an electronic signature incorporated or logically associated with a particular electronic communication or with particular electronic data, and
> (b) the certification by any person of such a signature, shall each be admissible in evidence in relation to any question as to the authenticity of the communication or data or as to the integrity of the communication or data.

13.78 Such a provision will make little significant change to current practice, particularly in Scotland, where the trend in the law of evidence has been towards removing technical barriers to admissibility and leaving matters concerning the weight to be afforded to a particular piece of evidence to the court. More significant will be provisions in clause 8. This provides ministers (including Scottish ministers) with a general power to modify any statute or statutory instrument:

> in such manner as he may think fit for the purpose of authorising or facilitating the use of electronic communications or electronic storage (instead of other forms of communication or storage) for any purpose mentioned in subsection (2).
> (2) Those purposes are–

(a)   the doing of anything which under any such provisions is required to be or may be done or evidenced in writing or otherwise using a document, notice or instrument;
(b)   the doing of anything which under any such provisions is required to be or may be done by post or other specified means of delivery;
(c)   the doing of anything which under any such provisions is required to be or may be authorised by a person's signature or seal, or is required to be delivered as a deed or witnessed;

(d) the making of any statement or declaration which under any such provisions is required to be made under oath or to be contained in a statutory declaration;

(e) the keeping, maintenance or preservation, for the purposes or in pursuance of any such provisions, of any account, record, notice, instrument or other document;

(f) the provision, production or publication under any such provisions of any information or other matter;

(g) the making of any payment that is required to be or may be made under any such provisions.

13.79 The power is not to be invoked unless the minister is satisfied that the use of electronic communications provides at least an equal measure of certainty and security as can be garnered through the use of more traditional requirements.

13.80 A vast range of transactions might be affected by this power. It was indicated in Parliament that for England and Wales:

> The Lord Chancellor is exploring, with the assistance of the Law Commission and the Land Registry, what is necessary to allow conveyancing in particular to be done electronically.

13.81 Much publicity has been given to the recognition of electronic signatures, but the power will also extend to permitting firms to supply accounts in electronic form and to give shareholders notice of meetings by e-mail. The task of updating the statute book will be a massive one. It has been estimated that there are in the region of 40,000 references to paper signatures, documents and records. In some cases amendment might not be required. In the recent Scottish case of *Rollo v HM Advocate* 1996 SCCR 875, evidence relating to the appellant's involvement in a drug dealing had been discovered by police stored on a electronic notepad seized during a search conducted under a warrant empowering the recovery of any 'document directly or indirectly relating to, or connected with a transaction' (prohibited under the Misuse of Drugs Act 1971). Holding that the device in question was a document, Lord Milligan ruled that:

> the essential essence of a document is that it is something containing recorded information of some sort. It does not matter if, to be meaningful, the information requires to be processed in some way such as translation, decoding or electronic retrieval.

13.82 A similar conclusion was reached in the case of *Alliance and Leicester Building Society v Ghahremani* [1992] RVR 198, where the deletion of part of a word-processed file held on a computer was held to constitute contempt of court when this was done subsequent to the making of a court order for discovery of documents. Although these cases concerned the criminal law, there would appear no reason to doubt that information held on a computer storage device will be classed as a document for civil law purposes.

13.83 Concerns were expressed in Parliament that the provisions of clause 8 might be used to compel persons doing business with the government to engage in electronic communications. Subsection 6 provides, however, that any order made 'may not require the use of electronic communications or electronic storage for any purpose'.

Conclusions

13.84 There seems little doubt that, as the information society develops, more and more transactions will be conducted within an electronic environment. There is little doubt either that electronic documents and signatures can provide the same level of authenticity and durability as may be achieved using paper records. In some respects, what has been occurring in the legal debate concerning the recognition of electronic signatures is typical of many human reactions to information (and other forms of) technology. History is littered with examples of documents and signatures being forged. Whilst not welcomed, this appears to be accepted as a fact of life in an imperfect world. Where computers become involved, the demand sometimes appears to be that perfection should be attained.

13.85 In respect of the Electronic Communications Bill, the most significant impact may be seen in respect of the provisions allowing electronic communication of documents. In the public sector, the government has set targets for 25% of government services to be delivered electronically by 2001, 50% by 2005 and 100% by 2008. Another target is for 90% of low-value government procurement to be conducted electronically by April 2001. Whilst the removal of unnecessary legal barriers is to be welcomed, there are also concerns at the prospect of a world of information 'haves' and 'have nots'. When 90% of low value government contracts are awarded electronically, a supplier without access to the Internet will be at a considerable disadvantage. It is speculated that the Inland Revenue might encourage taxpayers to submit returns electronically. Whilst this may be justified on the basis of a reduction in processing costs, the losers may again be those without Internet access.

13.86 As indicated above, provisions relating to the interception and decryption of electronic communications sent through a TTP were dropped from the Electronic Communications Bill. It is anticipated that a further Bill will be brought forward amending the present law on interception of communications to make provision in this regard. Whether any such measures will be effective is perhaps open to doubt. The role of trusted third parties primarily arises where those communicating have no strong basis to trust each other. Whilst it may be debatable whether those conspiring to commit criminal or terrorist acts will necessarily trust each other, there is even less cause to speculate that they will trust some independent (and presumably law-abiding) agency.

Chapter 14

The consumer and electronic commerce

Introduction

14.0 Until the emergence of the Internet, international trade was largely the province of the commercial operator. Save for the few souvenirs and bottles of duty-free which a holidaymaker might bring back into the country, almost all of the average consumer's interactions with business would take place in the confines of a single country. The world is changing and the growth in electronic has transformed the situation, especially in relation to contracts for information products such as books, music CDs, software and increasingly also for other products. To a considerable extent, a global marketplace exists and for consumers armed with credit cards and Internet access, the location of a supplier becomes irrelevant. It is also increasingly the case that more sophisticated and potentially privacy threatening contracts may be entered into on an international basis – financial services, insurance etc. Sensitive data may be involved in many instances. More than 100 websites offer to supply Viagra tablets, other sites offer medical products, such as contact lenses, beta blockers and Prozac.

14.1 Since around the 1970s the notion of consumer protection has entered the legal lexicon. The unrestricted operation of the doctrine of freedom of contract, it is argued, produces unacceptable results where consumers are unable, either by reason of technical expertise or bargaining power, to negotiate in any meaningful fashion concerning the terms under which goods or services are supplied. All too often the choice is between accepting the supplier's terms and conditions or doing without the goods or services sought. In the attempt to strengthen the consumer's position the legislature has intervened, principally to lay down minimal levels of legal protection which must be provided in any consumer contract. Two European directives are of particular relevance in this field. The first, adopted in 1997 and requiring to be implemented in the member states by June 2000 is Directive 97/7 on 'the protection of consumers in respect of distance contracts' (the Distance Selling Directive). Given its date, the directive largely predates the growth in consumer transactions over the Internet but its general provisions are of considerable significance. More directly relevant is the proposal for a Directive on Electronic Commerce. This measure is expected to be adopted in early 2000 and contains a number of provisions which are designed to further the cause of consumer protection.

The Distance Selling Directive

14.2 The market for distance selling through catalogues is a well-established one, especially in remote areas where retail outlets are few and far between. The sector is particularly well established in the US and it is anticipated that businesses with experience of these forms of transactions will be well placed to benefit from the move to electronic commerce. Over the past decade, the telephone, fax machine and, most recently, e-mail and the WWW have been used to solicit consumer contracts. The directive applies to all forms of distance selling but contains some provisions relating specifically to the use of electronic communications. A number of these have been supplemented by the terms of the draft Electronic Commerce Directive. The preamble makes its rationale clear:

> Whereas the introduction of new technologies is increasing the number of ways for consumers to obtain information about offers anywhere in the Community and to place orders; whereas some Member States have already taken different or diverging measures to protect consumers in respect of distance selling, which has had a detrimental effect on competition between businesses in the internal market; whereas it is therefore necessary to introduce at Community level a minimum set of common rules in this area. (Recital 4)

14.3 The directive defines the term 'distance contract' as:

> Any contract concerning goods or services concluded between a supplier and a consumer under an organized distance sales or service-provision scheme run by the supplier, who, for the purpose of the contract, makes exclusive use of one or more means of distance communication up to and including the moment at which the contract is concluded. (art 2(1))

Annex 1 contains an illustrative list of communication technologies. In addition to traditional categories, such as letters and press advertisements, reference is made to the use of systems of videotext, electronic mail and facsimile transmission.

14.4 The directive's provisions commence at the stage where the consumer's entry into a contract is solicited with its principal requirement being that promotional techniques must pay due regard to the consumer's privacy, conform to the 'principles of good faith' and provide 'clear and unambiguous information' regarding the nature of any product or service, its price and the identity of its supplier. In the case of telephone communication, the supplier is obliged to make its identity, and the fact that the call is commercial in nature, clear at the commencement of a call.

14.5 The directive also provides that two forms of technology – automated calling systems and fax machines – may be used only with the prior consent of the consumer: what might be referred to as an 'opt-in' system. Automated calling systems involve the use of a computer system to call numbers and on answer play a pre-recorded message to the recipient. Although reportedly used extensively in the US, such technologies are effectively prohibited in the UK, as their use would require a licence from Oftel which has indicated objections to the practice. In the case of other forms of communication, it is provided that these are to be made only when the consumer has not indicated a clear objection to receipt of solicitations. The operation of an 'opt-out' system would be compatible with this requirement.

14.6 The rationale behind the selection of specific prohibited technologies is not clear. Recital 17 of the directive asserts that the consumer's right to privacy should extend to 'freedom from certain particularly intrusive means of communication'. It is difficult to argue, however, that a pre-recorded telephone message is intrinsically more intrusive than other forms of telephone canvassing. An aspect of the technology which has drawn criticism is that once the message has started playing it cannot be stopped. Although the recipient may put his or her phone down, the message will continue, effectively stopping any other calls being made to or from the recipient's telephone. Incidents have been reported where a pre-recorded call has been received as the recipient was about to make an emergency call. Unsolicited faxes also are unlikely to be seen as invasive of privacy and a perhaps more persuasive basis for restricting these lies in the fact that the recipient of a fax incurs cost in terms of the paper and ink used for its reproduction. This was possibly more of a factor with previous generations of fax machines which required the use of special (and expensive) paper.

Unsolicited e-mails – the problem of spam

14.7 If fax transmissions are restricted, either on privacy protection or cost grounds, it would appear that a similar case could be made out for e-mail messages. The increasing commercialisation of the Internet has let to a massive increase in the practice generally referred to as 'spamming'. It has been estimated that in the US some 3.4 trillion (equivalent to 9.4 billion per day) e-mails were transmitted in 1998. Of these, 2.7 trillion were classed as commercial in nature, 96% of which could be characterised as involving spam. To give a point of comparison, the US postal service carried 107 billion letters and parcels in the same year.

14.8 Spamming can take two main forms. One of the largest and oldest components on the Internet is the collection of Usenet discussion groups. Running into tens of thousands, these provide a forum for on-line discussion on every conceivable topic (and a few fairly inconceivable ones). In essence, Usenet is a form of e-mail with the distinction being that messages are sent to subscribers to a group rather than to individuals. A message sent to one group may readily be copied – a practice referred to as 'cross-posting' – to others. Although this is a quite legitimate practice when the content of a message might be of interest to a range of readers, the technology is also vulnerable to those who wish to post commercial communications across a wide range of unrelated groups. At its height it was estimated that:

> spam posts had risen to the point they were actually out numbering legitimate Usenet posts. On an average day where 500,000 new messages were being sent via Usenet propagation, over 300,000 were spam messages.

A daily full feed of news is greater than 9 gigabytes of material. News is resent, propagated, by many servers. If 30% of Usenet propagation is comprised of spam, thousands of servers are routinely loading the Internet with 3+ Gigabytes of useless material each day.

14.9 A US husband and wife law firm, Canter and Seigel, have gone down in Internet history as the first persons to engage in spamming. Their crime was to post messages advertising their services as immigration lawyers to virtually every newsgroup in existence. Retaliation took a variety of forms, including the mail-bombing of their account by aggrieved users. Most Internet service providers have policies designed to deter subscribers from engaging in spamming and evidence of such activity will result in denial of service. Even at today's reduced levels, however, it is calculated that some 30% of articles and 20% of volume on Usenet are made up of spammed posts.

14.10 A factor exacerbating the problems of spam is the proliferation of Internet service providers providing individuals with access to the Internet. Most department stores now offer some form of Internet access, often free of charge. It is very easy for a person to set up an account with a service provider, engage in spamming and, if the account should be terminated, transfer activities to another site. It is also possible to send messages from Internet cafés without the requirement that the user enter into any form of contract with a service provider.

14.11 A further form of spamming involves commercial communications being sent by e-mail to large numbers of individuals. Often, e-mail details can be culled from newsgroup postings using software packages to automate the process. A number of organisations offer to supply lists of e-mail addresses, frequently divided into categories so that, for example, somebody wishing to promote child care products could obtain lists of those who have contributed to newsgroups discussing family-related matters.

14.12 Beyond the fact that commercial communications sent over the Internet can reach large numbers of people, the great attraction for the promoter is the low cost. In terms of the connection time required, it takes very little longer to send a message to 10,000 recipients than to a single person. Costs will, however, be incurred by the 10,000 recipients who will often have to pay telephone and Internet connection charges. In terms of impact upon the recipient, unsolicited commercial e-mail is today perhaps more inconvenient and expensive than unsolicited faxes.

14.13 The Distance Selling Directive makes no explicit reference to e-mail, a result perhaps explained by the fact that it was first drafted in 1992. E-mail solicitations will have to conform with the provisions of art 10(2), referred to above, which require that messages not be sent to a consumer who has expressed the clear wish not to receive such communications. The draft Electronic Commerce Directive is more explicit, providing in art 7 that:

> Member States shall lay down in their legislation that unsolicited commercial communication by electronic mail must be clearly and unequivocally identifiable as such as soon as it is received by the recipient.

14.14 This provision is comparable to the distance selling provisions requiring that the commercial nature of telephone selling should be made clear at the outset of a call. In the case of e-mail, an indication in the header of a message would appear to be necessary, allowing the user to decide whether to read further. In many cases, however, such notification will not save the consumer on-line time and costs. Many e-mail packages will download all the text of waiting messages before presenting the results to the user who may then choose to read messages and compose any replies off line. The more effective remedy is undoubtedly to stop messages being sent in the first place. Here the draft directive provides that:

> ... Member States shall take measures to ensure that service providers undertaking unsolicited commercial communications by e-mail consult regularly and respect the opt-out registers in which national persons not wanting to receive such commercial communications can register themselves.

14.15 Implementation of this provision would require the establishment of an e-mail preference system along the lines of the current telephone and mailing preference systems. Although this provision makes explicit reference to an 'opt-out' system, in its second consultation paper on implementation of the Distance Selling Directive, the Department of Trade and Industry suggest that the directive leaves it open to member states to adopt either an 'opt-out' or an 'opt-in' approach.

> The Government appreciates that there are arguments for both opt-out and opt-in approaches to unsolicited e-mail, and we would welcome views on either option. There are two alternative draft implementing Regulations, which implements Article 10.2 in respect of e-mail by means of opt-in and opt-out.

The paper continues to identify a variety of approaches already adopted within the EU:

> Some countries already ban unsolicited commercial e-mail (eg Austria). The draft EU E-commerce directive does not prevent this, and is neutral on opt-in or opt-out, leaving the Distance Selling Directive to regulate this. However, where Member States permit such e-mail, the draft E-commerce directive requires them to ensure that service providers established on their territory make unsolicited e-mail clearly identifiable as such as soon as it shows up in the recipient's in-tray, in recognition of the additional communication costs of the recipient and the need to promote responsible filtering initiatives by industry. We understand that a number of Member States (eg Austria, Italy, Germany and Sweden) either have or are likely to implement the e-mail provision of the Distance Selling Directive by opt-in, although others (eg Belgium) have gone for opt-out.

14.16 Significant UK precedents exist for the implementation of an opt-out scheme in the form of the mailing and telephone preference services. The latter operates on a statutory basis in accordance with the requirements of the European Directive concerning the processing of personal data and protection of privacy in the telecommunications sector. Enforcement is in the hands of the Data Protection Commissioner. The Direct Marketing Association has indicated the intention to adopt a voluntary e-mail preference service based on a scheme operating in the US – generally considered to be the home of 'spam'. Implementation of the directive, however, will again serve to establish a statutory scheme.

14.17 Although the DTI paper identifies benefits and disadvantages from both opt-in and opt-out schemes, the balance of the argument appears to lie in favour of an opt-in approach. One point which may carry considerable weight is the suggestion that attempts to opt out of the receipt of junk e-mail are sometimes misused by unscrupulous sellers. Sending a request not to receive e-mail indicates that the address used is accurate and in use, factors which make it valuable to the compilers and users of e-mail lists.

14.18 A further practical difficulty arises from the fact that many e-mail solicitations originate from outwith the EU. Although a breach of one or more national data protection or distance selling regimes may well have occurred, it is unlikely that jurisdiction can be effectively claimed unless the advertiser has an establishment or resources within the EU.

The provision of information to the consumer

14.19 Assuming that discussions between supplier and consumer extend beyond the initial contact, there is clear need to ensure that the latter is made aware of the terms and conditions associated with a particular contract. The directive provides for two approaches, the first which is outwith the scope of the present study, requiring the grant of a 'cooling-off' period following the conclusion of the contract. More relevant are provisions requiring that the consumer be given information as to terms. Article 4 specifies the items of information which must be given. These relate primarily to the identity of the supplier, the nature and cost of the goods or services and any arrangements for delivery. These are relatively easily satisfied in traditional mail order or catalogue sales, but in respect of electronic communications it is stated that:

> Whereas information disseminated by certain electronic technologies is often ephemeral in nature insofar as it is not received on a permanent medium; whereas the consumer must therefore receive written notice in good time of the information necessary for proper performance of the contract.

14.20 Whilst the comment regarding the transient nature of information displayed on, for example, a website is basically true, the text of an e-mail message can be as locatable as any written message. It would seem somewhat Luddite were a party engaging in electronic commerce to be required to supply confirmation details on paper. Article 5 of the directive requires that conformation be supplied in writing or 'in another durable medium available and accessible to him'.

14.21 It may be that the transmission of an e-mail which may be stored on the consumer's computer would satisfy this requirement. This is the view which has provisionally been adopted by the Department of Trade and Industry, which has commented in its second consultation paper:

> We consider that confirmation by electronic mail would meet the definition of confirmation in 'another durable medium available and accessible to [the consumer]', where the order has been made by means of e-mail.

The Electronic Commerce Directive

14.22 Within the European Union, a proposal for a directive on 'legal aspects of electronic commerce' was introduced in November 1998. The proposal was debated in the European Parliament and, following its comments, an amended proposal was introduced in September 1999. The scope of the measure is broad ranging. It applies to what are referred to as 'Information Society Services'. These are defined as:

> any service normally provided for remuneration, at a distance, by electronic means and at the individual request of a recipient of services.

14.23 For the purposes of this definition three key requirements apply:

- 'at a distance' means that the service is provided without the parties being simultaneously present;

- 'by electronic means' means that the service is sent initially and received at its destination by means of electronic equipment for the processing (including digital compression) and storage of data, and entirely transmitted, conveyed and received by wire, by radio, by optical means or by other electromagnetic means;

- 'at the individual request of a recipient of services' means that the service is provided through the transmission of data on individual request.

14.24 It is specifically provided that the definition is not to apply to radio or television broadcasting services. A television 'shopping channel' will, therefore, not be governed by the directive. Annex five provides a further, indicative, list of excluded services. These serve essentially to illustrate the three fundamental requirements of the legislation, although there appear to be a number of anomalous situations.

In some cases limitation of the scope of the directive is explicable by virtue of the fact that other items of legislation will cover particular forms of transaction but others are more difficult to explain.

14.25 One of the major topics covered by the draft directive relates to the topic of formation of contract. This was discussed in Chapter 13 and the issues identified there will be relevant also in consumer contracts. The other topic which raises specific consumer questions applies where buyer and seller are located in different legal jurisdictions.

Choice of law issues

14.26 As has been stated frequently, location is irrelevant in electronic commerce. It is also the case that the largest body of sites offering to supply goods or services is in the US. A consumer located in the UK and wishing to engage in electronic commerce is almost inevitably going to require to deal with US-based companies. International trade, which hitherto has been almost exclusively the preserve of large commercial operators, is assuming a significant consumer dimension.

14.27 In any situation where buyer and seller are located in different jurisdictions, two key legal issues will arise. The first is to determine which legal system will govern the transaction and the second to determine which courts will be competent to hear disputes arising from the transaction. In many cases it will be the case that the parties make explicit contractual provision for both matters. In a contract between parties in Scotland and France, for example, it might be provided that French law will govern the transaction but that disputes may be raised in the French or the Scottish courts, the latter being required to decide the case according to the relevant principles of French law.

14.28 In general, parties have (subject to the legal systems chosen having some connection with the subject matter of the contract) complete freedom to determine choice of law issues. Different rules apply where consumers are involved. Problems arise also where the parties fail to make explicit provision for issues of jurisdiction. In this case the matter may fall to be decided by the courts.

14.29 As discussed above in the context of contract formation, the question when and where a contract is concluded is a major factor in determining which legal system is to govern the transaction. Where transactions are conducted over the Internet, the question is not always easy to answer. The Global Top Level Domain name .com gives no indication where a business is located. Even where the name uses a country code such as .de or .uk there is no guarantee that the undertaking is established in that country. It is relatively common practice, based in part upon security concerns, to keep web servers geographically separate from the physical undertaking. A website might, for example, have an address in the German (.de) domain. Its owner, however, might be a UK-registered company.

14.30 The question whether an Internet based business can be regarded as having a 'branch, agency or establishment' in all the countries from which its facilities may be accessed is uncertain. The OECD has pointed out, in the context of tax harmonisation, that the notion of permanent establishment, which is of major importance in determining whether an undertaking is liable to national taxes, may not be appropriate for electronic commerce.

14.31 Within Europe, two international agreements, the Brussels and Rome Conventions presently make special provision for consumer contracts. The latter provides that a supplier with a 'branch, agency or establishment' in the consumer's country of residence is to be considered as domiciled there. Further, consumers may choose to bring actions in either their country of domicile or that of the supplier, whilst actions against the consumer may be brought only in the consumer's country of domicile.

14.32 The Brussels Convention builds on the Rome Convention's provisions and provides that an international contract may not deprive the consumer of 'mandatory rights' operating in the consumer's country of domicile. The scope of mandatory rights is not clear cut but, given the emphasis placed on the human rights dimension in many international instruments dealing with data protection, it is argued that any attempt contractually to deprive consumers of rights conferred under the Council of Europe Convention and the EU Directive would be declared ineffective on this basis.

14.33 More recent developments may complicate matters. The draft Electronic Commerce Directive provides that transactions entered into by electronic means should be regulated by the law of the state in which the supplier is established. This approach is justified on the basis of supporting the development of the new industries, Recital 8 stating that:

> ... in order to effectively guarantee freedom to provide services and legal certainty for suppliers and recipients of services, such Information Society services should only be subject to the law of the Member State in which the service provider is established.

14.34 At the same time, however, the Commission are proposing, in the form of a regulation 'on jurisdiction and the recognition and enforcement of judgments in civil and commercial matters', amendments to the Brussels and Rome Conventions which would have the effect of subjecting all consumer contracts to the law of the consumer's domicile. This approach is justified on the basis that the consumer is regarded as the weaker party in any contract with a business organisation.

14.35 There appears to be an inescapable conflict between choice of law provisions designed to favour the development of electronic commerce by making more predictable the nature of the liabilities incurred by service providers and giving priority to the interests of consumers by maximising their access to local courts and tribunals. The draft regulation states that:

> The Commission has noted that the wording of Article 15 has given rise to certain anxieties among part of the industry looking to develop electronic commerce. These concerns relate primarily to the fact that companies engaging in electronic commerce will have to contend with potential litigation in every Member State, or will have to specify that their products or services are not intended for consumers domiciled in certain Member States.

14.36 The intention was announced to review the operation of art 15 two years after the regulation's entry into force. In the shorter term, public hearings on the subject were announced and were held in Brussels in November 1999. The hearings attracted an audience of several hundred persons and produced several hundred pages of comments and suggestions. No consensus was – or perhaps could be – reached and the position remains one where different Commission Directorates appear to be promoting different policies.

Alternative dispute resolution

14.37 One possible palliative for jurisdictional problems is to try to obviate the need for formal legal proceedings. Two provisions in the Electronic Commerce Directive seek to facilitate this. Article 16 requires member states and the Commission to encourage the drawing up at Community level of codes of conduct designed to contribute to the implementation of the substantive provisions of the directive. Such codes, which will be examined by the Commission to ensure their compatibility with Community law, might provide a valuable unifying force throughout the EU. Article 17 obliges member states to:

> ... ensure that, in the event of disagreement between an Information Society service provider and its recipient, their legislation allows the

effective use of out of court schemes for dispute settlement, including appropriate electronic means.

14.38 Although a number of on-line dispute resolution services have been established, these have mainly been in the US and do not appear to have attracted significant custom – one site was even reduced to offering parties payment in order to induce them to use its facilities. In the UK the 'Which Web Trader' scheme, operated by the Consumers Association, requires participating traders to observe a code of practice but, in the event of a dispute with a consumer, makes it clear that recourse will have to be sought through the courts.

Liability of intermediary service providers

14.39 Almost invariably, a contract concluded or performed over the Internet will require the intervention of parties other than those directly involved with the contract. A number of Internet service providers may be involved in the transmission and delivery of communications. Again, third parties may provide computer storage space for a supplier's website. A further and more complex relationship may occur when an organisation provides a 'portal' through which users may be directed to a range of independent electronic commerce sites. Examples, some of which have been referred to in previous chapters, include *The Times* newspaper with its 'Trading Place' network of e-commerce suppliers, the Egg credit card company with its 'egg free' shopping zone and Amazon.com, which is increasingly trying to position itself as a one-stop shop by supplementing its own extensive list of offerings with links to third-party suppliers.

14.40 In such situations the issue may arise to what extent a host or portal operator will be liable for the acts or omissions of suppliers advertising on its facilities. The terms and conditions associated with the Egg site note that:

> The Egg Shopping Zone provides links which enable you to easily access retail websites operated by parties other than Egg. Egg does not control these retail websites and is not responsible for their contents. Egg cannot be held responsible in any way as to the content, reliability, quality, or fitness for purpose of any services, products, or information provided by third parties (this provision does not affect the Internet guarantee available to Egg Card holders when the Egg Card is used to pay for products and services in the Egg Shopping Zone).

Such disclaimers appear to be commonplace. Although the Mail Order Protection Scheme operating in the UK provides protection to consumers who order goods or services advertised in a newspaper or magazine by providing a right of recourse against the newspaper in respect of distance contracts entered into as a result of an advertisement published in the newspaper, this is a voluntary scheme and, to date, and has no electronic commerce equivalent.

14.41 The draft Electronic Commerce Directive contains provisions limiting the liability of what are referred to as intermediary service providers. Article 12 provides that an Internet service provider will not incur liability (except in respect of injunctions prohibiting the carriage of certain materials) in respect of the contents of material transmitted over the service where it provides merely a conduit for transmissions initiated and received by third parties. The immunity extends to the situation where the service provider makes transient copies of information for the purpose of its operations.

Conclusion

14.42 There seems little doubt that the level of consumer transactions conducted over the Internet will increase significantly over the coming years. The days are past when international trade was the province of merchants. Instead of 10,000 copies of a bestselling book being imported into the UK in a large container on a ship, 10,000 envelopes may make their way through the postal system to 10,000 individual consumers. As will be discussed in the following chapter, this phenomenon poses significant challenges to the tax authorities.

14.43 In order to increase consumer confidence in electronic commerce, there is need to ensure that appropriate legal rights are developed and, perhaps more important, that mechanisms exist for the redress of problems. As indicated above, it may well be that these will operate on an extra-legal basis. In particular, the involvement of large and reputable organisations to stand behind electronic transactions will provide significant consumer reassurance. One question may be whether this will come about through the entry into the electronic market of existing 'High Street' names or whether purely on-line business – such as Amazon will come to play the role. Sites such as Amazon, which initially supplied only a limited range of goods or services, now appear to be positioning themselves as 'one-stop' shops providing a vast range of products either themselves or through links to other operators.

Chapter 15

Tax and the Internet

Introduction

15.0 Although few things in life are inevitable, our exposure to death and taxes is generally claimed to constitute an exception to the general rule. Michael Faraday is reported to have answered a question concerning the utility of electricity: 'Sir, I do not know what it is good for. But of one thing I am quite certain, some day you will tax it.' As the scale of Internet usage and of electronic commerce grows, so attention is increasingly being paid to tax implications. The factor complicating the assessment and collection of taxes is (at least potentially) the global nature of electronic commerce. The question therefore arises where a business is to be regarded as established for fiscal purposes?

Principles of tax law

15.1 Although every state maintains its own system of taxation, considerable international harmonisation already exists, most notably in the form of the OECD Model Tax Convention. This provides the basis for more than 1,500 bilateral treaties between states providing for tax arrangements regarding each other's nationals. An OECD 'Discussion Paper on Taxation Issues' prepared by its Committee on Fiscal Affairs identified 'generally accepted tax principles of neutrality, efficiency, certainty, simplicity, effectiveness, fairness and flexibility' and affirmed that these should also apply in regimes established to deal with the new world of electronic commerce.

15.2 A similar view has been expressed in the UK in a joint policy paper prepared by the Inland Revenue and HM Customs and Excise. This indicated approval of the proposition that UK businesses required:

- certainty about tax rules;
- neutrality between electronic and conventional commerce;
- no double or unintentional non-taxation;

281

- compliance costs should be as low as possible;

- no new taxes on electronic commerce; and

- the use of modern technology by our tax administrations to improve the service they offer their customers.

15.3 This view was restated in *Electronic Commerce: The UK's Taxation Agenda*, published by the Inland Revenue and HM Customs and Excise in November 1999. This identified three areas where electronic commerce and communications offered both opportunities and posed challenges to tax authorities:

- tax administration;

- compliance and tax evasion issues;

- taxation rules per se.

15.4 Little consideration needs to be given to the first of these topics. It is not possible at present for individuals and companies to submit tax returns in electronic format. The future may bring the possibility of submitting tax returns electronically and the – perhaps not entirely welcome – prospect of taxpayers being able to engage in e-mail discussions with the tax authorities.

15.5 The remaining topics raise some issues of principle although most problems may be identified at the practical level. In most respects it is argued that the application of traditional provisions of tax law to electronic commerce will provide appropriate treatment for electronic commerce. The Inland Revenue have commented that:

> The Government does not believe that it is necessary at this stage to make any major changes to existing tax legislation and regulations or to introduce new taxes.

15.6 The notion that businesses should not be fiscally penalised for engaging in electronic commerce is one which receives widespread recognition. The United States Congress passed in 1998 the somewhat portentously titled 'Internet Tax Freedom Act'. Although much media publicity concerning the measure spoke in terms of a tax-free regime in cyberspace, the reality was somewhat less dramatic, with the statute restricting itself to a prohibition against the imposition of any new state or local taxation, either upon Internet access or which imposed multiple or discriminatory taxes on electronic commerce. As will be discussed below, the future of the tax moratorium is unclear, with a number of states expressing concern at the impact of electronic commerce on their tax revenues.

15.7 Whilst few changes may be required in relation to the principles of taxation policy, a number of issues may provide problems. Two types of tax can be identified. Direct taxes are imposed upon an individual or a company's income and capital. Indirect taxes are levied upon consumption, the most obvious example in the UK being the system of value added tax or VAT. Over the past 20 years there has been a significant shift from reliance on direct taxation to indirect taxation in part, on the basis that such taxes are seen as more socially progressive and easier to collect. As will be discussed, the emergence of the Internet is challenging the effectiveness of indirect tax regimes and might conceivably result in a reversal of the trend in tax policy.

Direct and indirect taxation

15.8 In most countries citizens are liable for payment of a range of direct and indirect taxes. In respect of income tax, perhaps the best known form of direct taxation, the emergence of the Internet will, especially for employed persons taxed under the PAYE system, have no significant effect in respect of liabilities. More difficult issues will arise in respect of direct taxation imposed upon businesses and individuals who generate income in respect of operations undertaken in two or more countries. Two issues arise. The first concerns the division between taxes based on the source of income and upon the residence of the taxpayer and the second concerns the issue where a business may be considered to be established?

Source and residence taxation

15.9 In the situation where income is earned in one country by an individual resident or undertaking established in another, the question inevitably arises where taxes fall due to be paid? Resolution of this issue is the prime rationale behind the raft of bilateral tax conventions negotiated under the auspices of the OECD Model Tax Convention. These typically identify their purpose as 'the avoidance of double taxation and the prevention of fiscal evasion'. Two approaches are possible, providing for income to be charged either on the basis of its source or the residence of the individual or organisation concerned. In the situation where there is an approximate balance of income flow between countries, there is little financial consequence whether income is taxed on the basis of source or residence, although matters become more difficult when this is not the case.

Establishment of electronic providers

15.10 In the situation where a person or business established in one country earns income in another, it is apparent that there will be two countries with a potential interest in taxing income. This might be taxed either at the point and in the country where it is earned or in the country of residence. One point which might be taken into account is that the rules of private international law do not permit enforcement of national tax obligations in another country. Different countries adopt different approaches and the prime purpose of tax treaties is to ensure that double taxation does not occur. Article 7 of the OECD Model Tax Convention provides that:

> The profits of an enterprise of a Contracting State shall be taxable only in that state unless the enterprise carries on business in the other Contracting State through a permanent establishment situated therein.

15.11 The notion of 'permanent establishment' is defined in art 5. It includes places of management, branches, offices, factories and workshops but specifically excludes:

> The use of facilities solely for the purpose of storage, display or delivery of goods or merchandise belonging to the enterprise;
> The maintenance of a stock of goods or merchandise belonging to the enterprise solely for the purpose of storage, display or delivery.

15.12 In the situation where a website permits customers to download data such as software, audio or visual works, the question may arise whether the database can be considered as a 'stock of goods or merchandise'. The commentary on the convention indicates that the exceptions (six in total) seek to distinguish activities which are preparatory or auxiliary to the purpose of a business from those which are more integral in their nature and significance. The OECD's Committee on Fiscal Affairs has undertaken to give more precise guidance concerning the application of art 5 within the context of electronic commerce. It is unclear, for example, whether maintaining a website in a particular jurisdiction to which orders for goods or services might be submitted would class as a permanent establishment. The activity might be regarded as coming within one or both of the exceptions listed above, but appears to be integral to the seller's business. Further complexities can be identified:

> ... a server may be located in a building situated in a country where the enterprise has no other presence. Alternatively, it could be located on a portable computer used in different places within that building or moved from city to city by an itinerant employee, Further difficulties would arise where a number of mirror sites on different servers located in different

countries would be used so that a customer could be directed to any site for any function depending on electronic traffic.

15.13 Many of these possibilities exist already. With the reduction in telecommunications costs, many global businesses routinely switch customers' telephone calls to an office in a convenient (for the business) time zone. Anyone, for example, wishing to book a British Airways plane ticket between Glasgow and London and telephoning the airline outwith UK business hours may find the call dealt with by an agent in the US or India. Again, it is common for popular websites offering users the possibility to download materials to maintain facilities in a range of countries. An example of the international potentialities of even a comparatively simple-seeming electronic transaction can be seen in the following example, involving a French company specialising in the supply of food products such as wine from Cahors and nougat from Montelimar. It is reported that:

> The site has an intercontinental architecture: stock and order management activities and supplier relationship management are situated in France: the import/export organisation is based in Hong Kong for tax reasons and the Web pages are also created in Hong Kong, 4 times more cheaply than elsewhere (slightly under 3 Ecus, as against 10 Ecus in France or the United States) . . . the site is hosted by an American server in Arizona essentially for reasons connected with bandwidth, freedom of encryption and the securitization of card payments. . . . The orders are delivered throughout the world by UPS.

15.14 Although all of the jurisdictional and taxation issues in this example are doubtless capable of resolution, it does appear that food shopping has never been so complex. Faced with the flexibility which the Internet provides it is to be expected that 'street-wise' traders will lose little time in structuring their electronic businesses in such a way as to minimise their liability for income tax.

Indirect taxes – taxes on consumption

15.15 The OECD has estimated that 30% of its member states' tax income now comes from indirect taxes. Two main forms of indirect taxation can be identified. Within Europe and all of the members of the OECD other than Australia and the US systems of value added tax operate. In the two other countries the system of sales tax applies. Additionally, of course, certain forms of goods will attract excise taxes upon being imported into a country. Principal examples will include alcohol and cigarettes.

15.16 In the situation where supplier and consumer are located in the same jurisdiction, the fact that a transaction is entered into or performed electronically should not impact upon liability for tax. More difficult issues arise where transactions occur across borders. This has been an issue of some significance in the US where each of the states possesses the freedom to impose sales tax on goods supplied for use or consumption within its territory. The tax collection structure can indeed devolve to the level of local communities to the extent that some 2,300 local taxes exist. Faced with the problems for businesses of dealing with 50 different state laws, the Uniform Commercial Code was drawn up in 1898. Amended on many subsequent occasions, it provides a common set of principles which, when adopted in State law, ensures a uniform regulatory structure across the states. Interstate commerce is regulated at the federal level, with the US constitution authorising Congress to 'regulate Commerce with foreign nations and among the several States'. In the case of *Freeman v Hewitt* 329 US 249 the Supreme Court ruled that:

> State taxation falling on interstate commerce ... can only be justified as designed to make such commerce bear a fair share of the cost of the local government whose protection it enjoys.

15.17 In the case of *National Bellas Hess, Inc v Department of Revenue of the State of Illinois* 386 US 753 the Supreme Court confirmed that this prohibited a state from requiring a mail order business established outwith its boundaries to collect and account for taxes due on purchases made by its citizens. The issue returned to the Supreme Court in 1992 in the case of *Quill Corp v North Dakota* 504 US 298 (1992). Once again, the constitutionality of a state tax law was at issue. The tax required to be collected and remitted by every 'retailer maintaining a place of business' in North Dakota. The word 'retailer' is defined as encompassing 'every person who engages in regular or systematic solicitation of a consumer market in the state'. It was argued on behalf of the North Dakota government that this definition was capable of applying to any organisation which advertised goods or services to its citizens. In the particular case this would apply to mail order sales but the principle would also clearly extend to electronic commerce. The Supreme Court of North Dakota refused to follow the case of *Bellas Hess,* arguing that 'the tremendous social, economic, commercial and legal innovations of the past quarter century have rendered its holding obsolete'. In particular it was argued that mail order sales had transformed from 'a relatively inconsequential market niche in 1967' to a market worth $183.3bn in 1989.

15.18 By a majority, the Supreme Court affirmed its earlier ruling in *Bellas Hess.* Whilst it recognised that a physical connection between a company and a state was not required to subject a corporation to state law, the constitutional prohibition against measures which might impede interstate commerce remained applicable to prohibit the imposition of an obligation to collect and remit sales and use taxes. It was suggested that the matter might be addressed by Congress, something that might appear a reasonable step given estimates that the annual loss of revenue to the states amounted to some $3.2bn. To date, however, no action has been taken and the enactment of the Internet Tax Freedom Act has, if anything, signalled a move in the opposite direction. The legislation provided for a two-year moratorium on the imposition of new state taxes. Proposals have been tabled in 1999 which would have the effect of making the moratorium permanent. Significantly, the proposal was initiated by a Senator from the State of New Hampshire, which is one of only two states which does not impose any form of sales tax. The continuance of the moratorium might well have the effect of making such a location economically attractive to organisations wishing to develop an e-commerce business.

European elements

15.19 To a considerable extent, the problems identified in the US with its systems of sales tax do not occur under the European Value Added Tax model. As indicated above, this style of tax is adopted by the overwhelming majority of OECD members. As opposed to the concept of a sales tax, which is levied once at the point of supply to the end user, VAT is chargeable at all stages throughout a supply chain. If a supply chain A-B-C-D can be identified, A will charge VAT on the supply of the goods or services to B. B will be entitled to reclaim this amount and must in turn charge VAT on the supply to C. The process will be repeated by C, with the effect that ultimately only the end user, D, will bear the cost of the tax.

15.20 As with other aspects of electronic commerce, a vital question will relate to the jurisdiction within which tax liabilities will arise. In the European Union, the 6th VAT Directive establishes a common set of rules for determining where tax liabilities will arise. Generally, the applicable regime will be that in which the supplier is established. Cultural, artistic and entertainment services are liable for tax at the place of performance, whilst services relating to intangibles or intellectual services, a concept which includes agreements relating to copyright, licensing or professional services are liable for VAT in the jurisdiction where the customer is established.

15.21 As has been discussed above, the concept of establishment can raise complex issues in the information age. As is pointed out by the OECD, with the liberalisation of telecommunications regimes, a large number of companies can offer telecommunications services in a country without necessarily being resident in that territory. Until the loophole was closed in 1997, it was indeed the case that Internet service providers (such as CompuServe and America Online) based outside the EU were not responsible for charging VAT to their customers, thereby obtaining a significant competitive advantage over EU-based providers. With effect from 1 July 1997, the rules relating to VAT liability in respect of telecommunications services within the EU have provided for the location of the customer to be the determinant factor in assessing liability to VAT.

15.22 One significant issue which arises in the EU concerns the distinction between goods and services in the case where these are provided by a supplier established outside the EU. An example would be the provision of books or software from a supplier established in the US. Where goods are imported into the EU, there is liability to pay the VAT due in the country of importation. There are thus no issues of principle, although concern has been expressed at the ability of customs authorities to cope with volume of transactions. The relevant international instrument concerned with such issues is the Kyoto Convention on the simplification and harmonization of Customs procedures prepared by the World Customs Organization. Discussions are currently taking place with a view to adopting provisions to deal with the expected upsurge in the number of small volume imports arising from the growth in electronic commerce. In a number of cases, agreements have been made between the customs authorities and package delivery firms under which the latter agree to notify the authorities of the value of goods being imported and the identity of the recipient in return for a guarantee of speedy processing of materials at the point of importation

15.23 More difficult issues arise with regard to the importation of services. At present, an EU consumer obtaining a service from an external supplier is not liable to pay VAT. A Commission Communication explains that this situation has arisen because the volume and value of such transactions has historically been very low. This situation is changing, not least because many information-based products, such as software and audio works, can readily be supplied in digital form over the Internet. The strange situation therefore arises that a consumer purchasing a disk-based copy of a software program from a US-based supplier will be liable to pay VAT on the importation, whilst a more Internet-wise consumer can obtain exactly the same result through downloading the software without incurring liability to tax. The Commission has commented that:

> Turn-over relating to EU final consumption attributable to e-commerce (i.e. delivered to private individuals as opposed to companies) is difficult to estimate. This may reach a figure of 5 billion ECU by the year 2001 for all types of electronic commerce – goods and services, ordered and paid for on-line, irrespective of the mode of delivery. Only a proportion of this total will be attributable to supplies from non-EU sources and only a further fraction of this will consist partly of 'direct' electronic commerce, i.e. services delivered on-line . . . If the predicted increase in such services supplied to final consumers, who at present pay no VAT, reaches a level which is economically significant it may be necessary, in conjunction with the business community, to design mechanisms to tax such supplied.

15.24 Consumers might be advised to make electronic transactions whilst the fiscal sun continues to shine. The UK's newly published taxation agenda indicates the intention to seek to close the loophole allowing consumer imports of services to escape liability to VAT, although short of an agreement by the external supplier either to collect and forward the tax or to supply details of the nature of the service provided and the identity of the recipient to the tax authorities. Short of an international agreement on the point, it is difficult to see what incentive there might be for the supplier to act as tax gatherer or to provide information identifying the recipient.

The European Single Market and electronic commerce

15.25 An interesting fiscal issue arose in the case of *R v Commissioners of Customs and Excise, ex p EMU Tabac SARL, the Man in Black Ltd and John Cunningham*, a dispute referred by the Court of Appeal for a ruling from the European Court of Justice. EMU is a company incorporated in Luxembourg and the Man in Black Ltd (MBL) in the UK. Both are subsidiaries of another company, the Enlightened Tobacco Company. Taking advantage of the fact that excise duties on tobacco are much lower in Luxembourg than in the UK, an operation was established whereby UK smokers could place cigarette orders with MBL, which would in turn make purchases from EMU and arrange for the cigarettes to be delivered to the UK. The UK tax authorities argued that the cigarettes were liable to tax on importation, whilst the companies argued that they were covered by the exemptions applicable in respect of imports made by private individuals. A transaction conducted through an agent, it was argued, had to be considered in the same light as a transaction carried out by the principal. As individuals could, under Single Market rules as established in Directive 92/12, themselves bring goods into the UK without liability to tax, the same result should apply to the present arrangement.

15.26 The European Court of Justice held that the UK was entitled to levy duty on the cigarettes. The provisions in art 8 of the directive sanctioning personal imports required that:

> transportation must be effected personally by the purchaser of the products subject to duty . . . [A]t no point did the Community legislature intend Article 8 to apply in the event of the involvement of an agent.

15.27 An alternative approach has now evolved, making use of the Internet. A Greek company has established a website offering to supply cigarettes and other tobacco products to UK consumers at Greek prices. The site claims:

> By taking advantage of the European Common Market! In the same way you can buy a U.K. specification car in the Netherlands cheaper than in the UK, or tobacco and alcohol cheaper in Calais, you can also avoid paying the over-taxation by buying your cigarettes and tobacco mail-order from us!

The response to the question whether the transaction is legal is unequivocal:

> Absolutely! One of the benefits of being part of the European Union in the U.K. is that it allows free movement of goods between member countries. There is only one restriction about the quantity. The maximum order for cigarettes is 4 cartons and for tobacco is 1Kg.

15.28 By avoiding the involvement of an agent it is clearly hoped to bring the transactions within the scope of art 8 of the directive. Conceptually, it is difficult to identify reasons why this should not be the case. If the Single Market is to be effective, there should not be a distinction between the situation where a UK citizen buys cigarettes whilst on holiday in Athens and where the order is made over the Internet. Clearly, transport costs will limit the range of goods which would be suitable for such operations, but it does appear that the existence of the Internet is making it more and more difficult for national governments to sustain tax regimes which are at variance with those in other states.

15.29 Evidence exists in other fields also that companies may choose to establish overseas operations to evade national tax regimes. A number of bookmakers have set up telephone call centres in countries, such as Gibraltar, which do not impose any equivalent to the UK's betting levy. Such an operation has the disadvantage that telecommunications costs may eradicate any tax savings. A number of companies have now established Internet-based betting operations.

Alternative forms of taxation

15.30 As the EU and OECD reports recognise, practical difficulties are likely to meet attempts to enforce tax systems in respect of electronic commerce. A number of alternative approaches have been canvassed, with some attention being paid to the notion of a 'bit tax'. In essence this would involve charges being levied upon Internet users dependent on the volume of data transmitted to or from their equipment. The notion of such a tax was first proposed in a paper produced by Arthur Cordell and Thomas Ide for the Club of Rome in 1994.

15.31 Within Europe, the report *Building the Information Society for Us All*, produced by a group of independent experts appointed by the Commission, suggested in 1996 that the Commission investigates:

> Appropriate ways in which the benefits of the Information Society (IS) can be more equally distributed between those who benefit and those who lose. Such research should focus on practicable, implementable policies at the European level which do not jeopardise the emergence of the IS. More specifically, the expert group would like the Commission to undertake research to find out whether a 'bit tax' might be a feasible tool in achieving such redistribution aims.

15.32 A more detailed argument in favour of the 'bit tax' concept was prepared by the chairman of the group Luc Soete. The proposal was generally poorly received with objections being raised both to the level of 'surveillance' which might be required to collect data for billing purposes and also on the grounds that, as well as catching commercial uses of the Internet, the tax would apply where, for example, a person distributed to friends and relatives copies of holiday photos taken with a digital camera. In some respects the arguments are similar to those which have been raised concerning proposals to impose a levy on the cost of audio cassette tapes, the proceeds going to compensate copyright holders for losses caused by unauthorised domestic copying. The objection has been made that those users (admittedly perhaps a small minority) who make non-infringing use of tapes, should not be required to make payments to copyright owners. The Commission have indicated that they do not intend to move in this direction it being stated that:

> While some commentators have suggested that there might be a need to look at alternative taxes such as a bit tax, the Commission is of the opinion that this is not appropriate, since VAT already applies to these transactions.

The question remains, however, whether systems of taxation primarily designed to operate in an economy dominated by tangible goods are well suited for the information society.

15.33 Arguments in favour of a 'bit tax' have also been advanced by the UN in a report, *Globalization With a Human Face,* published in July 1999. This advocated levying a tax on data sent over the Internet, with the funds used to support the development of a telecommunications infrastructure in the least developed countries of the world. Statistics produced by NUA Internet Surveys indicate a massive variation in access to, and use of, the Internet between the various regions of the world. Some 200 million people are estimated to make use of the Internet with the geographic breakdown:

Africa	1.72 million
Asia/Pacific	33.61 million
Europe	47.15 million
Middle East	0.88 million
Canada & US	112.4 million
Latin Americ	5.29 million

A tax of 1 cent per 100 e-mails, it was estimated, would yield an annual income of $70bn.

15.34 The UN proposal (coupled with a further proposal for a tax on income from patents) has not received a warm welcome in the developed world, where it was described by the leader of the US Republican Party in Congress as 'an unnecessary and burdensome tax on the Internet'. It is arguable also that the administrative procedures needed to collect the tax would consume most of the money raised.

Conclusions

15.35 The term 'globalisation' is one of the buzz-words associated with the expansion of international trade. Its impact will be felt on national tax regimes as well as on all other aspects of life and society. The Internet makes it possible for operators in almost every area of activity to deal directly with an end user, without the need for such traditional intermediaries as travel agents, import agencies, car dealers, tobacconists, off-licences and so on. From a fiscal perspective, such operators offered the advantage that responsibility for the collection of taxes and duties could be placed on them. It is much more straightforward to collect tax in respect of 10,000 items from one person than to proceed against 10,000 individual purchasers.

15.36 A further significant change arises from the ability of vendors to target customers in a particular state without the need to maintain any form of physical establishment. The Greek cigarette case described above provides an excellent example of such a situation. Other illustrations might refer to the ease with which Internet-based banks can transact with UK customers without the need for any UK branch structure. 'Offshore banking' is no longer the preserve of the wealthy. Further problems may arise with the emergence of 'smart cards', such as Mondex, which act as a kind of virtual wallet. A benefit claimed for these systems is that transactions are effectively anonymised. Users could download 'cash' from offshore bank accounts and pay for goods or services with the same anonymity as available with cash transactions. The supplier will, in turn, be able to upload credit to a similar bank account. Whilst it might be argued that this is no different from the present situation, where goods might be paid for with paper money, logistical and security problems will make most customers wary of carrying too much money, whilst the supplier may be wary of retaining too much money in biscuit tins or under bedding. With electronic cash, however, the carrying of large amounts of digital money poses no logistical or security problem. This is altogether a benefit for the black economy to the extent that it has been suggested that, for many people, paying tax will be an optional matter. A hopeful conclusion for some individuals, perhaps, but one with dire consequences for the employment prospects of the Chancellor of the Exchequer and for those who, due to the nature of their employment, will have to bear the burden of a shrinking tax base.

Index

295